AF600221

POPE URBAN II AND CANON LAW

This dissertation was approved by Stephan G. Kuttner, J. U. D., S. J. D., J. C. D., LL. D., as director, and by the Right Reverend Clement V. Bastnagel, S. T. L., J. U. D., and the Reverend Frederick R. McManus, A. B., J. C. D., as readers.

THE CATHOLIC UNIVERSITY OF AMERICA
CANON LAW STUDIES
No. 403

POPE URBAN II AND CANON LAW

A DISSERTATION
Submitted to the Faculty of the School of Canon Law of The Catholic University of America in Partial Fulfilment of the Requirements for the Degree of Doctor of Canon Law

BY

REVEREND FRANCIS J. GOSSMAN, B. A., S. T. L., J. C. L.
A Priest of the Archdiocese of Baltimore

THE CATHOLIC UNIVERSITY OF AMERICA PRESS
WASHINGTON, D. C.
1960

Nihil Obstat:

CLEMENS V. BASTNAGEL, S. T. L., J. U. D.
Censor Deputatus

Washingtonii, D. C., die 6 aprilis, 1960.

Imprimatur:

✠ FRANCISCUS P. KEOUGH, D. D.
Archiepiscopus Baltimorensis

Baltimorae, Md., die 11 aprilis, 1960.

PRINTED IN THE UNITED STATES OF AMERICA
BY J. H. FURST COMPANY, BALTIMORE, MARYLAND

TO MARY
THE IMMACULATE MOTHER
OF GOD

FOREWORD

Canon Law as it exists today may be looked upon as an institution with deep roots in the past. The legal and theological traditions which it embodies link the Church of today with Christ, Its Founder, and at the same time reflect the history of that Church down through the ages. It is remarkable that in a history-conscious world the medieval background of Canon Law has been largely neglected until very recent years.

But if the law of the Church has deep roots in the past, it is not at all surprising that history has left its mark on ecclesiastical jurisprudence. Very few periods of medieval history have been studied as intensively and by such a large group of eminent scholars as the age of the Gregorian reforms. From the canonical viewpoint, however, there are many elements of this reform deserving closer scrutiny; for the Gregorian reform movement was itself an incentive for canonical thought. The present study has for its purpose to examine the contribution to canonical thought made by Pope Urban II (1088-1099), the second successor of Gregory VII.

Blessed Urban II lived and reigned in an era in which the Church was sorely troubled within and without. History gives the assurance that as man and monk, priest and Pope, Urban met the challenge of his time with an abundance of spiritual and intellectual acumen. He undertook to carry out the ideas of Gregory, to be his *pedisequus,* as he himself put it. Both Urban and Gregory sought that "*libertas et puritas ecclesiae*" which the Church so desperately needed. In the pursuit of this objective Urban met with remarkable success; he waged a winning struggle with the emperor, Henry IV, and restored indispensable prestige to the papacy.

Although history remembers Urban II principally for his part in beginning the Crusades, a study such as this gives some indications of a different kind of contribution. The Pope saw in Canon Law one of his chief weapons against the abuses of his day. In his efforts of reform Gregory VII had given the impetus to a canonical revival. Taking the initiative from his predecessor, Urban made Canon Law a tool for the Church's reform.

A sincere and humble expression of thanks is due to His Excellency, the Most Reverend Francis P. Keough, D. D., Archbishop of Baltimore, for the opportunity to pursue graduate studies in Canon Law; and to the members of the Faculty of the Graduate School of Canon Law of the Catholic University of America for their guidance, helpfulness and encouragement. In a research study such as this, the cooperation of many individuals and institutions was necessary, especially for the acquisition of microfilms. Special thanks are extended to Mlle. Jeanne Vielliard, directress of the Institut de Recherche et d'Histoire des Textes, Paris, and Dr. John T. Gilchrist, Lecturer in History at the University of Adelaide in South Australia. Grateful acknowledgment should be extended to the staff of the Mullen Library of the Catholic University of America and the microfilm division of the Library of Congress for the use of microfilms of the Vatican Library, Rome, and to the directors of the National Libraries of Munich and Vienna for their most generous cooperation in obtaining research materials. A final word of deepest gratitude must in all justice be given to Dr. Stephan Kuttner, whose constant interest and genuine direction were responsible for this study. Without his encouragement and assistance this work would never have been begun, let alone finished.

TABLE OF CONTENTS

PART II

A Compendium of the Canonical Thought of Pope Urban II

Chapter I

Chapter II

Chapter III

INTRODUCTORY CHAPTER

This study consists of two parts. The first part is a catalogue of the acts of Pope Urban II as they have been found in the canonical collections made between the years of Pope Urban's pontificate and the completion of the *Decretum Gratiani,* that is from the year 1088 until about 1140. After determining that approximately fifteen collections from this period contained no relevant material, twenty-four canonical collections were searched to discover exactly what canonical thought was taken from the acts of Urban II. In the majority of cases it was necessary to consult microfilmed manuscript copies of the collections, because very few of the canonical works of the pre-Gratian period have been edited. Each canon discovered has been indicated in the collection in which it is first found, and is there identified according to its actual source. A brief résumé of the content has been included along with the identification. Each successive time that a canon has appeared, the reader has been directed back to the place in the collection where that canon first appeared. Any relation with the *Decretum* of Gratian has been noted, and at the conclusion of Part I there is included an appendix treating the canons of Urban II found in the *Decretum.* There is also another appendix which shows by a chart the recurrence of canons and offers some observations on the interrelation of the various collections among themselves and with the *Decretum* of Gratian.

The first part of this study is, then, a reasonably accurate report of the weight which contemporary canonists attributed to the canonical ideas of Pope Urban II. It had been hoped that two other collections might be included in the first part of this work, the *Summa Haimonis* and the *Collectio Atrebatensis,* but circumstances prevented the acquisition of films of the manuscripts or of other information.

The second part of this work is a survey of the canonical thinking of Urban II as found both in and outside of the collections examined in Part I. Part II has for its purpose an examination of the content of the canonical thought of Urban II. There is a very obvious difference in the objective of each part. Part I is a study of the formal aspect of the canons, insofar as they have been absorbed into canonical collections, while Part II has for its principal aim to study the content of the ideas expressed both in and outside of the collections. For there is a considerable number of letters and decrees which, so far as research has indicated, never were assumed into any of the collections. In order to obtain a representative idea of the volume and content of Urban's canonical thought in its entirety, it has been necessary to search outside of the collections.

This search began with a study of the correspondence of Urban. Since the complete register of Urban's correspondence has been lost, it was necessary to go the best existing substitute. These substitutes are the *Regesta Pontificum Romanorum* of Philip Jaffé (1819-1870), and the *Italia* and *Germania Pontificia* together with the *Papsturkunden* series, begun by Paul Kehr (1860-1944).[1] By combining the sources of each of these works one can compile as complete a record as possible of the papal correspondence; in this way it is possible to reconstruct Urban's register in accord with the most recent results of historical research. From papal correspondence it was natural to turn to the councils convoked by Urban II. By combining the content of conciliar canons with the ideas expressed in the papal correspondence, Part II of this study presents a compendium of the canonical thought of Urban II. In the second part the ideas expressed are identified as coming from within or outside of the canonical collections.

In a general way the sources from outside of the collections present no major problems. There is, it is true, the fact that some of Urban's correspondence and acts have been lost; this loss is

[1] The *Regesta* of Jaffé attempts to catalogue every known papal letter from the beginning of the Church to the year 1198. Paul Kehr began a new search of local archives throughout Europe in an effort to discover still more papal correspondence. The results of his search in Italy and Germany are found in *Italia* and *Germania Pontificia.* For the other countries of Europe, the final *regesta* has not been completed, but the complete reports of most of the archival investigations have been published separately. The additional source material which these investigations have uncovered serves as a very useful supplement to information already available in Jaffé's tabulation.

unfortunate, but not unusual for the period. But there are several problems concerning the acts of the councils convoked by Urban.

The first difficulty, in this regard, concerns the acts of the Council of Piacenza, held in March, 1095. There are two different accounts of the acts of this council. The first was given by Bernold of Constance (1054-1100) in his *Chronicon* (begun in the year 1072 or 1073 and going to 1100) and consists of nine canons.[1a] The wording of this version is clearly that of a résumé or an abbreviation; Bernold himself declares as much.[2] The second version of the decrees of Piacenza appears to be a reconstruction of the canons.[3] It is from this latter group of fifteen canons that excerpts have been taken by Gratian and other collectors before him.[4] The second series of canons is essentially the same as that given by Bernold, except that in the second group greater detail is given to the matters of simony and ordination *extra ecclesiam*.[5] Both series have been accepted as authentic.[6]

[1a] Bernold's account of the Council of Piacenza is found under the year 1095 in his *Chronicon*; a critical edition of this passage is in the *Monumenta Germaniae Historica, Scriptores*, Vol. V (ed. G. Pertz, Leipzig: Verlag Karl W. Hiersemann, 1925), pp. 461-464. This same passage is found in J. Mansi, *Sacrorum Canonum Nova et Amplissima Collectio* (53 vols. in 60, Parisiis, Arnhem, Lipsiae, 1901-1927), XX, 801-803; hereafter cited Mansi.

[2] "Haec autem inter alia in illa sinodo constituta sunt. . . ."—*Monumenta Germaniae Historica, Scriptores*, V, 461.

[3] This series of canons is found in the *Monumenta Germaniae Historica, Leges*, Sectio IV, *Constitutiones et Acta Publica Imperatorum et Regum*, Vol. I (ed. L. Weiland, Hannoverae: Impensis Biblica Hahniani, 1893), pp. 560-563; in the introductory remarks the editor lists fifteen manuscripts which contain the series of canons, with some individual differences; his remarks are prefaced by this observation: ". . . Ea, quae nobis in codicibus servata sunt, pro Breviario tantum Gestorum habenda sunt, quod in duobus vel fortasse tribus recensionibus ferebantur." Mansi, following *Codex Ms. Vaticanus Latinus 1208*, lists the series of fifteen canons, XX, 805-807.

[4] C. 2, D. LXX: this canon is not found in any of the pre-Gratian collections examined by the writer; c. 4, D. LXXVI, found in Part I of this study at n. 11 of the Italian Collection in Three Books; c. 108, C. I, q. 1; c. 5, C. I, q. 3, and c. 1, C. I, q. 5, found in the Collection in Seven Books, n. 2; and c. 5, C. IX, q. 1, found in the *Polycarpus*, n. 5. For other collections in which these same canons are also found, the reader is requested to consult the chart in Appendix II of Part I.

[5] C. Hefele-H. Leclercq, *Histoire des Conciles* (11 vols. in 21, Paris:

The acts of the Council of Clermont (1095) present much the same difficulty as those of Piacenza; here, however, there are as many as eight different recensions of the acts. The original acts of Clermont have also perished.[7] The best and most widely diffused list of canons came from Lambert, Bishop of Arras († 1115).[8] The merit of Lambert's recension arises from the fact that he was personally present at the Council of Clermont; even in his own day Lambert was regarded as a reliable witness and as an authority concerning the Council of Clermont.[9] Lambert's list of thirty-two canons was thus given first place by canonists and historians; Berardi (1719-1768), referring to it, called it the "*vulgata editio.*"[10]

With all its merits Lambert's series of canons is not regarded as complete. There is enough evidence from other sources to show that several matters were given special attention, yet Lambert's listing of canons is either deficient in details or completely silent concerning such matters.[11] The recension of Clermont as given by the *Codex Cencii* complements Lambert's list of canons.[12] The

Letouzey et Ané, Editeurs, 1907-1952), V, I, 388-395, especially pp. 391-392; hereafter this work will be cited Hefele-Leclercq, *Conciles.*

[6] A. Fliche-V. Martin, eds., *Histoire de l'Église,* Vol. VIII, A. Fliche, *La Réforme grégorienne et la Reconquête chrétienne* (*1057-1123*) (Paris: Bloud et Gay, 1944), p. 265, note 7; this work will hereafter be cited Fliche, *Histoire.*

[7] Mansi, XX, 884; Hefele-Leclercq, *Conciles,* V, I, 399.

[8] Mansi, XX, 816-819. "On peut dire qu'en général, le *codex Lamberti* donne le meilleur texte et le plus grand nombre de canons. . . ."—Hefele-Leclercq, *Conciles,* V, I, 400.

[9] Cf. the quote of Gabriel Cossart in Mansi, XX, 905, where it is indicated that Lambert testified to the legislation of the Council of Clermont at the Council of Beauvais, held in 1114 (Mansi, XXI, 121-126). Cossart was a Jesuit canonist, who in 1671 and 1672, completed the collection begun by Philip Labbé, entitled *Sacrosancta Concilia.*

[10] *Gratiani Canones genuini ab apocryphis discreti* (3 parts in 4, Venetiis: ex typographia Petri Valvasensis, 1777), I, 441; hereafter cited as Berardi, *Canones.*

[11] Hefele-Leclercq claim that Lambert's *codex* is inferior in certain particulars, *Conciles,* V, I, 400; cf. also pp. 401 and 403 for examples of omissions from Lambert's text of the canons.

[12] This conclusion is implicitly affirmed by Hefele-Leclercq when the

Codex Cencii consists of a list of ten cannons with the inscription, "*Concilum Claromontanum Anno MXCV. ex Cencii Camerarii volumine MS.*"[13]

An account which is of relatively recent discovery and which holds a recognized place among the more reliable series of canons of the Council of Clermont is found in the Collection of Saint-Germain-des-Prés.[14] The canons as found in this manuscript of Wolfenbüttel are for the most part the same as those of Lambert; there are, however, six additional canons, which are found at the beginning of the thirty canons of this recension. The numbering is different from Lambert's version, although the same general order is found in both accounts. Sdralek mentions that the authenticity of the Wolfenbüttel version of Clemont is substantiated by other sources.[15] Several canons found in this version are repeated in other collections before Gratian. The *Correctores Romani* quote a canon found in this version of Clermont.[16]

additions made to the thirty-two canons of Lambert come only from the *Codex Cencii.* The fact that Gratian cites the Council of Clermont only from a source which is agreement with the *Codex Cencii* adds to the authority of this list of canons. Cf. Hefele-Leclercq, *Conciles,* V, I, 400-403.

[13] Mansi, XX, 901-903. This series obviously came from a manuscript of the library of Cencio Savelli, the camerlengo to Popes Celestine III and Innocent III; he later became Pope Honorius III (1216-1227). An extensive search did not unearth any further information about the manuscript of Cencio, but Baluze (1630-1718) edited another codex containing the same ten canons. Baluze ascribed his series of canons to an old manuscript from the monastery of Saint-Sauveur, at Aniane in the diocese of Montpellier; when he edited the manuscript it was kept in the Colbertine Library. For the text and some observations, see the notes of Baluze to chapter XXXI of Book VI of the work of Petrus de Marca, *De Concordia Sacerdotii et Imperii* (4 vols., Neapoli, 1771), III, 207-208. The manuscript of Cencio appears to offer a real problem, since in none of the studies of the library of Cencio does a manuschipt of the Council of Clermont appear. The manuscript from the Colbertine Library used by Baluze is very likely that found today in *codex ms. Bibliothèque Nationale, fonds latins, 3881.*

[14] This version has been edited by Max Sdralek, *Wolfenbüttler Fragmente,* in the series *Kirchengeschichtliche Studien herausgegeben von Dr. Knöpfler, Dr. Schrörs, Dr. Sdralek* (Münster i. W.: Verlag Heinrich Schöningh, 1891), Band I, Heft, II, pp. 133-136 and 24-25. Hereafter cited as Sdralek.

[15] Pp. 24 and 25.

[16] Cf. the *notationes Correctorum* at c. 2, D. LXXVI; the canon there

The remaining versions of the acts of Clermont are best described as a grouping of fragments by various authors.[17] Occupying first place among these fragmentary series of canons are those of Ordericus Vitalis (1075-ca. 1143), found in his *Historia Ecclesiastica,* written between the years 1120 and ca. 1143.[18] Given equal authority with Ordericus' fragmentary canons is the equally abbreviated series of canons of William of Malmesbury (ca. 1080-ca. 1143); William's series is included in his *De Gestis Regum Anglorum,* which was finished by 1125.[19] These two summaries of the canons of Clermont stem from a common tradition of the acts of that council, for they resemble each other very closely; there are only three canons found in Ordericus' summary which are not found in William's account.[20]

Each of these summaries is primarily a historical account of the Council of Clermont. The authors themselves attempted only a

quoted is found in the Wolfenbüttel manuscript; it is called canon 1 of Clermont, but the *Correctores* do not indicate their font. Other canons from this manuscript are found in the second Collection of Châlons-sur-Marne and in the Collection in Ten Parts; cf. the chart found in Appendix II of Part I.

[17] Cf. Hefele-Leclercq, *Conciles,* V, I, 399. P. Jaffé, *Regesta Pontificum Romanorum ab condita ecclesia ad annum post Christum natum MCXCVIII* (editionem secundam correctam et auctam auspiciis Gulielmi Wattenbach, curaverunt S. Loewenfeld, F. Kaltenbrunner, P. Ewald, 2 vols., Lipsiae, 1885-1888), I, 681, after JL 5586. This work is cited as JK, JE or JL, depending upon the period assigned to the editors; thus Kaltenbrunner, to the year 589; Ewald, from 590-881; Loewenfeld, from 882-1198; for reference to a letter, the consecutive numbers of this work are cited; where reference is not to a letter, either the page reference is given, or a reference is made to information included after a certain letter.

[18] Auguste le Prevost (ed.), *Orderici Vitalis Historiae Ecclesiasticae Libri Tredecim* (5 vols., Parisiis: apud Julium Prenouard et Socios, 1840-1855), III, 464-465, contains an account of the Council of Clermont including an abbreviation of the canons enacted; this series of fragmentary canons is also included in Mansi, XX, 885-886.

[19] William Stubbs, ed., *Willelmi Malmesbiriensis Monachi De Gestis Regum Anglorum,* Rerum Britannicarum Medii Aevi Scriptores (Rolls Series) (2 vols., London, 1889), II, cxx (of the preface) and II, 391-393, for William's record of the Council of Clermont with his summary of the canons; this summary can also be found in Mansi, XX, 904-905.

[20] Mansi, XX, 905.

summary of the statutes enacted; their own words imply that an abbreviated form was their primary aim.[21] What was the exact source which these two historians drew upon can only be surmised. Apparently it was noticeably different from the account transmitted by Lambert of Arras. The wording and the numbering of the accounts of Ordericus and William bear little resemblance to the version of Lambert; the content is closely related. The divergent wording and arrangement is explained by the frequent paraphrasing of the various collectors. Although the two accounts of Ordericus and William are shorter than Lambert's version, they both stand up well in a comparison with Lambert's account. There are differences in particulars at times, but the general pattern is evident.

The version of François Belleforest (1530-1583)[22] consists of twelve canons, translated from the author's French, in which some of decrees of Clermont are found in a very abbreviated form. Belleforest wrote his *Grande Annales de France* in 1579, but did not cite the source whence he drew his series of canons. This recension does not seem to be held in such high regard; no study of this group of canons has been made.[23]

There is another manuscript which contains the same canons as Lambert's series, but in a different arrangement, together with ten additional canons. These ten canons are proper to this manuscript, which is usually called simply the "*vetus membrana*." [24]

[21] Ordericus has, "Decreta vero concilii, apud Clarummontem habiti sunt hujuscemodi: . . ."—Mansi, XX, 885. William of Malmesbury speaks about "*quaedam meis sermonibus pro compendio brevians. . . .*"—quoted by W. Levison, "Aus Englischen Bibliotheken II: Englische Handschriften des *Liber Pontificalis*," *Neues Archiv*, XXXV (1909-1910), 393, note 4; the author here describes a version of the acts of Clemont which are very similar to the account given by William of Malmesbury; he notes that both Ordericus and William seem to have used a common source which apparently has perished. Whether that common source was an officially recognized collection no one can say. This article is hereafter referred to as Levison.

[22] Mansi, XX, 820-821.

[23] There are some notes along with the Latin rendering in Mansi, XX, 820.

[24] The canons of the "*vetus membrana*" were apparently first discovered by Pierre Pithou (1539-1596), the French canonist. The first to edit this manuscript was Gabriel Cossart, in his continuation of P. Labbé's *Sacrosancta Concilia* (15 vols. in 16, Parisiis, 1672), X, 594.

Finally J. Pflugk-Harttung (1848-1919) discovered a list of "... *praecepta Urbani Papae, data in Avernensi concilio.*" [25] This series of nineteen canons seems to be a very poor rendering of the decrees of Clermont. The very general outlines of the canons of Clermont are found in this series, but they are so far removed from what is regarded as the original, that very little authority is conceded to this recension.[26]

To sum up the facts as they exist concerning the Council of Clermont, it should be noted, first, that there are many discrepancies among the various series of canons and summaries of canons. These differences point to the lack of a single common tradition. There were apparently several different traditions from a time shortly after the actual conclusion of the council itself.

The nature of the evidence is so diverse, especially in origin, that conclusions can, at best, be only hypothetical. While it is true that several of the series purport to be the acts of the council (e. g. the *codex Lamberti,* the series from the Collection of Saint-Germain-des-Prés and the *Codex Cencii*), several of the groups are very evidently not intended to give the entire acts of the council, but only a summary of the matters dealt with (e. g. the summaries of Ordericus Vitalis, William of Malmesbury and François Belleforest). There are still other groups of canons, which remain especially doubtful (e. g. the "*vetus membrana,*" the series discovered by Pflugk-Harttung). The mixture of source material from both canonical fonts and historical chronicles adds to the problem, since each of these disciplines approaches the same subject from a different point of view, uses different methods, and ultimately has a diverse objective.

[25] *Acta Pontificum Romanorum inedita* (3 vols., Vol. I, Tübingen: Verlag und Druck von Franz Fues, 1881; Vols. II and III, Stuttgart: Verlag von W. Kohlhammer, 1884-1886), II, 161 (hereafter cited Pflugk-Harttung, *Acta inedita*). Through correspondence with Professor Walther Holtzman, Director of the Deutsches Historisches Institut in Rome, the writer was made aware of an additional manuscript of the twelfth century containing the decrees of the Councils of Piacenza and Clermont "in a form quite different from the others." There was not enough time to make a study of this manuscript, but any future study should not neglect it. The manuscript is one of the Bodleian Library: Selden Supra n. 90 (Summary Catalogue 3478), folio 24v-27r.

[26] Hefele-Leclercq, *Conciles,* V, I, 399-400.

The marked discrepaincies together with the diverse nature of the evidence lead one to conclude that no safe reconstruction of the original acts of Clermont seems as yet possible. Historians and canonists have pointed out the divergence among the various series of canons, but no real effort has been undertaken to formulate a critical reconstruction of the acts. When one examines the evidence, it is not unusual that no one has ever made a serious attempt at a critical text; the almost total lack of any positive indications, except from the *codex Lamberti* and that of Cencius, presents poor prospects for any real clarification.

These two series of canons, together with the series found in the Collection of Saint-Germain-des-Prés, which is basically the same as Lambert's recension, do present some reliable evidence. For one thing, besides the fact that Lambert was present at the council, his group of canons is substantially found in at least three of the pre-Gratian collections, namely the Collection of Saint-Germain-des-Prés, the second Collection of Châlons-sur-Marne and the Collection in Ten Parts. Almost every canon found from Clermont in these collections is textually concordant with the series attributed to Lambert. It is for this reason particularly that Lambert's series is consistently put in first place.[27]

The *Codex Cencii* has in its favor the fact that fragments corresponding to it are quoted in Gratian and in several of the pre-Gratian Collections. In fact the only canons in Gratian from the Council of Clermont textually concur with what is known today as the *Codex Cencii*. These canons, together with those of Lambert, therefore, are unique in enjoying a solid tradition in the canonical collections. This evidence is not alone sufficient for labeling these two series as the authentic acts of Clermont, but their absorption into collections made shortly after the council itself is surely a point in their favor.

None of the other series of canons has such strong arguments

[27] Hefele-Leclercq, *Conciles*, V, I, 400-404; Fliche, *Histoire*, VIII, 281-283; S. Runciman, *The History of the Crusades* (3 vols., Cambridge: at the University Press, 1951-1954), I, 106-113, especially p. 109, note 1; K. Setton-M. Baldwin, eds., *A History of the Crusades*, Vol. I, *The First Hundred Years* (Philadelphia: The University of Pennsylvania Press, 1955), p. 237, note 36.

to recommend it. However, the summaries of Ordericus Vitalis and of William of Malmesbury were certainly written at a time not distant from the actual council. Although time is in their favor, fragments from these two summaries are nowhere incorporated into the collections. Nevertheless scholars generally consider these two abridgments as faithful summaries of the original decrees of Clermont.[28] These two summaries resemble each other very closely and come from a common source; in their comparison with Lambert's series of canons, the recensions of Ordericus and William present greater similarity than any other group.

The remaining series of canons do not have much corroborative evidence to support them. What is more, no critical evaluation has ever been undertaken. Such a critical investigation of all the source material along with a scientific reconstruction of the acts of Clermont would be a very useful project, both in itself, and for the purposes of this study. But to undertake such a task here would be to go beyond the limitations of this dissertation. Even the schematic presentation of the problem, as it has been given in this introductory chapter, is enough to indicate that a complete study of the matters is not only desirable, but necessary. A critical study of this nature would necessarily go into some detail and length.

On the basis of the information and evidence available at present, the following conclusions seem justified. The series of canons from Lambert and the *Codex Cencii* may be accepted, as they have been, as the most complete record of the enactments of the Council of Clermont. With reference to the canons of this council the summaries of Ordericus Vitalis and William of Malmesbury can be regarded as reliable contemporary abbreviations which were primarily historical in origin. The summary of François Belleforest and the ten canons proper to the "*vetus membrana*" should really be given further examination in whatever claims they may have, but with reference to the present study it seems warranted to by-pass such further consideration. Likewise the nineteen decrees discovered by Pflugk-Harttung are so markedly divergent from the more commonly acceptable series of canons, that it seems preferable to omit consideration of these in the present study. The true

[28] Cf. Levison, p. 393, note 4; Setton-Baldwin, *A History of the Crusades*, I, 237, note 36.

scientific value of each of these series, the appraisal of which has not been undertaken in the present study, is yet to be determined; on the other hand, the recensions which have been accepted do have the merit of being commonly regarded as a reasonably complete record of the legislation enacted at Clermont.

A final question remains to be considered. This question concerns the council convoked by Urban at the Lateran Palace, sometime in the year 1097. There is no doubt that Urban convoked such a council.[29] There is, however, some doubt about the decrees of this council. Pflugk-Harttung (1848-1919) proposed a list of ten canons, which he claimed came from this Lateran Council.[30] Hefele (1809-1893)-Leclercq (1869-1945) rejected this series of canons on the basis that the decrees could not have been enacted before the Second General Council of the Lateran in 1139. No canon from this series has been discovered in any of the collections. With more reserve, Fliche (1884-1951) concluded that the question of the authenticity of the proposed canons is insoluble from the evidence which is at present available.[31] Because of the evident doubt which pervades this series of canons, they have not been given consideration in this study.

In conclusion it can be said of the acts and correspondence of Urban II that the *lacunae* are unfortunate. The discrepancies and perplexities posed by the acts of the Council of Clermont are enough to lead one to hope for a reliable and critical reconstruction of this council—a wish which was voiced over fifty years ago.[32]

[29] Hefele-Leclercq, *Conciles*, V, I, 453.

[30] *Acta inedita*, II, 167-168; cf. Hefele-Leclercq, *Conciles*, V, I, 454-456.

[31] *Histoire*, VIII, 329, note 1.

[32] Levison, p. 393, note 4.

PART I

THE CANONS FROM URBAN II FOUND IN THE CANONICAL COLLECTIONS FROM 1090 UNTIL THE TIME OF THE *DECRETUM GRATIANI*

PART I

CANONS FROM URBAN II FOUND IN THE CANONICAL COLLECTIONS FROM 1090 UNTIL THE TIME OF THE *DECRETUM GRATIANI*

The purpose of this part of the dissertation is to examine the legislation of Urban II as it is found in the canonical collections of the period from his election until the completion of the *Decretum* of Gratian, i. e., from the year 1088 until ca. 1140. In this way it is possible to arrive at an objective evaluation of Urban's contribution to the legal thinking of his time, not merely from the judgment of the modern scholar looking backward, but in the estimation of the contemporaries of the Pope himself. In other words, the contribution of Urban to Canon Law will be measured by the content and quantity of his canonical thought which was actually absorbed into one or more of the collections of his time. The method followed in Part I of this study has been chosen as the best way to assess in the objective terms of his contemporaries the contribution made to canonical thought by Urban II. The purpose here is not to examine Urban's legal ideas from the viewpoint of a modern scholar, as will be done in Part II, but to strive for the evalutation given by the canonists who had a rôle in the development of Canon Law in the pre-Gratian period.

Accordingly this part of the study is a catalogue of the decretals and the canons of Urban II which were included in the canonical collections made between 1088 and 1140. Every effort has been made to identify and classify each entry. Where some explanation is required, this has been included. Only major textual variations have been noted. The actual entry includes merely the opening and the closing words; these are given as they occur in the text under consideration. The complete text of a canon is given only when its source is unknown. The various collections which contain relevant material have been arranged in an order that seeks to be both logical and chronological. Basically this arrangement evolves into a two-fold division of collections, the one evincing strong Gregorian influences, and the other showing dependence upon the works of Ivo of Chartres.

The Collection of *Codex Ms. Vaticanus Latinus 4977*

This collection was compiled toward the end of the eleventh century. Although it has some Gregorian material, it cannot be considered as imbued with the reform spirit.[1]

This collection actually begins only with folio 24r and therefore the first four canons herein given do not form a part of the collection. Fournier (1855-1935)-Le Bras (b. 1891) maintain that the first twenty-three folios contain a résumé of the Collection in Seventy-four Titles.[2] But if the observation of Fournier-Le Bras is correct, the fact that there are four canons of Urban II is left unexplained, since the Collection in Seventy-four Titles antedates the pontificate of Urban II by at least twelve years.[3] Wherever possible the location of the text will be given according to the numerical indication of *liber* (or *pars*), *titulus* and *capitulum*. In the present collection, however, the texts have been so set down as to make counting quite confusing, since some of the canons run the entire width of the folio and others are in columns.

1) folio 1v

De neptis tue . . . de uiro est sentiendum

JL 5399, to Sancho I, king of Aragon (1063-1094), (July 1, 1089), (given at Rome), c. 3, C. XXXI, q. 2. A forced espousal enjoys no valor, unless both of the parties concerned given full consent to it.

[1] P. Fournier-G.-Le Bras, *Histoire des collections canoniques en Occident depuis les Fausses décrétales jusqu'au Décret de Gratien* (2 vols., Paris: Recueil Sirey, 1931-1932), II, 125-127 (hereafter cited Fournier-Le Bras, *Histoire*); P. Fournier, *Un groupe de Receuils canoniques Italiens des X*[e] *et XI*[e] *Siècles* (Paris: Imprimerie Nationale, 1915), pp. 116-118. To these add A. Van Hove, *Prolegomena*, Vol. I, Tom. I of the *Commentarium Lovaniense in Codicem Iuris Canonici*, editum a Magistris et Doctoribus Universitatis Lovaniensis (2. ed., Mechliniae: H. Dessain, 1945), p. 316 (hereafter cited Van Hove, *Prolegomena*); A. Stickler, *Historia Iuris Canonici Latini*, Vol. I, *Historia Fontium* (Augustae Taurinorum: apud Custodiam Librariam Pontif. Athenaei Salesiani, 1950), p. 160 (hereafter cited Stickler, *Historia*).

[2] *Histoire*, II, 125, footnote 2.

[3] Stickler, *Historia*, pp. 167-168, esp. footnote 2 on the latter page. See also Van Hove, *Prolegomena*, p. 323, and Fournier-Le Bras, *Histoire*, II, 15-16.

2) folio 5r

Eos qui post . . . interdictione mulctentur

Canon 12, Council of Melfi, Sept. 10, 1089, Mansi, XX, 724, c. 10, D. XXXII. Any cleric in sacred orders who attempts to live as a married person is to be removed from benefice and office; permission is given to put into bondage the wives of such clerics who disregard this regulation. The bishop who consents to such behavior is to be suspended.

3) folio 5r (this canon follows the one above)

Erubescunt impii . . . deus iudex est

JL 4575 (this letter belongs to Alexander II, but is here inscribed, *Item gradensi patriarche dominico* and, since it follows the preceding canon of Urban, is attributed to Urban II), to Dominic, patriarch of Grado, 1065, c. 11, D. XXXII. All clerics in sacred orders, who publicly cohabit with women, are to be removed from every office, dignity and honor; those who do so secretly are left to the judgment of God, since the Church does not judge occult matters in the external forum. In the text of the canon as found in this collection there is no mention of subdeacons; in c. 11, D. XXXII mention of subdeacons is included. The erroneous inscription of this canon is also found in Gratian.

4) folio 5r-5v (this canon follows the one preceding)

Ad sacros ordines . . . uirginem uxorem habuerit

Canon 3 (here and in Gratian this canon bears the incorrect inscription: *Item meldensi sinodo presidens ait*), Council of Melfi, Sept. 10, 1089, Mansi, XX, 723, c. 12, D. XXXII. Every candidate for sacred orders must be either a virgin or of proven chastity; if the candidate has been married previously he must be the husband of a single wife and she a virgin (cf. I Tim. III: 2 and Tit. I: 6). It is of particular interest to note that the three last-mentioned canons are found together in Gratian and that the exact inscriptions, including all of the errors, are found in both places. The evidence suggests some dependence by Gratian upon this or a similar collection; the similarity must certainly be due to something other than coincidence. Chance scarcely offers an adequate explanation for the fact that three canons appear in this collection and in Gratian's *Decretum* in the identical arrangement and with the same erroneous inscriptions. The entire context of both places is alike; in the present collection there are found in consecutive order chapters 8, 9, 10, 11, 12, 13, 15 and 16 of D. XXXII in Gratian.

5) folio 50r (at the foot of the folio)

Gregorii papae et urbani papae.

Siue per bonos sacerdotes. siue per malos christi domino sacrificium offertur. sacrificium nec crescit nec minuitur. quando sacrificat sacerdos. sed angelus dei. qui ibidem adstat. quem oculi humani uidere non possunt. quique illud inuisibiliter sanctificat custodit et benedicit.

This text, which harmonizes with the policies of both Urban II and Gregory VII, cannot be identified. It is not found among the known sources of Urban II, nor has it been discovered among those of Gregory VII.

The Collection in Two Books

The Collection in Two Books was compiled about the year 1085 at Rome, under Gregorian influence. It follows the arrangement of the Collection in Seventy-four Titles with other sources added. The canons of Urban II are added at the end of the collection by a later canonist.[4]

1) folio 196r (six folios from the end of the manuscript)

Discretioni nostre uidetur . . . mysteria reconciliabis

JL 5378, to Anselm, archbishop of Milan, 1088. The manner of reconciling those ordained by excommunicated bishops is related.

[4] The collection is found in *codex ms. Vaticanus latinus 3832;* cf. Fournier-Le Bras, *Histoire,* II, 127-131; Van Hove, *Prolegomena,* p. 325; Stickler, *Historia,* p. 175.

2) folio 196r-196v (follows the above entry)

Quia te speciale . . . uitam perducat eternam

JL 5393, to Gebhard, bishop of Constance, April 18, 1089, given at Rome. Portions of this letter are in c. 110, C. XI, q. 3, and c. 4, C. IX, q. 1. This letter contains what became the accepted teaching about excommunication for the ages to come. The letter classifies those guilty of association with the excommunicated according to various grades. The question of ordination by excommunicated bishops is to be handled by a council (actually this matter was treated at Piacenza in 1095). Gebhard is requested to fill vacant abbeys and bishoprics and is appointed apostolic legate.[5] Excerpts of this letter appear with frequency in the collections of this time, but this is the only instance in which the entire text is found in a collection. These two excerpts are 1) *Excommunicationis questione . . . metus incutiatur* and 2) *Ut ab excommunicatis . . . precipua est concedendum,* which is found in c. 4, C. IX, q. 1. This last passage is also found in chapter 4 of the letter of Urban to Pibo, bishop of Toul, JL 5409. It is not too unlikely that the papal chancery kept records of its replies; thus when a similar question arose, the answer was frequently couched in similar or identical language because of recourse to these records.

The *Collectio Britannica*

This collection favorable to the reforms of Gregory VII was made in Italy about the year 1090. It is especially important for the number of papal letters which it contains. The name *Britannica* derives rather from the British Museum, where the manuscript is preserved, than from the origin of the collection.[6]

[5] Cf. Fliche, *Histoire*, VIII, 211; F. Mourret, *A History of the Catholic Church*, Vol. IV (St. Louis: B. Herder Book Company, 1941), pp. 245-246 (hereafter cited Mourret, *History*).

[6] P. Ewald, "Die Papstbriefe der Brittischen Sammlung," *Neues Archiv*, V (1879-1880), 277-414, 501-596, and especially 352-366 (hereafter referred to as Ewald) together with S. Loewenfeld, *Epistolae Pontificum Romanorum ineditae* (Lipsiae: Viet et Comp., 1885). Cf. also Fournier-Le Bras,

1) Ewald, p. 352

Notum facimus . . . viris religiosis. Post triduum . . . pontificem elegerunt

JL 5349, to Hugh, abbot of Cluny, March 13, 1088, given at Terracina. In these two fragments of a larger letter Urban announces his election as Roman Pontiff.

2) Ewald, pp. 352-353

De me ita . . . atque consentio

JL 5348 (simply inscribed *Item* in the *Britannica*), to the German hierarchy, March 13, 1088, given at Terracina. In this portion of a longer letter Urban asserts that it is his intention to pursue the same policy as Gregory VII, whose principles Urban ratifies and approves. In JL 5348 some effort has been made to establish the exact identification of the addressees, namely, Gebhard, archbishop of Salzburg, the bishops, Altmannus of Passau, Meinhard of Würzburg, Adalbert of Worms, Wigoldus of Augsburg and Gebhard of Constance, the dukes Welpho of Bavaria, Berthold of Suabia, Berthold of Zähringen and all the faithful of Germany.

3) Ewald, p. 353

Dilectissimus filius . . . gratia possumus

JL 5352, to Willelmus, abbot of the monastery of St. Benedict at Fleury-sur-Loire, April-June, 1088. Refusal of a privilege because custom forbids that a favor be made when the recipient or his representative is absent.

4) Ewald, p. 353

Multa videntur . . . templo purificaverit

JL 5353, to Peter, bishop of Terracina, April-June, 1088. Good faith on the part of the culprits prevents many of the present evils from being formally sinful.

5) Ewald, pp. 353-354

Audivimus unde . . . est confirmare

JL 5354, to Bonizo of Sutri, April-June, 1088. Regarding

Histoire, II, 155-163; Van Hove, *Prolegomena*, pp. 326-327; Stickler, *Historia*, p. 175.

Bonizo's uncanonical election to the see of Piacenza, Urban desires that everything be put in order so that the election might perdure.

6) Ewald, p. 354

Si potest fieri . . . pace laudamus

JL 5355, to Herman, cardinal priest of the church of the *Quatuor Coronati,* April-June, 1088. Urban requests that everything possible be done to keep Bonizo in the see of Piacenza.

7) Ewald, p. 354

Sutrinus episcopus . . . solempniter intronizetur

JL 5356 (inscribed: *Urb. m. . . .*; Loewenfeld fills in the inscription thus: *M[ediolanensi archiepiscopo ?]*, April-June, 1088. Another appeal that Bonizo receive the support needed to remain as bishop of Piacenza.

8) Ewald, p. 354

Item. In Adversana civitate preter consuetudinem veterem a domino Urbano papa episcopus factus est propter dissensionem Neapolitane et Capuane ecclesie, inter quas lis fuerat, utrilibet Adversana deberet ecclesia subiacere.

This is the first of a series of historical notes that is interspersed within the framework of canons in the *Collectio Britannica.* Some of these notes which appear later in the present collection have appeared in other places, while some of them, such as the one now under consideration, appear in this one place only.[7] This historical note serves as background for the next letter. Its origin belongs either to a

[7] These historical entries are taken, it seems, from the papal register of Urban. In L. Duchesne's edition of *Le Liber Pontificalis*, Tome II (Paris: Ernest Thorin, Editeur, 1892), p. 294, footnote 6, reference is made about ". . . une suite de notices historiques relevées mot à mot dans le registre d'Urbain II . . . des exposés narritifs étaient intercalés entre les lettres. . . ." Actually this observation is made concerning the note that forms n. 11 of the present collection, but if this argument is valid for other historical notes of the collection, it is valid here.

summary made by the compiler of the *Britannica* or to an excerpt from the papal register, as was explained above.

9) Ewald, pp. 354-355

Patrem vestrem . . . reverentia suscipite

JL 5357, to the clergy of Aversa, (July,) 1088. Urban announces that he has consecrated Wimundus as bishop of Aversa because the discord between Naples and Capua has needlessly delayed the bishop's elevation beyond an acceptable limit of time.

10) Ewald, p. 355

Venerabilis viri . . . consecrationis imposuimus

JL 5358, to Iordanus, prince of Capua (here inscribed, *Urb. Iordano*; to this title Jaffé has completed the inscription thus: *Iord*[*ano principi Capuano*]), (July,) 1088. Urban repeats his message given in the preceding letter. Note that the name of the newly consecrated bishop is spelled Guimundus here and Wimundus in letter n. 9 above.

11) Ewald, p. 355

Hoc tempore Anselmo . . . obviam concurrente

This is the second of the historical notes placed in the midst of the canons of this collection. It concerns the reconciliation of Anselm, archbishop of Milan. The exact text, word for word, can be found in the *Liber Pontificalis* [8] and in the *Urbani Papae II Vita* of Peter of Pisa.[9] The account of Urban's life is exactly the same in both of these biographies; the life of Peter of Pisa was incorporated in the *Liber Pontificalis*. The final words as found in Peter's text, *Pallium fraternitati . . . benedictione transmittimus,* are not included in the note as found in the *Britannica,* but it is found in effect in the following letter.

[8] Duchesne, *Le Liber Pontificalis*, II, 293, and footnote 6.

[9] Peter's account can be found in I. M. Waterich, ed., *Pontificum Romanorum Vitae,* Tomus I, *Iohannes VIII-Urbanus II* (Lipsiae: Sumptibus Guilhelmi Engelmanni, 1862), pp. 572-573. Hereafter cited Watterich, *Vitae.*

12) Ewald, p. 356

Sicut pium . . . humiliter obedisti. Nos de reversione . . . benedictione transmittimus

JL 5359, to (Anselm,) archbishop of Milan, (July,) 1088. Urban restores to Anselm the fullness of episcopal orders and grants him the unusual favor of the pallium, although Anselm is unable to come or to present his representative to receive it.[10]

13) Ewald, p. 356

(S)citis namque . . . compage seiunctus

JL 5360, to the clergy and people of Milan, (July,) 1088. One who separates himself from the Church is a heretic, as St. Ambrose himself had asserted.

14) Ewald, p. 356

Ex presenti dispositionis . . . Aversana amitteret

JL 5361, to (John,) the archbishop of Naples, (July,) 1088. Urban explains that he consecrated Guimundus as bishop of Aversa because the needs of the Church forbade further delays.

15) Ewald, pp. 356-357

Nuper autem . . . possessio redderetur

JL 5362, to Guimundus (bishop of Aversa), (July,) 1088. Urban returns Aversa as suffragan to the see of Naples.[11]

16) Ewald, p. 357

Sane quod super . . . moribus adiuvare

JL 5363, to Guimundus, bishop (of Aversa), (July,) 1088, c. 3, C. XXIV, q. 2. It is not necessary to refuse offerings in the name of a deceased person who, though sinful, was not excommunicated. In this case a soldier had died in the act of plundering and was for this reason thought to be

[10] Cf. letter n. 3 of the *Britannica*, where a favor was denied to an absent abbot.

[11] Concerning the disputes about who was to fill the sees of Aversa and Piacenza, see Fliche, *Histoire*, VIII, 222-223.

excommunicated *ipso facto.* Because this excommunication was not in effect *nominatim* and because of previous promises of amendment, Urban absolved the man and instructs Guimundus that there is no need to refuse prayers and offerings made in the name of such a deceased.

17) Ewald, p. 357

Hoc tempore . . . depositus fuerat

Another historical notice forming a résumé of the relations at this time between Bernard, archbishop of Toledo, and Urban II.[12]

18) Ewald, pp. 357-358

Bernardo episcopo . . . habere censuimus. Inter ea vero . . . non ferendum

JL 5367, to Aldefonsus, king of Galicia in Spain, (Oct. 15,) 1088, (given at Anagni). Urban commends to the king Bernard, archbishop of Toledo, who has recently been appointed primate of Spain and given the pallium; the king is requested to free the bishop of Santiago de Compostela.[13]

19) Ewald, p. 358

Auditum nostrum . . . disquirendus adveniat

JL 5368, to the clergy and faithful of Santiago de Compostella, (Oct. 15,) 1088, (given at Anagni). Urban voices his disapproval of the acceptance of Peter by the people of Santiago, while their lawful bishop, Didacus, has been imprisoned. The diocese is put under interdict until the lawful shepherd is freed.

20) Ewald, p. 358

Pervenit ad aures . . . scelere responsurus

JL 5369, to Peter, the invader (of the diocese of Santiago

[12] For further information about this pericope see, Duchesne, *Le Liber Pontificalis*, II, 293, and footnote 7; Watterich, *Vitae*, p. 573; and Hefele-Leclercq, *Conciles*, V, I, 340, note 2.

[13] Aldefonsus is Alphonse VI, king of Castile; cf. Fliche, *Histoire*, VIII, 203.

de Compostela), (Oct. 15,) 1088, given at Anagni. Peter is summoned to the presence of the Roman Pontiff.

21) Ewald, p. 358

Toletanum siquidem . . . gravia terminabitis

JL 5370 (in the *Britannica* there is no inscription; Loewenfeld supplies it), to the archbishops of Tarragona and the rest of Spain, (Oct. 15,) 1088, (given at Anagni). Urban announces that primacy has been bestowed upon the see of Toledo.[14]

22) Ewald, p. 358

Toletano episcopo . . . datione contradidimus. Et omnia monasterio . . . habuisse noscuntur.

JL 5371 (in the *Britannica* no inscription is cited), to Hugh, abbot of Cluny, (Oct. 15,) 1088, (given at Anagni). Urban announces that Bernard, archbishop of Toledo, has been named primate and has been given the pallium; Urban takes under his special protection all the lands subject to Cluny.

23) Ewald, pp. 258-259

Ideo non rectis . . . clementes extitimus. Discretioni nostre . . . ministeria reconciliabis

JL 5378; cf. the Collection in Two Books, n. 1.

24) Ewald, p. 359

Quia consuetudo . . . eligere valeatis

JL 5379, to Bernard, abbot of the monastery of St. Martin of Tours, at Marmoutier. Because illness prevents his coming, the abbot is to send the prior of another monastery in order to receive certain privileges in the name of Bernard from the papal court.

[14] Concerning the addressee of this letter, cf. J. P. Migne, *Patrologiae Cursus Completus, Series Latina* (221 vols., Parisiis, 1844-1864), CLI, 290, footnote 8; this work is hereafter listed as *PL.*

25) Ewald, p. 359

Quamvis de electione . . . sufferentes tolleramus

JL 5380, to Peter, bishop of Pistoia, 1088. For the present Urban tolerates the uncanonical election and consecration of Peter.

26) Ewald, p. 359

Vendentes et ementes . . . habere permittas

JL 5381, to Herman, bishop of Metz, 1088. All power is suspended for simoniacal and married clerics in major orders.

27) Ewald, pp. 359-360

Cum annis essem . . . non complevi. In preterito . . . unum mancusum

This is not a letter of Urban II; rather it is from the hand of Sancho II Ramire, king of Aragon, written to assure the Pope of the king's fidelity as a vassal of the Holy See. Cf. JL 5398.

28) Ewald, p. 360

Hainricus Suessionensis . . . idem actum est

This text is an account of the oath taken by Henry, bishop of Soissons. The same text can be found in the life of Urban II by Peter of Pisa, although the section in the middle of the oath is not found in Peter's account.[15]

29) Ewald, p. 360

Si verum esse . . . tantum in domino

JL 5382, to Iordanus, prince of Capua, 1088, c. 1, C. XXXI, q. 2. A case of forced marriage is settled on the basis of the actual intention of the parties. Where there has been no consent, there can be no valid bond; therefore either party can marry again.

[15] Watterich, *Vitae*, p. 573; Duchesne, *Le Liber Pontificalis*, II, 294, note 8.

30) Ewald, pp. 360-361

Debent subditi . . . manum extendere. Multa ecclesie . . . moderanter dissimulant. Multa etiam . . . testimonio comprobantur. Scripsistis nobis . . . aliqua deposuimus. Porro Daibertum . . . dare potuit.

JL 5383, to Peter, bishop of Pistoia, and Rusticus, abbot of the monastery at Vallombrosa, 1088; part of this letter is in c. 24, C. I, q. 7. A request for obedience and trust; Urban explains that the extreme straits of the Church may well be the reason for some changes of policy. Finally Urban explains the case of a deacon ordained contrary to Canon Law by a heretical bishop; the deacon is to be re-ordained. This last part of the canon concerns the very disputed point of whether ordination by one guilty of the heresy of simony is valid or not.[16]

31) Ewald, p. 361

Porro de libertate . . . hactenus habuerunt

JL 5384, to (Hugh,) the abbot of Cluny, 1089. The special exemption given to all the lands held by Cluny does not in any manner restrict the rights already enjoyed by certain bishops.

32) Ewald, pp. 361-362

Sed te sub . . . distuleris. De presbiterorum . . . manum imponas

JL 5385, to Rainaldus, archbishop of Reims, 1089. Urban rebukes this archbishop for neglecting to obtain papal confirmation of the pallium bestowed *sede vacante* by the cardinals. The second portion of this letter permits the sons of priests to be ordained, so long as they are of good morals.

33) Ewald, p. 362

Nosti frater . . . exigente restitueres. Nosti enim . . . debent intuitus

JL 5386, to Anselm, archbishop of Milan, 1089. Anselm is given the pallium and all clerics promoted by his simoniacal

[16] Cf. *infra*, pp. 160-161 where this question is discussed.

predecessor, Theobald, are confirmed in their rank, provided that they themselves are not guilty of simony.

34) Ewald, p. 363

Eorum qui in . . . non exsufflamus

JL 5387 (to the count of Salerno; all that remains of the mutilated inscription of this letter is "*. . . mlis . . . tano;*" Loewenfeld notes that Ewald has incorrectly supplied the inscription thus: *Comiti Saleritano*), 1089. The Masses of canonically ordained priests are still regarded as valid, even if they depart from the fold. Concerning the problem of the inscription, see the note at JL 5387 and Loewenfeld, *Epistolae Pontificum Romanorum ineditae,* p. 62, letter n. 127 and footnote a.

35) Ewald, p. 363

Notificamus tibi . . . aliquam iniungatur

JL 5388, to (Cyriacus,) the bishop of Genoa, 1089, c. 3, C. XXXV, q. 6. Concerning the value of testimony given under oath about the close relationship of the partners in a marriage, Urban says that, if blood relatives or suitable witnesses will swear that the impediment of consanguinity was present, then the parties should be forced to separate; that, if this relationship is asserted, but not under oath, then the parties are to be left together.

36) Ewald, p. 363

Quod de monasterio . . . bona consumere

JL 5389, to Pontius, bishop of Rodez, France, 1089. Urban writes of the appointment of an apostolic nuncio.

37) Ewald, p. 363

Quia simpliciter . . . officio confirmamus

JL 5390, to Peter, bishop of León, Spain, 1089, c. 14, D. LVI. Urban dispenses a bishop, born out of wedlock, on the grounds that his life and morals were upright.

38) Ewald, pp. 363-364

Diu excommunicationis . . . metus incutiatur. Ut ab excommunicatis . . . recuperari debeant. Si quem vero . . . ministerio sequestramus

JL 5393, cf. Collection in Two Books, n. 2. The three parts of this entry are part of the larger letter found in the Collection in Two Books, n. 2.

39) Ewald, p. 364

Auctoritas nostre . . . mancipere procurent

JL 5396, to the clergy and people of Bergamo, April-June, 1089. Urban explains the manner of expiating for the crime of simony.

40) Ewald, p. 364

Audivimus te . . . venire permittas

JL 5397, to William Rufus, king of England, April-June, 1089. Urban expresses his regret that William II of England has expelled the bishop of Durham and forbidden the latter to come to the papal court; Urban demands that the bishop and his accusers, if there are any, come to the pontiff.[17]

41) Ewald, p. 364

Fili in Christo . . . modo dubitaveris. De neptis tue . . . coniunxit invitam.

JL 5399, cf. Collection of *Codex Ms. Vaticanus Latinus 4977,* n. 1. This canon adds in its first part Urban's heartfelt congratulations upon learning of the full support of Sancho I, king of Aragon (1063-1094).

42) Ewald, p. 364

Si quem lapsorum . . . intererit estimandum

JL 5404, to (. . . *no*) bishop, July, 1089. The rehabilitation of major clerics is left to the decision of the bshop concern-

[17] Cf. Norman F. Cantor, *Church, Kingship and Lay Investiture in England, 1089-1135* (Princeton, New Jersey: Princeton University Press, 1958), p. 51. Hereafter referred to as Cantor, *England.*

ing probity of life. The name of the addressee has not survived. All that the manuscript has is ". . . *no episcopo.*"

43) Ewald, p. 365

Mandamus fraternitati . . . precipicio demergantur

JL 5405, to William, archbishop of Rouen (the manuscript has "(.) . . *mo . . . gensi archiepiscopo*"; Loewenfeld has supplied the addressee thus: *Willelmo Rotomagensi*), (July,) 1089. Urban commutes the penalty of those sent into exile for the benefit of their families; one year in exile was made the maximum sentence. For the remaining time a lesser penance could be enjoined.

44) Ewald, p. 365

Eo tempore Artaldus . . . sacerdotio repellar

This is not a letter or canon of Urban, but another historical note. This note is found in Gratian, c. 2, C. VIII, q. 3, where the word "*Alanesis*" was mistaken for "*Arelatensis.*" Since Narbonne is mentioned, it is clear that Arles is a mistake, because Arles is not in the metropolitan province of Narbonne. Actually the diocese mentioned is Elne in the province of Narbonne, whose seat was later transferred to Perpignan. This historical note is of interest in that it is the only such passage which recurs with frequency in the collections of Urban's time. Ewald notes that this notice is not from Petrus Pisanus, but there is no indication about whence the text was drawn.

45) Ewald, p. 365

Quod vero Alanensis . . . non rennuant

JL 5407, to Dalmatius, archbishop of Narbonne, July-Sept., 1089. Urban commands that the clergy of Elne bear no arms, and that they refrain from treating benefices as though they were hereditary possessions; the clergy are to obey Artaldus their lawful bishop.

46) Ewald, p. 365

Clericis igitur . . . precepta custodiant

JL 5408, to the clergy of Elne, July-Sept., 1089. Urban repeats his message of letter n. 45.

47) Ewald, p. 366

a) *Anno dominicae incarnationis 1089, pontificatus domni Urbani pape secundo, indictione XII, IV Idus Sept. congregata est apud Melphiam Apuliae urbem, eius iussu sinodus episcoporum LXX, abbatum XII.*

This historical note is from the Chronicle of Bernoldus.[18]

b) *Sanctorum patrum . . . presbiterum consecretur*
Canon 1-4, Council of Melfi, Sept. 10, 1089, Mansi, XX, 721-723. These canons forbade simony and clerical incontinence; major clerics were permitted to continue in a marriage with a wife who had been a virgin; and the canonical age for the major Orders was established at 14 or 15 for the subdiaconate, at 24 or 25 for the diaconate, and at 30 for the priesthood. Canon 3 of this pericope is in c. 12, D. XXXII; cf. Collection of *Codex Ms. Vaticanus Latinus 4977,* n. 4.

After the canons of Melfi, there follows:

Responderunt Iusta et canonica definitio ab omnibus observetur. Eodem die talia sunt decreta coram sinodo promulgata.

This canon follows:

Nullus laicus . . . est offeratur
Canon 5, Council of Melfi, Mansi, XX, 723. The permission of the Pope or the local bishop is needed to bestow one's tithes on a monastery or a community of canons regular.

After this canon others follow:

Illud summopere . . . regulariter commendatus
Canons 8-10, Council of Melfi, Mansi, XX, 723. Lay investiture and vagrant clerics and monks were forbidden.

Next this pericope is found:

Responsum est ab omnibus. Fiat. Sextum demum die, postquam diutius est de moribus ecclesie disputatum, adiunxit . . .

[18] Found in Watterich, *Vitae,* p. 579 and Mansi, XX, 725.

Then the next series of canons is found:

Ne gravamen aliquod . . . opportunitate ferat

Canons 11-16, Council of Melfi, Mansi, XX, 723-724. As Loewenfeld notes,[19] the version of the Council of Melfi as given in Mansi does not agree completely with that of the *Britannica.*

In last place there is the following note:

Interim dum agerentur hec Rogerius dux domno Urbano iuravit. Cuius iuramenti tenor infra scriptus est.[20]

The Collection of Turin in Seven Books

This collection contains more than 1400 chapters; it was composed about the year 1100 by a promoter of the Gregorian reform. The Collection in 74 Titles forms the chief source for the present collection.[21]

1) Fournier-Le Bras, *Histoire,* II, 165, footnote 3, in Book V of the collection

Extraordinaria pollutio . . . et damnabilis

JL 5730, to Hugh, bishop of Grenoble, 1088-1099, c. 11. C. XXXV, q. 2. Serious sins of impurity, so long as they do not terminate in sexual intercourse, do not give rise to the impediment of affinity; only carnal *copula* is the basis of such impediments.[22]

The *Polycarpus*

The collection which is known as the *Polycarpus* was made between 1104 and 1106 by Gregory, cardinal of the church of

[19] Jaffé, *Regesta Pontificum Romanorum,* I, 664.

[20] Cf. the citation in Jaffé, *Regesta Pontificum Romanorum,* after JL 5408.

[21] Cf. Fournier-Le Bras, *Histoire,* II, 163-167; Van Hove, *Prolegomena,* p. 327; and Stickler, *Historia,* p. 187.

[22] Since the manuscript of this collection was not available, it was necessary to rely on the report given by Fournier-Le Bras in the place cited above in the previous footnote.

St. Chrysogonus, Rome. It has exerted considerable influence upon later collections, and itself shows marked Gregorian tendencies.[23]

1) folio 58r lib. 3, tit. 10, cap. 24

Illud quoque precipimus . . . unquam exigatur

Canon 13, Council of Piacenza, March 1-7, 1095, Mansi, XX, 806. Nothing may be demanded for confirmation, baptism or burial, on the grounds that such a practice would be simony.

2) folio 100r lib. 4, tit. 31, cap. 82

Due inquid [inquit ?] leges . . . non estis sub lege

JL 5760, a decree of Urban II (there is no addressee), 1088-1099, c. 2, C. XIX, q. 2. This canon attributes to Urban the contention that, since the religious life is a higher vocation than that of the secular clergy, a cleric can enter religion, even though his bishop is unwilling. This canon is called a forgery by Berardi.[24]

3) folio 100v lib. 4, tit. 31, cap. 83

Mandamus et mandantes . . . in choro maneat

This canon is not from Urban II, although it is found here under his name; it is from chapter 25 of Anselm of Havelburg's treatise, *Liber de Ordine Canonicorum Regularium* (*PL,* CLXXXVIII, 1109). This text is ascribed to Urban II in Gratian at c. 2, C. XIX, q. 3.[25] The canon contains a prohibition from becoming monks on the part of canons

[23] For this collection *codex ms. Vaticanus latinus 1354* was used. Cf. Fournier-Le Bras, *Histoire,* II, 169-185; Van Hove, *Prolegomena,* p. 327; Stickler, *Historia,* pp. 178-179; A. Theiner, *Disquisitiones Criticae in praecipuas canonum et decretalium collectiones* (Romae: in Collegio Urbano, 1836), pp. 342-345 (hereafter cited Theiner, *Disquisitiones*).

[24] *Canones,* II, 2, 368-369.

[25] *Corpus Iuris Canonici* (ed. Lipsiensis 2. post Aemilii Ludovici Richteri curas . . . instruxit Aemilius Friedberg, 2 vols., Lipsiae: ex Officina Bernhardi Tauchnitz, 1879-1881; editio anastaticè repetita, Lipsiae: Tauchnitz, 1928), c. 2, C. XIX, q. 3, footnote 3 (hereafter cited, Friedberg). Cf. Berardi, *Canones,* II, 2, 376, from whom Friedberg got his information.

regular. Such a transfer is allowed them only in the event of an earlier public lapse. All those who have transferred contrary to this prescript are ordered to return and to do penance.

4) folio 140v lib. 6, tit. 10, cap. 14

Compatimur infirmitati tue . . . et dampnabilis

JL 5730; cf. the Collection of Turin in Seven Books, n. 1.

5) folio 172r lib. 7, tit. 10, cap. 14

Ordinationes ab heresiarchis . . . aliquid seueritati

Canon 8-12, Council of Piacenza, March 1-7, 1095, Mansi, XX, 806, c. 5, C. IX, q. 1. This canon has no inscription here in the *Polycarpus*. The entire group of canons from the Council of Piacenza concerns the abuses connected with sacred ordination. Among the evils reprobated are ordinations by bishops guilty of simony, and the invasion of another's see; those who had permitted themselves to be ordained by an unworthy prelate could be tolerated, so long as they had not knowingly sought ordination from a simoniac, and provided that the candidates' lives were otherwise irreproachable. This group of canons was repeated as canons 8-11, Council of Rome, April 24-30, 1909, Mansi, XX, 963.

The First Collection of Prague

This collection was compiled during the pontificate of Urban's successor, Paschal II (1099-1118); it depends heavily upon the *Polycarpus* and was composed by one favoring the reforms of Gregory VII. A second redaction was made between 1123 and 1154; it includes materials taken from the works of Ivo of Chartres.[26]

[26] Cf. F. Schulte, "Über drei in Prager Handschriften enthaltene Canonen-Sammlungen," in *Sitzungsberichte der philosophisch-historischen Classe der kaiserlichen Akademie der Wissenschaften* (of Vienna), LVII (1868), Heft 1, 175-221; hereafter cited Schulte. See also Van Hove, *Prolegomena*, p. 328; Stickler, *Historia*, p. 188.

1) Schulte, p. 211 cap. 281

Sane quod super . . . moribus adiuvare

JL 5363, cf. *Collectio Britannica,* n. 16.

2) Schulte, p. 211 cap. 282

Excommunicatorum interfectoribus . . . flagitio contraxerunt

JL 5536, to Godfrey, bishop of Lucca, 1088-1095, c. 47, C. XXIII, q. 5. Those who have killed heretics out of zeal for the Church of Christ should make satisfaction; but they are not to be considered guilty of homicide.

The Collection in Seven Books

Collected in central Italy sometime between 1112 and 1120, this collection displays dependence upon several earlier works; among them one can count the *Polycarpus,* the *Decretum* of Burchard of Worms, the Pseudo-Isidorian decretals, the collection of Anselm of Lucca and the *Liber de Vita Christiana* of Bonizo of Sutri. The texts show a marked Gregorian influence, although there are included those later texts which mitigated the earlier rigor of the reform.[27]

1) folio 81r lib. 3, tit. 79, cap. 5

Mandamus et mandantes . . . in choro maneat

Here inscribed: *Urbanus papa II;* this canon is falsely attributed to Urban. Cf. the *Polycarpus,* n. 3.

2) folio 88r lib. 4, tit. 9, cap. 9

Ea que a sanctis . . . habere non patimur

Canons 1-7, Council of Piacenza, March 1-7, 1095, Mansi, XX, 805. These canons are in Gratian as follows: canons 1 and 2 are found in c. 5, C. I, q. 3; canons 3 and 4 are found in c. 108, C. I, q. 1; canons 5, 6 and 7 are found in

[27] The *codex ms. Vaticanus latinus 1346* was the source of this section of the report. See Fournier-Le Bras, *Histoire,* II, 185-192; Van Hove, *Prolegomena,* p. 328; Stickler, *Historia,* p. 187; and Theiner, *Disquisitiones,* pp. 345-355.

c. 1, C. I, q. 5. This entire group of seven canons forms an elementary platform against the simony which was rampant during Urban's pontificate. The first two canons deal with simony in a general way and state that every simoniacal contract is void; the last five enactments concern simony in connection with holy orders and ecclesiastical benefices. These same canons are repeated again in the last council held by Urban at Rome, April 24-30, 1099; cf. the *Polycarpus,* n. 1, with the observations made in that place and Mansi, XX, 961.

3) folio 114r lib. 5, tit. 30, cap. 6

Due inquit leges . . . non estis sub lege

JL 5760; cf. the *Polycarpus,* n. 2.

4) folio 132v lib. 6, tit. 25, cap. 8

A die septuagesime . . . nullo modo contrahantur

Canon 4, Council of Benevento, March 28, 1091, Mansi, XX, 739. This canon forbids the celebration of marriage during the "closed times;" to wit, from Septuagesima until the octave of Easter, and from the beginning of Advent until the octave of the Epiphany. The transmission of this canon involves several complications, and therefore some remarks need to be made here. This canon is found in Gratian at c. 10, C. XXXIII, q. 4, but is ascribed to the Council of Lérida, Spain, held in 546. This same canon is found on folio 103r in the Collection in Nine Books (*codex ms. Vaticanus Bibl. Cap. S. Petri C. 118*) and is also ascribed to the same Spanish council in this collection. The problem is to discover the actual origin of the canon. If one examines the canons of the Council of Lérida, one will find the present canon placed at the end of the list of canons and put into a special section labeled "*fragmenta.*" (cf. Mansi, VI, 616). A notation is placed beside the canon indicating that the canon is from the *Decretum* of Burchard of Worms. And if one checks the fourth canon of Liber IX in Burchard's *Decretum,* one finds the canon in question with the remark that it was taken from canon 3 of the Council of Lérida.

Here, however, it is necessary to observe that Burchard of Worms adulterated the inscriptions of the texts, when he put them into his *Decretum,* in an attempt to add the authority of antiquity and thus to gain wider acceptance for them.[28] In his research Fournier established that the canon under discussion actually is derived from chapter 112 of the *Capitula* of Herardus, archbishop of Tours, written in 858 (*PL,* CXXI, 771). Therefore, on the basis of Fournier's study, it is safe to say that Burchard took the substance of Herardus' text and placed it into his *Decretum* with the false inscription linking it to the Council of Lérida. There is, however, more to the matter, since the same enactment, couched in somewhat different words, is found in the Council of Seligenstadt, convened in the year, 1023, which was approximately one year after the completion of the *Decretum* of Burchard. The problem, then, is to determine how the text, substantially identical with that found in the *Decretum,* was assumed into the Council of Seligenstadt. Again it is Fournier who has solved the difficulty, for he has noted that Burchard was very influential in the convocation of the latter council.[29] Fournier admits that the striking similarity between the present canon and that found in Seligenstadt, and also between other canons of Burchard and this council,

[28] P. Fournier has shown by extensive examination and comparison that Burchard used many apocryphal inscriptions from councils, and that he preferred to cite those of the Carolingian epoch; one example he gives is the Council of Lérida. Cf. Fournier, "Études critiques sur le Décret de Burchard de Worms," *Nouvelle Revue Historique de Droit Français et Étranger,* XXXIV (1910), 78, 314 and 578.

[29] P. Fournier, "Le 'Decret' de Burchard de Worms. Ses caractères, son influence," *Revue d'Histoire ecclésiastique,* XII (1911), 687, footnote 1. The actual citation in the footnote mentions that canon 3 of the Council of Seligenstadt parallels the *Decretum* of Burchard, X, 4. This reference must be an error in which X, 4 was printed instead of IX, 4, because X, 4 is completely out of context (it deals with sacrificing to idols), while IX, 4 concerns the same material as canon 3 of the Council of Seligenstadt, namely, the celebration of marriage during the so-called "closed times." This error in numbers is surely the fault of a typesetter and the same identical mistake has been repeated to the letter and number in Fournier-Le Bras, *Histoire,* I, 418, footnote 1.

testify to the influence of Burchard at that council. The present canon has had a rather interesting background; it began with Herardus of Tours, was incorporated into the *Decretum* of Burchard (and there ascribed to the Council of Lérida) and then was repeated in the Council of Seligenstadt. The canon was finally reiterated in the Council of Benevento by Urban II.

5) folio 188r canon added after the conclusion of the collection

Ordinationes que . . . aliquid seueritati

Canons 8-12, Council of Piacenza, cf. the *Polycarpus,* n. 5. This collection concludes with folio 166r; the present canon is found among many canons that have been added to the collection.

The Recension " Bb " of the Collection of Anselm of Lucca

This second edition of Anselm's collection was made at Lucca sometime during the years 1109 to 1118 by a follower of the Gregorian reform movement. The collector made additions, changed some rubrics and filled in gaps.[30]

1) folio 162v lib. 6, cap. 150

Presbiterorum filios . . . fuerint conuersari

Canon 14, Council of Melfi, Sept. 10, 1089, Mansi, XX, 724; c. 1, D. LVI. The sons of priests are to be removed from the sacred ministry of the altar, unless they prove themselves by entering a house of canons regular or of monks.

2) folio 166r lib. 6, cap. 175

Nullus episcopus . . . iurare compellat

JL 5759, a decree of Urban II, 1088-1099, c. 23, C. XXII, q. 5. No bishop is to demand that his clerics make an oath

[30] Fournier-Le Bras, *Histoire,* II, 193-195; P. Fournier, "Observations sur diverses recensions de la collection canonique d'Anselme de Lucques," *Annales de l'Université de Grenoble,* XIII (1901), 427-458, esp. 450-454; Van Hove, *Prolegomena,* p. 328; Stickler, *Historia,* p. 187; Theiner, *Disquisitiones,* p. 367. This collection is found in *codex ms. Vaticanus Barb. latinus 535.*

to himself except concerning the ecclesiastical charge of the cleric.

3) folio 199r lib. 7, cap. 185

Nullus omnino laicus . . . die illo accipiat

Canon 4, Council of Benevento, March 28, 1091, Mansi, XX, 739. From Ash Wednesday everyone, including all laymen, are forbidden to eat meat; every man, woman and cleric is to receive ashes upon his head on this day.

4) folio 205v-206r addition to lib. 7; the cap. is unnumbered, but it would be 229

Due inquit leges . . . non estis sub lege

JL 5760, cf. the *Polycarpus*, n. 2.

5) folio 206 follows the above cap.

Mandamus et mandantes . . . in choro maneat

Inscribed *Idem urbanus papa II*, this canon is not Urban's. Cf. the information given at the *Polycarpus*, n. 3.

6) folio 208v added at the end of lib. 7

Statuimus ne . . . cautione suscipiat

JL 5763, to the monastery of St. Ruf, at Valence, 1092-1099, c. 3, C. XIX, q. 3. A canon regular who wished to enter the monastic life needed the permission of his chapter to do so. Attention should be called to the error in the footnotes of Friedberg's *Decretum* of Gratian. In footnote 13 at c. 3, C. XIX, q. 3, the source of the canon is given as "Jaffé no. 4313." But this number in Jaffé is the famous canon, *Due sunt leges*. Perhaps since both of these canons appear on the same page in Friedberg, he confused the Jaffé numbers. At any rate the information given above is the correct source according to the second edition of Jaffé's *Regesta*. However, in this same second edition of Jaffé, JL 5763 is said to be found in "*Gratiani decr.* c. XIX, qu. 3, c. 2." This information is also erroneous, since this entry is located at chapter 3 of the third question, not at chapter 2.

The Recension " C " of the Collection of Anselm of Lucca

The third revision of Anselm's collection was completed either about the year 1115 or 1125, probably in southern Italy. Many spurious canons found their way into this collection, which is Gregorian in tone.[31]

1) folio 172v-174r lib. 3 after cap. 131

Saluator post dictum . . . coronam uitae

JL 5743, to Lucius, *prepositus* of the church of St. Iuventius (the present manuscript has " *Vincentius* ") in Pavia, 1088-1099. Portions of this letter are found at c. 8, C. I, q. 3; c. 12, C. I, q. 3, and c. 6, D. XXXII. This is a very long letter on the subject of simony.

2) folio 413v added at the conclusion of lib. 8

Sane quia monachorum . . . iura seruentur

Canon 4 (according to the *Codex Cencii*), Council of Clermont, Nov. 18-28, 1095, Mansi, XX, 902; c. 6, C. XVI, q. 2. This canon lays down the rules for parish churches under monastic control. The bishop was to appoint, with the abbot's consent, the chaplain who exercised the actual care of souls. The spiritual ministry was directly under the control of the bishop; the temporal administration was under the supervision of the abbot. At the Council of Nîmes this text is found again as canon 1 (July 8-12, 1096, Mansi, XX, 933). The Council of Nîmes was for the most part a repetition and an explanation of the decrees of the Council of Clermont.[32] This canon is found at the conclusion of the eighth Book in an entirely different script. Reference to it may be found in Friedberg at c. 2, C. IX, q. 2, *palea,* footnote 14, but in another connection. Cf. n. 27 of Appendix II to this section.

[31] This recension may be found in *codex ms. Vaticanus latinus 4983.* Cf. Fournier-Le Bras, *Histoire,* II, 195-198, Van Hove, *Prolegomena,* p. 328; Stickler, *Historia,* p. 188; and Fournier, *art. cit.* in *Annales de l'Université de Grenoble,* XIII (1901), 427-458, esp. 443-449.

[32] Hefele-Leclercq, *Conciles,* V, I, 447-449 together with 399-404.

3) folio 583v lib. 12, cap. 74

Ut ab excommunicatis . . . est precipua concedendum

JL 5393, this is one of the excerpts of the letter reported in the Collection of Two Books, n. 2.

4) folio 583v-584r lib. 12, cap. 75

Discretioni nostrae uidetur . . . misteria reconciliabis

JL 5378; cf. the Collection in Two Books, n. 2.

The Italian Collection in Three Books

Compiled by a Roman or one imbued with the Roman spirit of reform about the year 1112, this collection drew upon all of the important contemporary collections. These include the Pseudo-Isidorian decretals, the Collection in 74 Titles, that of Anselm of Lucca, the *Polycarpus,* the *Decretum* of Burchard of Worms, and other collections of the time which were favorable to the reform movement.[33]

1) folio 19v lib. 2, tit. 1, cap. 40

Presbiterorum filios . . . fuerint conuersari

Canon 14, Council of Melfi, cf. the Recension " Bb " of the Collection of Anselm of Lucca, n. 1.

2) folio 25r lib. 2, tit. 5, cap. 35

Due inquid [inquit ?] leges . . . non estis sub lege

JL 5760, cf. the Polycarpus, n. 2.

3) folio 25r lib. 2, tit. 5, cap. 36

Mandamus et mandantes . . . in choro maneat

This is not a canon of Urban II; cf. the *Polycarpus,* n. 3. The canon follows the preceding canon; the first is inscribed: *Dominus papa urbanus in cap. sancti rufi;* the present canon, which is the second in the series, is marked *Eiusdem.*

[33] *Codex ms. Vaticanus latinus 3831* was used in the investigation of this canonical collection. Cf. Fournier-Le Bras, *Histoire,* II, 198-203; Van Hove, *Prolegomena,* p. 328; and Stickler, *Historia,* p. 179. This collection also bears the title: *Liber romani ordinis vel canonum.*

4) folio 34r lib. 2, tit. 8, cap. 13

Exteriores ecclesie . . . possidere existimat

JL 5743; this is one of the portions of the longer letter found in the Recension "C" of the Collection of Anselm of Lucca, n. 1. This particular fragment can be found at c. 12, C. 1, q. 3. In the "*notationes correctorum*" at this place it is stated that the opening words of this canon are probably a *dictum Gratiani.* This conjecture appears to be false, since the exact canon is found here as in Gratian, including the part that is Urban's and the part that is not his.

5) folio 34v lib. 2, tit. 8, cap. 27

Ea que a sanctis . . . esse decernimus

Canons 1-4, Council of Piacenza; this canon forms the first part of that reported in the Collection in Seven Books, n. 2.

6) folio 34v lib. 2, tit. 8, cap. 28

Quicumque sane . . . non patimur

Canons 5-7, Council of Piacenza; cf. these same canons as mentioned in the Collection in Seven Books, n. 2. There is some mix-up among the paging of the manuscript at this point. The present canon begins on what is folio 34v, but it is concluded on what would be called 34r; these two folios are not photographed alongside of each other. The only way to be certain of the order of the folios at this point is to check the canons at the beginning and end of each folio.

7) folio 34r (see the preceding note about the mix-up in pagination) lib. 2, tit. 8, cap. 29

Ordinationes que . . . aliquid seueritati

Canons 8-12, Council of Piacenza; there are treated in the *Polycarpus,* n. 5.

8) folio 35r lib. 2, tit. 9, cap. 3 (numbering doubtful because of pagination)

Qui aliorum errorem . . . heresiarcha dicendus est

This *capitulum* is inscribed *ex decretis urbani pape;* the text does not belong to Urban I. It is found in Gratian at c. 32, C. XXIV, q. 3, and is there inscribed *Item Urbanus Papa.* In footnote 384 at this place, Friedberg calls this text a "*caput incertum.*" Berardi prefers to consider the canon as genuine; according to him similar ideas are to be found in canon 13, Council of Toulouse, held in 1056 under Pope Victor II (Mansi, XIX, 849) and Urban's letter to Gebhard, bishop of Constance, which Berardi erroneously claims was written to the German hierarchy.[34] In his list of canons, however, Theiner (1804-1874) prefers to identify the present text as belonging to Urban I.[35] As a conclusion one may consider this canon as doubtfully belonging to Urban II, until something certain is proved.

9) folio 35r lib. 2, tit. 9, cap. 4

Quorum uero uices . . . super omnem terram

The source for this canon is unknown; in the present manuscript it lacks an inscription, but comes after the preceding canon; it is also found in Gratian under Urban's name (at c. 6, D. LXVIII, *Item Urbanus*). Friedberg (in footnote 77) says only that this is a "*caput incertum.*" But Theiner maintains that this fragment belongs to Urban II.[36] Berardi prefers Paschal II to Urban. That part of the canon which begins, "*Pro patribus . . .*" is part of St. Augustine's commentary on Psalm 44, which somehow became mixed into the text.[37]

10) folio 103v-104r lib. 3, tit. 7, cap. 69

Illud quoque precipimus . . . unquam exigatur

Canon 13, Council of Piacenza; cf. the *Polycarpus,* n. 1.

11) folio 106v-107r lib. 3, tit. 8, cap. 36

Statuimus etiam ut . . . more solito fiat

Canon 14, Council of Piacenza, March 1-7, 1095, Mansi,

[34] *Canones*, III, 457.

[35] *Disquisitiones*, appendix, p. 117, s. v. *Qui aliorum.*

[36] *Disquisitiones*, appendix, p. 127, s. v. *Quorum vero.*

[37] *Canones*, II, 2, 371.

XX, 806; c. 4, D. LXXVI. The rules for the fasting of the four Ember weeks are given. This is the first canon of Council of Piacenza which is not repeated at the April synod of Rome in 1099. The first 13 canons of Piacenza are found as the first 12 of this Roman synod. The present canon appears only in the place cited above.

12) folio 119r lib. 3, tit. 11, cap. 128

Post susceptum uero . . . prohibet iungi

JL 6436 (Paschal II; actually this canon is here inscribed: *Urbanus episcopus in sancta sinodo placentie*), to Bonussenior, bishop of Reggio-Emilia, April 26, 1100-1115, given at the Lateran, c. 5, C. XXX, q. 3 (where the canon is ascribed to Paschal II). The rules of spiritual and carnal affinity for marriage are given. The canon certainly belongs to Paschal II.[38]

The Collection in Nine Books

This collection is a revision of the preceding Collection in Three Books. It was made about the year 1125 in the same place as its exemplar. The scribe has so arranged this collection that space has been left within the body of canons for new legislation to be added in its proper place.[39]

1) folio 14v at the very end of lib. 1

Nullus in episcopatum . . . fieri permittimus

Canon 1, Council of Benevento, March 28, 1091, Mansi, XX, 737; c. 4, D. LX. This canon is found with no inscription. Every candidate for the episcopate must be in sacred orders, namely the diaconate and the priesthood; for special reasons a subdeacon was eligible.

[38] Cf. Berardi, *Canones*, II, 2, 382-383; Kehr, *Italia Pontificia* (8 vols. in 9, Berolini: apud Weidmannos, 1906-1935), letter n. 474, V, 367; P. Gams, *Series Episcoporum Ecclesiae Catholicae* (Graz: Akademische Druck -u. Verlagsanstalt, 1957), p. 763.

[39] This collection is found in *codex ms. Vaticanus Bibl. S. Petri C. 118.* Cf. Fournier-Le Bras, *Histoire*, II, 203-208; Van Hove, *Prolegomena*, p. 328; Stickler, *Historia*, p. 179; Theiner, *Disquisitiones*, pp. 383-397.

2) folio 17r lib. 2, tit. 14, cap. 11

Presbiterorum filios . . . fuerint conuersari

Canon 14, Council of Melfi, cf. the recension " Bb " of the Collection of Anselm of Lucca, n. 1.

3) folio 23r lib. 2, tit. 37, cap. 25

Due inquit leges . . . non estis sub lege

JL 5760; see the *Polycarpus*, n. 2.

4) folio 23r lib. 2, tit. 37, cap. 26

Mandamus et mandantes . . . in choro maneat

Inscribed *eiusdem*, after the preceding canon of Urban II, the present canon is erroneously attributed to him; cf. the *Polycarpus*, n. 3.

5) folio 23v lib. 2, tit. 37, cap. 32

Statuimus ne . . . cautione suscipiat

JL 5763; cf. the recension " Bb " of the Collection of Anselm of Lucca, n. 6.

6) folio 30r lib. 3, tit. 46, cap. 1 (*unicum*)

Questi sunt preterea . . . missas audiunt

As found here the present canon is not ascribed to Urban II; there can be little doubt, however, that it was repeated in substance by Urban at the Council of Melfi, Sept. 10, 1089, Mansi, XX, 725. This canon is found at c. 46, C. XVI, q. 1; in Gratian the inscription is: *in Magontiensi Concilio*. Actually this *capitulum* is canon 19 of the second Council of Chalon-sur-Saône, held in the year 813, Mansi, XIV, 97. Cf. especially the note of the *Correctores* at c. 46, C. XVI, q. 1, in which they note that a certain Vatican *codex*, containing two councils of Urban II, has a very similar canon: *Perlatum est . . . missas audiunt, et infantes eorum baptizantur.*

7) folio 31r lib. 3, tit. 53, cap. 1

Ea que a sanctis . . . esse decernimus

Canons 1-4, Council of Piacenza; cf. the Collection in Seven Books, n. 2 and the Italian Collection in Three Books, n. 5.

8) folio 31r lib. 3, tit. 53, cap. 2

Quicumque sane . . . habere non patimur

Canons 5-7, Council of Piacenza; cf. the last part of the three sections mentioned in n. 2 of the Collection in Seven Books and the Italian Collection in Three Books, n. 6.

9) folio 31r-31v lib. 3, tit. 57, cap. 2

Exteriores ecclesie . . . possidere existimat

JL 5743; concerning the first part of this canon especially, cf. the Italian Collection in Three Books, n. 4.

10) folio 33v lib. 3, tit. 62, cap. 8

Sane quia monachorum . . . iura seruentur

Canon 4, Council of Clermont according to the *Codex Cencii*; cf. the recension " C " of the Collection of Anselm of Lucca, n. 2.

11) folio 33v-34r lib. 3, tit. 62 cap. 9

Saluator predicit . . . coronam uite

JL 5743; cf. recension " C " of the Collection of Anselm of Lucca, n. 1. Note that the opening words of this letter are found in various forms; this can be explained by way of scribal errors.

12) folio 58v lib. 5, tit. 17, cap. 2

Curatos wigoni comiti . . . deo quam hominibus

JL 5724, to the bishops of Embrun, Gap and Die, France, 1088-1099, c. 5, C. XV, q. 6. The opening word of this canon should be *Iuratos*. Urban forbids soldiers to serve under the leadership of an excommunicated count.

13) folio 91r lib. 7, tit. 50, cap. 7

Illud quoque precipimus . . . unquam exigatur

Canon 13, Council of Piacenza; cf. n. 1, of the *Polycarpus*.

14) folio 92v lib. 7, tit. 60, cap. 12

Statuimus etiam ut . . . more solito fiat

Canon 14, Council of Piacenza, cf. the Italian Collection in Three Books, n. 11.

15) folio 101v-102r lib. 8, tit. 47, cap. 21

De neptis tue . . . de uiro est sentiendum

JL 5399, cf. the Collection of *Codex Ms. Vaticanus Latinus 4977,* n. 1.

16) folio 102r lib. 8, tit. 47, cap. 22

Si uerum esse . . . tantum in domino nubat

JL 5382, cf. the *Collectio Britannica,* n. 29.

17) folio 103r lib. 8, tit. 47, cap. 49

Notificamus ut tres . . . aliquam iniungatur

JL 5388, cf. the *Collectio Britannica,* n. 35. Note that the word, *tibi,* has been omitted from the opening words.

The Collection of *Codex Ms. Vaticanus Latinus 3829*

The author of this compilation has gathered together in chronological order decretals of the Roman Pontiff from Pope Linus to Paschal II (1099-1118). This was an attempt to show the historical development of pontifical legislation made during the pontificate of Gelasius II (1118-1119) probably in Italy. There is much taken from the Pseudo-Isidorian collection.[40]

1) folio 279v at the end of the collection in a rustic hand

Ut ab excommunicatis . . . precipua est concedendum

JL 5393, this is one of the excerpts of the letter considered in the Collection of Two Books, n. 2.

2) folio 280v sole canon on this folio at the end of the collection

Conuenit troie . . . non prohibeantur

Canon 1, Council of Troia, March 11, 1093, Mansi, XX, 789-790; c. 4, C. XXXV, q. 6. This canon concerns the separation of spouses who are suspected of being impeded from marriage by close ties of consanguinity. If the parties make a confession of the fact, or if persons will swear concerning

[40] Fournier-Le Bras, *Histoire,* II, 210-218; Van Hove, *Prolegomena,* p. 329; Stickler, *Historia,* p. 188.

the impediment, cohabitation must cease; if no such evidence can be obtained, the parties are to be left in peace; if they know within themselves that the allegation is true then they are guilty of a serious offense, and are *ipso facto* excommunicated.

3) folio 283v at the conclusion

Porro eos qui ecclesiam . . . canonum preiudicio

JL 5740, to Vitalis, priest of Brescia, 1088-1099, c. 2, C. I, q. 5. A cleric guilty of selling churches is by special dispensation of Urban permitted to retain his ecclesiastical office, if he has otherwise repented in a house of canons regular or in a monastery, where he has proved himself otherwise commendable.

The Collection of *Codex Ms. Bibl. Taurinensis 903*

There is something of a dispute concerning the date of this collection. Texts have been taken from every possible source, and often haphazardly. The collection has exerted very little if any influence upon others. It is a Gregorian collection.[41]

1) Pflugk-Harttung, *Zeitschrift für Kirchenrecht,* p. 365 folio 20

Presbiter non amplius . . . nec expellatur

In his *Acta inedita,* II, 3, n. 8, Pflugk-Harttung reports this canon under the name of Urban I; the contents, however, so he notes, place the canon in the milieu of Urban II. This canon demands that only one church be in the charge of a cleric, just as a man is allowed but one wife. The bishop controls appointments to benefices.

[41] Pflugk-Harttung maintains that this collection is a falsification made during the twelfth or thirteenth century after the fashion of the Pseudo-Isidorian decretals; cf. Julius von Pflugk-Harttung, "Eine grosse Fälschung in Canones," *Zeitschrift für Kirchenrecht*, XIX (Neue Folge, IV), 361-372. Fournier-Le Bras express doubt concerning the opinion of the German scholar in *Histoire*, II, 218-222, esp. 220-221. Cf. also Van Hove, *Prolegomena*, p. 328: Stickler, *Historia*, p. 188; Pfulgk-Harttung, *Acta inedita*, II, *passim*, with texts from this collection.

2) Pflugk-Harttung, *Zeitschrift für Kirchenrecht,* p. 366 folio 64

Nemo coniungat . . . de viro sentiendum est

JL 5399, cf. the Collection of *Codex Ms. Vaticanus Latinus 4977,* n. 1. But note that the opening sentence of the present canon is different from that in the Vatican *codex* cited above. This canon is reported in *Acta inedita,* II, 166, n. 201, by Pflugk-Harttung.

The *Tripartita* of Ivo of Chartres

This noteworthy collection is actually composed of two separate parts. The so-called *collectio A* was compiled ca. 1093-1094; this was a chronological grouping of papal decretals from Clement I to Urban II, followed by a second section devoted to canons of councils and patristic texts. Shortly after the *Decretum* was finished by Ivo (ca. 1094), the *collectio B* was added to the *collectio A,* and in this way the *Tripartita* was born. The *collectio B* is an abbreviation of the *Decretum Ivonis,* containing 861 texts divided into 29 titles. It is thought that Ivo intended his *Tripartita* to lead the way toward a middle course between the rigors of the Gregorian Reform movement and the *Decretum* of Burchard of Worms. The *Tripartita* exerted considerable influence, particularly outside of Italy.[42]

1) folio 75r fragment 668 at the end of the first part of *collectio A*

Ut ab excommunicatis . . . precipua concedendum

JL 5393; this is one of the fragments referred to in the Collection in Two Books, n. 2.

[42] Fournier-Le Bras, *Histoire,* II, 58-66; P. Fournier, *Les Collections Canoniques attribuées à Yves de Chartres* (a separately published reprint from the *Bibliothèque de l'École des Chartes,* for the years 1896-1897, Paris: Librairie d'Alphonse Picard et Fils, 1897), pp. 1-40 (hereafter cited as Fournier, *Les Collections Canoniques*); Van Hove, *Prolegomena,* pp. 331-332; Stickler, *Historia,* pp. 180-184. The literature on the *Tripartita* and the other works is abundant; any of the works just cited will offer ample bibliography. For this collection the author consulted *codex ms. Paris, Bibliothèque Nationale 3858B.*

2) folio 75r this canon follows the above

Presentium portitorem . . . officio fungi

JL 4589 (a letter of Alexander II; here inscribed, *Item,* after the preceding letter of Urban II), to Albert (or Adalbero), bishop of Metz, 1063-1065, c. 3, C. I, q. 5. This is the decision of a case concerning a simoniacal ordination in which both the ordaining prelate and the one ordained knew nothing of the sum given. If the priest cannot easily be replaced, then he may remain at his post. This letter is attributed to Urban II by Gratian.[43]

3) folio 75r fragment 670; follows the preceding canon

Compatimur infirmitati tue . . . et dampnabilis

JL 5730; cf. the Collection of Turin in Seven Books, n. 1.

4) folio 131r cap. 22 in the second part of *collectio A*

Artaldus alanensis . . . sacerdotio me repellat

This historical note is, with a few textual variations excepted, identical with that reported in the *Collectio Britannica,* n. 44.

5) folio 131r-131v cap. 23 following the preceding canon

Super quibus consuluit . . . compatres effecti sint

JL 5741, to Vitalis, priest of Brescia, 1088-1099, c. 4, C. XXX, q. 3. In a case of necessity the parents, father and mother alike, may administer baptism to their own child. The children of any two who functioned as sponsors at the same baptism may intermarry, an exception of course being made with reference to persons for whom their parents acted as sponsors.

6) folio 131v cap. 24 follows the preceding canon

a. *Quod autem uxor . . . iniungi debet*

b. *Eos qui ecclesiam . . . canonum preiudicio*

These two different texts are put together to form a single canon. The first is JL 5742, to Vitalis, priest of Brescia,

[43] Cf. Fournier-Le Bras, *Histoire,* II, 62; Fournier, *Les Collections Canoniques,* p. 21.

1088-1099, c. 6, C. XXX, q. 4. This canon first forbids that two sponsors at baptism both receive the child from the font; that one receive the child is sufficient for both to become true sponsors. In the second part of this first letter Urban forbids that a man marry two who are sisters to each other or "*commatres*" to himself. The second letter is JL 5740 to the same addressee; cf. the Collection of *Codex Ms. Vaticanus Latinus 3829,* n. 3.

7) folio 158v tit. 10, cap. 41 (here begins *collectio B*)

Ut ab excommunicatis . . . est precipua concedendum

JL 5393; this canon is an excerpt from the larger letter listed in the Collection in Two Books, n. 2.

8) folio 158v tit. 10, cap. 42

Presbiterorum filios . . . fuerint conuersari

Canon 14, Council of Melfi; cf. the recension "Bb" of the Collection of Anselm of Lucca, n. 1.

9) folio 158v tit. 10, cap. 43

Statuimus ne . . . cautione suscipiat

JL 5763; cf. the recension "Bb" of the Collection of Anselm of Lucca, n. 6.

10) folio 158v tit. 10, cap. 44

Lugdunensis parrochie . . . canonum disciplina

JL 5723, to Hugh, archbishop of Lyons, 1088-1099, c. 10, C. IX, q. 2. Urban answers the query of Hugh; the latter may tolerate those of his clerics who had been ordained by other bishops, so long as there is no doubt about their ordination and good repute. This situation should not continue, as it is contrary to the sacred canons, and a suitable penance should be enjoined.

11) folio 167v-168r tit. 15, cap. 21

Si uerum esse . . . in domino nubat

JL 5382; see the *Collectio Britannica,* n. 29.

12) folio 168r tit. 15, cap. 22

De neptis tue . . . est etiam sentiendum

JL 5399; cf. the Collection of *Codex Ms. Vaticanus Latinus 4977,* n. 1.

13) folio 176r-176v tit. 16, cap. 8

Notificamus tibi . . . aliquam iniungatur

JL 5388; see the *Collectio Britannica,* n. 35.

14) folio 176v-177r tit. 16 cap. 14

Conuenit troie . . . non prohibeantur

Canon 1, Council of Troia; see the Collection of *Codex Ms. Vaticanus Latinus 3829,* n. 2.

15) folio 182v tit. 20, cap. 14

Excommunicatorum interfectoribus . . . flagitio contraxerunt

JL 5536; cf. the First Collection of Prague, n. 2.

The *Decretum* of Ivo of Chartres

This very ample collection consists of 3760 chapters, almost half of which are from the *Decretum* of Burchard of Worms. The *collectio A* of the *Tripartita* was also used in the present complilation. The order of materials within the collection has been criticized as unmethodical. Ivo was striving to compile an enchiridion useful in compiling other collections, rather than a well-ordered collection; in fact there are those who consider this *Decretum* as a preparation for the *Panormia* which was to follow. This work was completed during the year 1094, before the *collectio B* was finished.[44]

[44] A rather faulty edition of the *Decretum* can be found in *PL*, CLXI, 47-1022; to serve as a check upon this printed edition, *codex ms. Vaticanus Latinus 1357* was consulted. Wherever the printed text differs from the manuscript, the latter has been used. Cf. Fournier-Le Bras, *Histoire,* II, 67-85; Fournier, *Les Collections Canoniques,* pp. 40-91; Van Hove, *Prolegomena,* pp. 331-332; Stickler, *Historia,* pp. 180-184.

1) folio 67v-*PL,* CLXI, 312 pars 4, cap. 219
Canonum contemptores . . . obedire canonibus
JL 5611, Gerard, bishop of Thérouanne, 1088-1096. Those who defy the sacred canons are to be excommunicated.

2) folio -*PL,* CLXI, 350 pars 5, cap. 72 *in medio*
Nullus in episcopatum . . . licentia non fiat
Canon 1, Council of Benevento; cf. the Collection in Nine Books, n. 1. This canon is missing in the manuscript, folio 77v.

3) folio 124v-*PL,* CLXI, 532 pars 6, cap. 406.
Ut ab excommunicatis . . . precipua est concedendum
JL 5393; this is one of the excerpts mentioned in the Collection in Two Books n. 2.

4) folio 124v-*PL,* CLXI, 532 pars 6, cap. 407
Discretioni nostre uidetur . . . ministeria reconciliabis
JL 5378; cf. the Collection in Two Books, n. 1.

5) folio 124v-*PL,* CLXI, 532 pars 6, cap. 408
Nosse te uolumus . . . sententia subiacebit
JL 5722, to Rudolph, count, 1088-1099. No layman is to exercise power over a cleric; anyone who does so contrary to the law will be punished.

6) folio 124v-*PL,* CLXI, 533 pars 6, cap. 410
Presbiterorum filios . . . fuerint conuersari
Canon 14, Council of Melfi; cf. the recension " Bb " of the Collection of Anselm of Lucca, n. 1.

7) folio 124v-*PL,* CLXI, 533 pars 6, cap. 411
Statuimus ne . . . cautione suscipiat
JL 5763; cf. n. 6 of the recension " Bb " of the Collection of Anselm of Lucca.

8) folio 124v-*PL,* CLXI, 533 pars 6, cap. 412
Lugdunensis parrochie . . . canonum disciplina
JL 5723, which is the same as n. 10 of the *Tripartita* of Ivo.

9) folio 136v-*PL,* CLXI, 588 pars 8, cap. 23

Vi uerum esse . . . in domino nubat

JL 5382; this can be found in the *Collectio Britannica,* n. 29. Note that this canon, through a scribe's error, begins with the word *Vi* instead of *Si.* An attempt to correct the error is visible.

10) folio 137r-*PL,* CLXI, 589 pars 8, cap. 24

De neptis tue . . . est et sentiendum

JL 5399; this is reported in the Collection of the *Codex Ms. Vaticanus Latinus 4977,* n. 1.

11) folio 154v-*PL,* CLXI, 663 pars 9, cap. 33

Notificamus tibi . . . aliquam iniungatur

JL 5388; cf. the *Collectio Britannica,* n. 35.

12) folio 156r-*PL,* CLXI, 668 pars 9, cap. 53

Conuenit troie . . . non prohibeantur

Canon 1, Council of Troia; cf. the Collection of *Codex Ms. Vaticanus Latinus 3829,* n. 2.

13) folio 165v-*PL,* CLXI, 706 pars 10 cap. 54

Excommunicatorum interfectoribus . . . flagitio contraxerunt

JL 5536; cf. the First Collection of Prague, n. 2.

14) folio 200r-*PL,* CLXI, 836 pars 14, cap. 45

Qui excommunicationis questione . . . metus incutiatur

JL 5393; this is another fragment from the letter listed in the Collection in Two Books, n. 2.

15) folio 201v-*PL,* CLXI, 842 pars 14, cap. 68

(S)ane quod super . . . moribus adiuuare

JL 5363; same as n. 16 of the *Collectio Britannica.*

The *Panormia* of Ivo of Chartres

Divided into eight books, the *Panormia* consists of excerpts taken systematically from the *Decretum* of Ivo. Both the arrangement and the texts are taken from the *Decretum* for the most part. This collection has enjoyed great authority and wide use; it was a veritable encyclopedia of the canon law of that period. The *Panormia* followed about 1094-1095 closely upon the completion of the *Decretum.*[45]

1) Douai-folio 52r; Munich-folio 46v; *PL*, CLXI, 1130
lib. 3, cap. 5

Nullus in episcopatum . . . metropolitani licentia

Canon 1, Council of Benevento; cf. the Collection in Nine Books, n. 1. The text as found in Migne adds three extra words, *firmiter fieri permittimus,* to complete the sentence grammatically; the two manucripts both lack this conclusion, and the final sentence lacks a verb.

2) Douai-folio 56v; Munich-folio 52r; *PL*, CLXI, 1142
lib. 3, cap. 51

Presbiterorum filios . . . fuerint conuersari

Canon 14, Council of Melfi; cf. the recension "Bb" of the Collection of Anselm of Lucca, n. 1. This canon is inscribed in all three sources investigated: *ex decretis* (*decreto*) *gregorii VII et urbani II.*

3) Douai-folio 57r; Munich-folio 52v; *PL*, CLXI, 1142
lib. 3, cap. 53

Cenomagnensem electum . . . periculo consulatur

JL 4610 (a letter of Alexander II; in Migne this canon in inscribed, *Urbanus archiep. Bartolomaeo Turon;* in both manuscripts the inscription is the same except that there is no mention of Urban or any other sender), to Bartholomew, archbishop of Tours, 1066-1067, c. 13, D. LVI (where the canon is also ascribed to Urban II). Although the bishop-elect of Le Mans is the son of a priest, the Pope

[45] The *Panormia* exists in a printed edition in *PL*, CLXI, 1041-1344; two manuscripts were used to serve as a check against this printed text: *Douai, Bibliothèque municipale 584* and *Munich, Bayerische Staatsbibliothek lateinsche 4545*. Cf. Fournier-Le Bras, *Histoire*, II, 85-99; Fournier, *Les Collections Canoniques*, pp. 91-110; Van Hove, *Prolegomena*, pp. 331-332; Stickler, *Historia*, pp. 180-184.

accepts the election by way of exception, if everything else is in order.

4) Douai-folio 57r; Munich-folio 52v; *PL,* CLXI, 1142
lib. 3, cap. 54

Quia simpliciter . . . officio confirmamus

JL 5390; cf. the *Collectio Britannica,* n. 37.

5) Douai-folio 60r; Munich-folio 55r; *PL,* CLXI, 1148
lib. 3, cap. 81

Daibertum a negzelone . . . nil dare potuit

JL 5383 (in the Munich ms. this canon is attributed to Gregory VII); cf. n. 30 of the *Collectio Britannica.*

6) Douai-folio 62r; Munich-folio 57r; *PL,* CLXI, 1152
lib. 3, cap. 101

Eos qui post . . . interdictione mul(c)tentur

Canon 12, Council of Melfi; this canon is reported in the Collection of *Codex Ms. Vaticanus Latinus 4977,* n. 2. The Munich ms. begins with a scribal error: *Hos qui post.*

7) Douai-folio 62v; Munich-folio 57v; *PL,* CLXI, 1152
lib. 3, cap. 104

Nemo ad sacrum . . . uirginem uxorem habuerit

Canon 3, Council of Melfi; this canon begins slightly different from n. 4 of the Collection of *Codex Ms. Vaticanus Latinus 4977,* but there is no doubt that the two are merely slightly different versions of the same canon.

8) Douai-folio 64r; Munich-folio 59r; *PL,* CLXI, 1156
lib. 3, cap. 122

Vendentes et ementes . . . habere permittas

JL 5381; cf. the *Collectio Britannica,* n. 26.

9) Douai-folio 70r; Munich-folio 64r; *PL,* CLXI, 1168
lib. 3, cap. 154

Clerico quo iacente . . . et timore permaneat

JL 5474, to Guarnerius, bishop of Merseburg, 1088-1093, c. 37, D. L. A cleric who accidentally killed a young child is not to be suspended from his orders, but should do penance for his carelessness. In the Douai ms. a scribe has erroneously inscribed the canon, *Rabanus II.*

10) Douai-folio 102r-102v; Munich-folio 96r; *PL,* CLXI, 1234
lib. 5, cap. 107

Sanctis quippe . . . metus incutiatur

JL 5393; this canon is another canon taken from the long letter concerning excommunication written to Gebhard of Constance and listed in the Collection of Two Books, n. 2.

11) Douai-folio 103r; Munich-folio 97r; *PL,* CLXI, 1236
lib. 5, cap. 111

Iuratos wigoni milites . . . auctoritate persoluere

JL 5724; this canon is the same as that reported in the Collection in Nine Books, n. 12, but there is further development given to the notion that a human obligation ceases when it opposes the divine rights. This canon is exactly as it is in c. 5, C. XV, q. 6. In the Douai ms. the inscription has been put at the end of the text.

12) Douai-folio 104v-105r; Munich-folio 98v; *PL,* CLXI, 1240
lib. 5, cap. 123

Sane quod super . . . moribus adiuuare

JL 5363; cf. the *Collectio Britannica,* n. 16.

13) Douai-folio 121v-122r; Munich-folio 114r; *PL,* CLXI, 1272
lib. 6, cap. 108

Si uerum esse . . . in domino nubat

JL 5382; this letter may be found listed in the *Collectio Britannica,* n. 29.

14) Douai-folio 122r; Munich-folio 114r; *PL,* CLXI, 1272
lib. 6, cap. 109

De neptis tue . . . est etiam sentiendum (. . . etiam de uiro sentiendum)

JL 5399; with several inversions of the word order this canon is the same as that listed in the Collection of *Codex Ms. Vaticanus Latinus 4977,* n. 1.

15) Douai-folio 136v; Munich-folio 126v; *PL,* CLXI, 1301
lib. 7, cap. 86

Notificamus tibi . . . aliquam iniungatur

JL 5388; this canon may be found reported in the *Collectio Britannica,* n. 35.

16) Douai-folio 139v; Munich-folio 128v; *PL,* CLXI, 1308
lib. 8, cap. 9

Non enim eos . . . trucidasse contigerit

JL 5536; this canon is one sentence taken from the body of the canon reported in the First Collection of Prague, n. 2.

The First Recension of the *Collectio Caesaraugustana*

The *collectio Caesaraugustana* is based largely upon the *Decretum* and the *Tripartita* of Ivo of Chartres along with the collections of Anselm of Lucca and Deusdedit. The first recension receives its name from the city of Saragossa, Spain, for the text was found among the manuscripts kept in a Carthusian monastery there. It was compiled in Burgundy, Aquitaine or in the northern part of Spain sometime between the years 1110-1120. The author was a believer in the Gregorian Reform.[46]

1) folio 56r lib. 3, cap. 69

Nullus in episcopatum . . . metroplitani licentia

Canon 1, Council of Benevento; cf. the Collection in Nine Books, n. 1.

[46] This recension of the collection is found in *codex ms. Vaticanus latinus Barberinus 897.* Cf. Fournier-Le Bras, *Histoire,* II, 269-285; Fournier, *Les Collections Canoniques,* pp. 130-140; Van Hove, *Prolegomena,* p. 333; Stickler, *Historia,* p. 184; Theiner, *Disquisitiones,* pp. 356-359. Very recently R. Losada Cosme, of the University of Salamanca, who has been doing research on the *collectio Caesaraugustana,* announced the discovery of two new manuscripts of this collection to be considered as the oldest form of the collection. Cf. the note of Stephan Kuttner concerning news of canonical collections before Gratian in, "Bulletin for 1958 of the Institute of Research and Study in Medieval Canon Law," *Traditio,* XIV (1958), 509.

2) folio 66r-66v lib. 4, cap. 22

Ut ab excommunicatis . . . est precipua concedendum

JL 5393; an excerpt from the canon reported in the Collection in Two Books, n. 2.

3) folio 66v lib. 4, cap. 23

Presentium portitorem . . . officio fungi

JL 4589; this canon belongs to Alexander II, but just as in the *Tripartita,* n. 2, so here it is spoken of as coming from Urban II. Recall that this canon credited to Urban in Gratian at c. 3, C. I, q. 5.

4) folio 67r lib. 4, cap. 24

Porro eos qui ecclesiam . . . canonum iudicio

JL 5740; this canon first came into consideration in the Collection of *Codex Ms. Vaticanus Latinus 3829,* n. 3. The final word of the present canon should be *preiudicio.* Here it should be mentioned that the numbering of the manuscript folios is quite confusing. The pages actually run thus: 60, 61, 62, 63, 64, 65, 66, 67, 68 corrected into 69 and then the following numbers are repeated, 66, 67, 68, 69; only the numbers are out of order, not the pages. The present canon is found in the first series of numbers; the following canon is in the second series of pages.

5) folio 66v-67r lib. 4, cap. 33

Ea que a sanctis . . . depositione mulctetur

Canons 1-7, 12-13 and the canon found after canon 15, Council of Piacenza (but note that these canons are mistakenly credited to the Council of Clermont: *Urbanus Papa II in Concilio Clarimontis*), March 1-7, 1095, Mansi, XX, 805-807. The first seven canons of this council have already been dealt with in n. 2 of the Collection in Seven Books. Canon 12, which is the third paragraph in c. 5, C. IX, q. 1, states Urban's policy of dispensing from the general rigor of the law because of the extreme need of the Church; Urban made it clear that this compromise was temporary in character, as was the plight of the Church. The canon which is found after canon 15 in the acts of the council (*Item post alia. Illud summopere . . . depositione mulctetur*) forbids clerics from accepting investiture from a layman. Canon 13 has already been treated in n. 1 of the *Polycarpus*. All of the present canons were also repeated at the Roman Synod of April 24-30, 1099, Mansi XX, 961-963, except for the very last, beginning *Item post alia.*

6) folio 69r lib. 4, cap. 40

Daibertum ab Vezelione . . . nil dare potuit

JL 5383; except for the scribe's error in copying the proper name (which has suffered much at various hands in this period), this canon has been considered in the *Collectio Britannica*, n. 30. This *capitulum* lacks any inscription.

7) folio 88r-88v lib. 4, cap. 127

a. *Super quibus consuluit . . . compatres effecti sunt*
b. *Quod autem uxor . . . iniungi debet*
c. *Porro eos qui ecclesiam . . . canonum preiuditio*

These three canons are grouped to form a single continuous canon in the present collection. The first part, JL 5741, has been dealt with in the *Tripartita*, n. 5; the second section, JL 5742, is found in the *Tripartita*, n. 6. The final part, JL 5740, is also in n. 6 of the *Tripartita*, but it was already considered in the *Collectio* of *Codex Ms. Vaticanus Latinus 3829*, n. 3.

8) folio 88v-89r lib. 4, cap. 128

Conuenit troie . . . non prohibeantur

Canon 1, Council of Troia, is also found in the Collection of *Codex Ms. Vaticanus Latinus 3829*, n. 2.

9) folio 132r lib. 6, cap. 24

Iuratos hugoni milites . . . auctoritate persoluere

JL 5724; this canon has already come under consideration in the *Panormia*, n. 11 and the Collection in Nine Books, n. 12. The proper name in the opening words of the pericope has suffered many variations at the hands of the copyists.

10) folio 132r lib. 6, cap. 25

Illa omnia sacramenta . . . introitu segregamus

JL 5423, to the suffragans of the Church of Arles (,1089). The oath which was forced from the archbishop, Guibilinus, is null and void; those who have kept him in captivity are declared infamous.

11) folio 164r lib. 8, cap. 40

Due inquit leges . . . non estis sub lege

JL 5760; reported in the *Polycarpus,* n. 2.

12) folio 164r lib. 8, cap. 41

Mandamus et mandantes . . . in choro maneat

This canon is falsely attributed to Urban II; cf. the information given in the *Polycarpus,* n. 3.

13) folio 164v lib. 8, cap. 45

Statuimus ne . . . cautione suscipiat

JL 5763; cf. the recension "Bb" of the Collection of Anselm of Lucca, n. 6.

14) folio 165v lib. 8, cap. 54

Presbiterorum filios . . . fuerint conuersati

Canon 14, Council of Melfi, as included in the report of the recension "Bb" of the Collection of Anselm of Lucca, n. 1.

15) folio 165v lib. 8, cap. 55

Quia suppliciter . . . officio confirmamus

JL 5390; cf. the *Collectio Britannica,* n. 37.

16) folio 188r lib. 10, cap. 14

De neptis tue . . . de uiro sentiendum

JL 5399; reported in the Collection of *Codex Ms. Vaticanus Latinus 4977,* n. 1.

17) folio 189v-190r lib. 10, cap. 28

Si uerum esse . . . in domino nubat

JL 5382; cf. the *Collectio Britannica,* n. 29.

18) folio 205r lib. 10, cap. 129

Notificamus tibi . . . aliquam iniungatur

JL 5388; also reported in the *Collectio Britannica*, n. 35.

19) folio 292v lib. 15, cap. 62

Excommunicatorum interfectoribus . . . flagitio contraxerunt

JL 5536; an excerpt from the letter reported in the First Collection of Prague, n. 2.

The Second Recension of the *Collectio Caesaraugustana*

The second recension of the *Collectio Caesaraugustana* was compiled shortly after the first, sometime between 1123 and 1144. It contains many additions, interpolations and transpositions when compared with the first recension. Many of the omissions represent a compromise with the rigidness of the strict Gregorian position.[47]

1) folio 13v

Nullus in episcopatum . . . metropolitani licentia fiat

Canon 1, Council of Benevento; cf. the Collection in Nine Books, n. 1.

2) folio 15v

Ut ab excommunicatis . . . est precipua concedendum

JL 5393; an excerpt from the letter found in the Collection in Two Books, n. 2.

3) folio 15v

Presentium portitorem . . . officio fungi

JL 4589; this canon belongs to Alexander II, but it is here ascribed to Urban II. The canon passed into Gratian

[47] For this collection *codex ms. Vaticanus latinus 5715* was used; the canons are unnumbered, but each of the opening canons of the fifteen books is supposed to begin with a large capital letter. This practice was not consistently followed, and therefore the only sure way to identify a canon is by means of the folio on which it is found. Cf. Fournier-Le Bras, *Histoire*, II, 270, 281-284; Fournier, *Les Collections Canoniques*, pp. 130-140; Van Hove, *Prolegomena*, p. 333; Stickler, *Historia*, p. 184.

under the name of Urban in c. 3, C. I, q. 5. Cf. the *Tripartita,* n. 2.

4) folio 15v

Porro eos qui ecclesiam . . . canonum preiudicio

JL 5740; this canon has already been reported in the Collection of *Codex Ms. Vaticanus Latinus 3829,* n. 3. The last three canons are found in consecutive order, in the same manner as they are given in the first recension of the *Collectio Caesaraugustana,* nn. 2, 3 and 4.

5) folio 16v-17r

Ea que a sanctis . . . depositione mul(c)tentur

Canons 1-7, 12-13 and the unnumbered canon found after canon 15, Council of Piacenza; here inscribed: *Urbanus II in concilio clarimontis.* Cf. the first recension of this collection, n. 5.

6) folio 17r

Daibertum Aguezelone . . . nil dare potuit

JL 5383; this canon has been considered in the *Collectio Britannica,* n. 30. The second word, a proper name, has really suffered at the hands of the scribe; it should be something close to *Nezelone.*

7) folio 20v

Eos qui post . . . interdictione mul(c)tentur

Canon 12, Council of Melfi; this canon has been recorded in the Collection of *Codex Ms. Vaticanus Latinus 4977,* n. 2. With this *capitulum* the sources of Urban II in the second recension of this collection begin to show differences from the first recension.

8) folio 21r

Clericum quo iacente . . . et timore permaneat

JL 5474 (here inscribed: *Rabanus II, guararnerio merseburgensi episcopo*) ; cf. the *Panormia,* n. 9.

9) folio 26r

Nullus in episcopatum . . . vel metropolitani licentia

Canon 1, Council of Benevento; cf. the Collection in Nine Books, n. 1. This same canon, with its alternate ending, appears previously on folio 13v of this manuscript.

10) folio 27r

Ex concilio melfiano urbani pape (vr. pp.) Nullus in duabus ecclesiis preposituram obtineat et cuiuslibet honorem altero uiuente per aliquam occasionem nullus adquirat. Quod si quis fecerit illum honorem cui post mortem alterius putabat succedere nullatenus habeat et ad alterius ecclesiastici honoris ambitum non ascendat.

The text of this canon has not been found in the acts of Urban II as they exist today. The content of the canon is similar to what was said in canons 12, 14 and 31 of the Council of Clermont, Nov. 18-28, 1095, Mansi, XX, 817-818.

11) folio 37r

Iuratos Wigoni milites . . . auctoritate persoluere

JL 5724; cf. the Collection in Nine Books, n. 12 together with n. 11 of the *Panormia.*

12) folio 37r-37v

Illa omnia sacramenta . . . introitu segragamus

JL 5423; cf. the first recension of the *Collectio Caesaraugustana,* n. 10.

13) folio 50r

Due inquit leges . . . non estis sub lege

JL 5760; this *capitulum* is identified in the *Polycarpus,* n. 2.

14) folio 50v

Mandamus et mandantes . . . in choro maneat

This chapter is here found immediately following the preceding canon, but it has no inscription in this manuscript. Cf. the *Polycarpus,* n. 3.

15) folio 50v

Statuimus ne . . . cautione suscipiat

JL 5763; cf. the recension "Bb" of the Collection of Anselm of Lucca, n. 6.

16) folio 51r

Presbiterorum filios . . . fuerint conuersari

Canon 14, Council of Melfi; this canon is found in the recension "Bb" of Anselm of Lucca, n. 1.

17) folio 51r

Quia suppliciter . . . officio confirmamus

JL 5390; cf. the *Collectio Britannica,* n. 37.

18) folio 53r

Litterarum presentium . . . illi restituas

JL 5734, to Bernard, archbishop of Toledo, 1088-1099. Concerning the unusual case of a man who claims that he received no orders between the time he was made an exocrist and the time he was ordained to the priesthood, Urban expresses surprise. A year of penance is prescribed; and then, if the life of the cleric warrants it, he is to receive all the orders which were omitted.

19) folio 58v

Nullus episcopus . . . regulariter commendatus

Canon 10, Council of Melfi, Sept. 10, 1089, Mansi, XX, 723. This canon demands that roving monks be not accepted without letters from their abbots.

20) folio 60v

De neptis tue . . . de uiro sentiendum

JL 5399; cf. the Collection of *Codex Ms. Vaticanus Latinus 4977,* n. 1.

21) folio 62v

Si uerum esse . . . in domino nubat

JL 5382; cf. the *Collectio Britannica,* n. 29.

22) folio 71r

Notificamus tibi . . . aliquam iniungatur

JL 5388; this canon is found in the *Collectio Britannica,* n. 35.

23) folio 71r

Conuenit troie . . . non prohibeantur

Canon 1, Council of Troia; cf. the Collection of *Codex Ms. Vaticanus Latinus 3829,* n. 2.

24) folio 71r-71v

a. *Super quibus consuluit . . . compatres effecti sunt*
b. *Quod autem uxor . . . iniungi debet*
c. *Porro eos qui ecclesiam . . . canonum preiudicio*

JL 5741, 5742 and 5740 in that order form this single canon, in the same manner as in the first recension of the *Collectio Caesaraugustana,* n. 7; cf. also the *Tripartita,* nn. 5 and 6. The last three canons of this collection (nn. 22-24) are found in sequence.

25) folio 72r

Compatimur infirmitate tue . . . et damnabilis

JL 5730; this canon is reported in the Collection of Turin in Seven Books, n. 1. In this manuscript the canon closes with a date: *data troie XI kal. mai.*

26) folio 85r

De romanorum presulum ueneracione. Vr. II. festiuitates romanorum pontificum celebres habeantur martirum in VIIII vel confessorum in tribus lectionibus preter quosdam qui pro sui excellentia celeberrimi. sicut siluester et gregorius. et aliquid [sic]. *Illi etiam sancti specialiter unenerandi sunt in officiis missarumque solemniis qui sunt* [ms.: *est*] *sanctis apostolis in mensa domini speciales conuiue nominati in canone positi sunt. Ut quorum meritis precibusque protectionis auxilio nos muneri cotidie deprecamur. anniuersarias solemnitates eorum precipue celebrare studeamus.*

This canon is here ascribed to Urban II; it is not found in any of the acts of Urban which have come down to the present time. This could be one of the many interpolations of the present collection. The source of this canon is not known.

27) folio 101r

Sane quia inter . . . iustitiam gerat

Canon 16, Council of Melfi, Sept. 10, 1089, Mansi, XX, 724. False penitence (i. e., penance done for one sin while others are ignored) is reprobated.

28) folio 108r

Excommunicatorum interfectoribus . . . flagitio contraxerunt

JL 5536; this is an excerpt from the letter in the First Collection of Prague, n. 2.

29) folio 121r

Quia monachorum . . . iura seruentur

Canon 4, *Codex Cencii,* Council of Clermont; cf. the recension " C " of the Collection of Anselm of Lucca, n. 2.

30) folio 121r

Item ibidem. Si uero laici decretis canonicis resistentes ecclesias uiolenter tenere presumpserint. ipsi excommunicentur. In ecclesiis uero illis. nullum diuinum officium fiat. nullus ibi oret. bannus non ponatur. mortuis non sepeliatur. baptismi tamen gratia ibi non negetur. infirmis remedio penitentie et communionis subueniatur.

This canon follows the preceding, which bears the inscription: *ex decretis urbani pape in concilio clarimontis.* It is not found in the acts of Clermont or anywhere else in the acts of Urban as they exist today.

The Collection of Saint-Germain-des-Prés

Composed of nine books, the present collection was the work of the Bishop of Thérouanne between 1096 and 1099. About 1120 the same author added some matter dealing with the Gregorian Reform. He depended upon Ivo of Chartres, especially his *Tripartita*. This collection is especially of interest because of the canons of the Council of Clermont which it contains; these 30 canons are the first thing to be treated in this collection.[48]

1) Sdralek, p. 132 folio 45v pars 1

Ieiunium quatuor . . . eiusdam excepta

This first canon and the 29 which follow are from the Council of Clermont; the canons of this council exist in this collection in a form not found anywhere else. The first five canons are completely different from any attributed to the Council of Clermont, held Nov. 18-28, 1095. The present canon gives the rules for fasting on Ember days. The substance of these regulations is the same as in the Collection in Three Books, n. 11, but the text has many variations that indicate two different formulations of the same regulations. Though found nowhere else, this canon also exists in the Second Collection of Châlons-sur-Marne, n. 45 (folio 167r); the only difference is that in the Châlons ms. the opening word is *Primum*.[49]

2) Sdralek, p. 133 folio 45v pars 1

Iudicatum est . . . aliqui accipiant

This canon has not been found anywhere else. It is here called canon 2 of the Council of Clermont. This canon

[48] Max Sdralek, *Wolfenbüttler Fragmente*, Band I, Heft, II. Cf. also Fournier-Le Bras, *Histoire*, II, 285-296; Van Hove, *Prolegomena*, p. 333; Stickler, *Historia*, p. 185.

[49] Concerning the present version of the acts of Clermont, see Sdralek, pp. 23-25. He claims that there is preserved in the present collection a new and different version of the canon's of Clermont. Four of the canons as found here were not passed down by Lambert of Arras, whose account is the most complete. The canons as found in the Collection are from an independent but genuine tradition.

forbids bishops from exacting the *redemptio altarium;* this practice, which consisted of entrusting the altars left vacant by the death of the beneficiary to the monastery for the payment of a certain sum, was declared simoniacal. A similar prohibition is found in other accounts of Clermont.[50]

3) Sdralek, p. 133 folio 45v pars 1

In ecclesiis ubi . . . conversatio pendeat

Canon 3, Council of Clermont, according to this collection. N. 10 of the Collection in Nine Books contains relevant information about the content of the present canon, namely with reference to the chaplain in religious churches who is to serve the parochial needs of the people. This chaplain is to be subject to the bishop in matters concerning the *cura animarum.* The present canon sets up the rule that these religious churches are to have a *capellanus* for caring for the people and is reported at the end of Lambert's account of the Council of Clermont, Mansi, XX, 819. The canon has been included in the Decretals of Gregory IX at c. 1, X, *de capellanis monachorum et aliorum religiosorum,* III, 37.

4) Sdralek, p. 133 folio 45v pars 1

Interdictum est . . . licentia pape

Canon 4, Council of Clermont, Nov. 18-28, 1095, according to this collection. This canon declares that every candidate for the episcopacy must be at least a deacon; a subdeacon may be chosen with the approval of the Roman Pontiff. This canon is similar in its content to that of canon 5 of Clermont according to Lambert's account, Mansi, XX, 817. The same rule had previously been announced at the Council of Benevento, March 28, 1091, Mansi, XX, 737.

[50] Cf. canon 7 of Lambert of Arras' account, Mansi, XX, 817; canon 3 of the *Codex Cencii,* Mansi, XX, 902 along with Hefele-Leclercq, *Conciles,* V, I, 401; this provision is repeated at the Council of Nîmes, July 8-12, 1096, Mansi, XX, 933 and Hefele-Leclercq, *Conciles,* V, I, 448. The Collection in Nine Books, n. 10 concerns this same canon 1 of the Council of Nîmes, but the subject under consideration there is different.

5) Sdralek, p. 134 folio 45v pars 1

Ut omnes . . . qui non bellant

Canon 5, Council of Clermont, according to this collection. This interesting canon extends the *pax Dei* even to animals. This idea is completely new and is nowhere else found in Urban's acts.[51]

6) Sdralek p. 134 folio 45v pars 1

Sanctitum est . . . pace permaneant

Canon 6 of the Council of Clermont according to the numbering of this collection. This canon is exactly identical with the first sentence of canon 1 as Lambert has it, Mansi, XX, 816. This canon extends the peace of God to include every day for monks, clerics and women and those in their company. For others only four days were embraced in the *pax*. This canon thus consecrated all the previous attempts to extend the peace to all Christendom since the beginning of the eleventh century.[52]

7) Sdralek, p. 134 folio 45v pars 1

Tribus diebus . . . fuerit puniatur

In this account, this is canon 7 of the Council of Clermont; In the version of Lambert it is the rest of canon 1, Mansi, XX, 816. The days on which the peace is in force for others are established.

8) Sdralek, p. 134 folio 45v pars 1

Quicumque pro . . . ei reputatur

Canon 8 of Clermont in the present account; this is a verbal restatement of canon 2 in Lambert's rendering, Mansi, XX, 816. Those going upon the first Crusade are granted what would today be called a plenary indulgence, so long as they had no ulterior motives.

[51] Cf. Sdralek, p. 24.

[52] Fliche, *Histoire*, VIII, 283.

9) Sdralek, p. 134 folio 45v pars 1

Ut nullus fiat . . . nisi levita

Canon 9 in this account of Clermont; this is the first sentence of canon 3 of Lambert and resembles c. 1, D. LX, Mansi, XX, 817. No one can be a dean or archpriest unless he is a priest; no one an archdeacon unless he is at least a deacon.

10) Sdralek, p. 134 folio 45v pars 1

Ne aliquis clericus . . . episcopum eligatur

Canon 10 of Clermont according to the present collection's count; this canon is substantially, though not verbally, the same as canons 4 and 5 according to Lambert, Mansi, XX, 817. Clerics must not bear arms; a candidate for the office of bishop has to be at least a subdeacon.

11) Sdralek, p. 134 folio 46r pars 1

Ut nullus sibi . . . statutum est

Canon 11 in the present collection; the wording is close to that of Lambert, canon 6, Mansi, XX, 817. Buying of benefices and prebends is forbidden; those who are guilty must answer to the bishop for their crime.

12) Sdralek, p. 134 folio 46r pars 1

Ut nullus deinceps . . . canonicatu arceatur

Canon 12 of the Council of Clermont; this is identical with canons 8 and 9 of Lambert's listing of canons, Mansi, XX, 817. No recompense is to be demanded for ecclesiatical burial; any priest, deacon, subdeacon or canon guilty of incontinence is to be deposed.

13) Sdralek, p. 134 folio 46r pars 1

In domibus clericorum . . . in ecclesia

Canon 13 of this version of the Council of Clermont; this corresponds to canons 10 and 11 according to Lambert, Mansi, XX, 817. Only such women as are permitted by the sacred canons are to dwell in the houses of clerics; the sons of concubines and clerics are not to be allowed to receive orders or any ecclesiastical honors.

14) Sdralek, p. 134 folio 46r pars 1

Ne filii clericorum . . . regulares fiant

Canon 14 of Clermont in this account; this canon repeats the provision given in the second part of the preceding canon concerning the offspring of clerics in major orders.

15) Sdralek, p. 135 folio 46r pars 1

Nulli clerico . . . possit habere

Canon 15 of Clermont in this collection; almost verbally identical with canon 12 of Lambert, Mansi, XX, 817. Holding two benefices in two cities is forbidden, because no one can have two titles.

16) Sdralek, p. 135 folio 46r pars 1

Ut omnis clericus . . . semper ordinetur

Canon 16 in the present enumeration is to be identified with canon 13 in Lambert's account of the Council of Clermont, Mansi, XX, 817. The title for ordinations is to be conserved and not changed.

17) Sdralek, p. 135 folio 46r pars 1

Ut nullus deinceps . . . geminos habeat

Canon 17 of Clermont; in Lambert's version this is canon 14, Mansi, XX, 817. No one can have two honors in one church.

18) Sdralek, p. 135 folio 46r pars 1

Ut nullus aliquem . . . laicorum accipiat

Canon 18 in this account of the acts of the Council of Clermont (Nov. 18-28, 1095) corresponds to the first sentence of canon 15 according to Lambert, Mansi, XX, 817. No ecclesiastical honor may be received from the hand of a layman.

19) Sdralek, p. 135 folio 46r pars 1

Interdictum est ne . . . honoribis faciant

Canon 19 of the present version is exactly alike with canon 16 in Lambert of Arras' account, Mansi, XX, 817. Lay investiture is absolutely forbidden.

20) Sdralek, p. 135 folio 46r pars 1

Ne episcopus vel . . . fidelitatem faciat

Canon 20 in the present collection; this is identified as canon 17 of the Council of Clermont by Lambert, Mansi, XX, 817. Fealty by a cleric to any layman, even to a king, is on all counts forbidden.

21) Sdralek, p. 135 folio 46r pars 1

Ut nullus presbiter . . . episcopi sui

Canon 21 of Clermont in the present collection is the same as the first sentence of Lambert's canon 18 of Clermont, Mansi, XX, 817. The bishop is to appoint the chaplain to care for laymen in monastic churches.

22) Sdralek, p. 135 folio 46r pars 1

Ne laici decimam . . . sibi retineant

The present canon 22 is identical with canons 19 and 20 as found in the codex of Lambert, Mansi, XX, 818. Laymen may not accept or keep titles or any ecclesiastical property.

23) Sdralek, p. 135 folio 46r pars 1

Ne aliquis laicus . . . reverti possint

Canon 23 in the present collection is to be identified as forming canons 21 and 22 in Lambert's record of Clermont, Mansi, XX, 818. Seizing another's patrimony is forbidden; culprits in this matter may not be admitted to the sacrament of Penance until they have made satisfaction; so also no person is to be admitted to Penance unless his contrition is universal.

24) Sdralek, p. 135 folio 46r pars 1

Ut nullus christianus . . . carnem comedat

Canon 24 of Clermont in the present version of that council is exactly the same as canon 23 of Lambert's account, Mansi, XX, 818. The eating of meat is forbidden throughout Lent.

25) Sdralek, p. 135 folio 46r pars 1

Ne fiant ordinationes . . . ordinationes fieri

Canon 25 in the present version is the same, with some few changes in wording, as canon 24 in Lambert's record of that council, Nov. 18-28, 1095, Mansi, XX, 818. Ordinations are to be held only during Ember weeks and on the Saturday of mid-Lent.

26) Sdralek, p. 135 folio 46r pars 1

Ut in sabbato . . . circa noctem

The Collection of Saint-Germain-des-Prés and Lambert's account of the Council of Clermont both number the present canon as 26, Mansi, XX, 818. On Holy Saturday the fast is to be protracted until nightfall.

27) Sdralek, p. 136 folio 46r pars 1

Ne aliquis communicet . . . et per cautelam

Canon 27 of the present account of the canons of Clermont resembles very closely that which Lambert designated as canon 28, Mansi, XX, 818. The Eucharist is ordinarily to be received under only one species.[53]

28) Sdralek, p. 136 folio 46r pars 1

Si quis ad . . . reddatur iusticie

Canon 28 of the present list of canons of the Council of Clermont corresponds to the wording of canons 29 and 30 in the acts as transcribed by Lambert, Mansi, XX, 818. Whoever seeks asylum at a cross along the roadside is to be given the same right of sanctuary as one who flees to a

[53] For further information and background concerning this canon and its connection with the heresy of Berengarius of Tours, cf. Mansi, XX, 894 ff.; see also Hefele-Leclercq, *Conciles*, V, I, 403, esp. footnote 1.

church. One who seeks such sanctuary after having committed a crime is to receive the just penalty for his crime, but is to be spared life and limb.

29) Sdralek, p. 136 folio 46r pars 1

Ne aliquis laicus . . . ab episcopis fiat

Canon 29 of this account of Clermont corresponds to canon 31 in Lambert's list, Mansi, XX, 818. Cf. c. 46, C. XII, q. 2, together with the notes of the *Correctores.* The laity must not despoil the goods of bishops or clerics during the life of the latter or also after their death.

30) Sdralek, p. 136 folio 46r pars 1

Si quis episcoporum . . . ab omnibus fiat

This 30th and last canon of the present collection of Clermont corresponds to canon 32 in Lambert's version, Mansi, XX, 818. Imprisonment and incarceration of bishops are to be considered sufficient for rendering the captor perpetually infamous.

31) Sdralek, pp. 39-41 folio 48v-49r pars 2

At this place are found the 18 official canons of the Council held at Rome. April 24-30, 1099, Mansi, XX, 961-964. Of these canons the first 12 are identical with those of Piacenza, Mansi, XX, 805-806. Canons 13 to 17 are the same as canons 2 to 7 of the Council of Melfi, Mansi, XX, 723. The 18th and last canon of the Council of Rome is different in form, though not in content, from the canon found in Mansi, XX, 964.[54]

32) Sdralek, p. 48, footnote 15 folio 53r pars 4

Statuimus ne . . . cautione suscipiat

JL 5763; already reported in the recension "Bb" of the Collection of Anselm of Lucca, n. 6. Here attention should be called to an apparent error in Sdralek's work. For the present entry all he has is JL 5760, which, he says, is also

[54] Cf. Sdralek, p. 41, for some few observations of the canons of the Council of Rome as found in the Collection of Saint-Germain-des-Prés.

found in Ivo's *Decretum,* pars 6, cap. 411. A quick check will reveal that the letter reported at the place indicated in Jaffé is different from the letter found in Ivo at the place cited. Sdralek has apparently fallen into the same error as Friedberg; in fact, he has probably been led into it by following Friedberg, who makes the identical error. It has already been explained, when this mistake was first encountered (in the recension "Bb" of the Collection of Anselm of Lucca, n. 6), that Freidberg may have mixed up his footnote apparatus; these two canons appear on the same page of Friedberg's edition of the *Decretum* of Gratian.

33) Sdralek, p. 48, footnote 15 folio 58v pars 4

Convenit Troiae . . . non prohibeantur

Canon 1, Council of Troia; cf. the Collection of *Codex Ms. Vaticanus Latinus 3829,* n. 2.

34) Sdralek. p. 48, footnote 15 folio 58v pars 4

Si verum esse . . . in domino nubat

JL 5382; cf. the *Collectio Britannica,* n. 29.

35) Sdralek, p. 48, footnote 15 folio 58v pars 4

Notificamus tibi . . . aliquam iniungatur

JL 5388; cf. the *Collectio Britannica,* n. 35.

36) Sdralek, p. 50 folio 59v pars 4

Eos qui post . . . interdictione mul(c)tentur

Canon 12, Council of Melfi; cf. the Collection of *Codex Ms. Vaticanus Latinus 4977,* n. 2.

37) Sdralek, p. 50 folio 58v pars 4

Nullus in episcopatum . . . licentia non fiat

Canon 1, Council of Benevento; cf. the Collection in Nine Books, n. 1.

38) Sdralek, p. 55 pars 5 letter n. 6

Memento carissime . . . se honorificabit

JL 5471, to Robert, Count of Flanders, Dec. 2, 1092, given

at Castraneto. Urban exhorts Robert to desist in his attacks on the clergy.

39) Sdralek, p. 56 pars 5 letter n. 8

Quoniam relatum est . . . omnino interdicimus

JL 5794, to John, archdeacon of the church at Arras, 1099. Urban confirms John's election to the see of Thérouanne.

The First Collection of Châlons-sur-Marne

The first collection of Châlons-sur-Marne is divided into eighteen parts; its arrangement and composition come close to the structure of the *Tripartita* of Ivo of Chartres. It was compiled between the years 1125 and 1130, probably in Châlons-sur-Marne.[55]

1) folio 2v pars 1, cap. inserted at the foot of the page after c. 9

Super quibus consuluit . . . compatres effecti sint

JL 5741; cf. the *Tripartia*, n. 5.

2) folio 3r pars 1, cap. continuation of the above on opposite page

a. *Quod autem uxor . . . iniungi debt*

b. *Porro eos qui ecclesiam . . . canonum preiudicio*

JL 5742 and 5740, as in the *Tripartita*, n. 6, form a single canon.

3) folio 41r pars 9, cap. 29

Ut ab excommunicatis . . . est precipua concedendum

JL 5393; this is a most frequently repeated excerpt from the letter of Urban to Gebhard of Constance, reported in the Collection in Two Books, n. 2.

4) folio 41v pars 9, cap. 30

Compatimur infirmitati tue . . . et dampnabilis

JL 5730; cf. the Collection of Turin in Seven Books, n. 1.

[55] Fournier-Le Bras, *Histoire*, II, 308-311; Fournier, *Les Collections Canoniques*, pp. 158-172; Van Hove, *Prolegomena*, p. 334; Stickler, *Historia*, p. 186. This collection is contained in *codex Châlons-sur-Marne, Bibliothèque municipale 47*.

5) folio 46r pars 9, cap. 56

Artaldus alanensis . . . sacerdotio me repellat

This historical notice, which turned up with some frequency in the pre-Gratian collections, was listed in the *Collectio Britannica,* n. 44.

6) folio 46v pars 9, cap. 58

Nullus in episcopatum . . . metropolitani licentia

Canon 1, Council of Benevento; cf. the Collection in Nine Books, n. 1.

7) folio 105r pars 18, cap. 51

Ne aliquis laicus . . . reuerti possint

Canon 23, Council of Clermont, Nov. 18-28, 1095, according to the version of the acts as found in the Collection of Saint-Germain-des-Prés, n. 23. There is a very close resemblance to canons 21 and 22 as found in Lambert's account, Mansi, XX, 818; but textually the present canon is almost identical with that found in the Collection of Saint-Germain-des-Prés.

The Second Collection of Châlons-sur-Marne

This collection is an attempt to increase and perfect the preceding collection, and is well over twice as large in size. The arrangement is rather methodical; for its 13 books the same sources as in the first collection were used. The work was compiled sometime between the years 1130 and 1139, probably by the same person as the first collection of Châlons.[56]

1) folio 27r pars 1, *de simonia,* cap. 6

Presentium portiorem . . . officio fungi

JL 4589; this letter is here attributed to Urban II; actually it is a letter written by Alexander II, as was indicated in the *Tripartita,* n. 2.

[56] Fournier-Le Bras, *Histoire,* II, 311-313; Fournier, *Les Collections Canoniques,* pp. 172-182; Van Hove, *Prolegomena,* p. 334; Stickler, *Historia,* p. 186. This collection is contained in *codex Châlons-sur-Marne, Bibliothèque municipale 75.*

2) folio 28v pars 1, *de simonia,* cap. 12

a. *Quod uxor . . . iniungi debet*

b. *Porro eos qui ecclesiam . . . canonum preiudicio*

JL 5742 and 5740; these two fragments have been put into a single canon, as in the *Tripartita,* n. 6.

3) folio 28v pars 1, *de simonia,* cap. 13

Daibertum a nezelone . . . nil dare potuit

JL 5383; cf. the *Collectio Britannica,* n. 30.

4) folio 29r pars 1, *de simonia,* cap. 15

Quicquid igitur . . . uires optinere censemus

Canon 2, Council of Rome, April 24-30, 1099, Mansi, XX, 961; this canon is the last half of c. 1, C. I, q. 3. Here this canon is inscribed: *ex conilio urbani pape II habito rome in ecclesie beati petri anno christi M XCIX. VI kal. mai cap. I;* this canon was first promulgated at the Council of Piacenza, canon 2, March 1-7, 1095, Mansi, XX, 805. Note that this is canon 2; in this collection it is called *cap. I.* For the content of this canon see the Collection in Seven Books, n. 2.

5) folio 29r pars 1, *de simonia,* cap. 16

Si qui tamen . . . et scientia commendat

Canon 3, Council of Rome, April 24-30, 1099, Mansi, XX, 961; this canon forms the first half of c. 108, C. I, q. 1. This canon is actually inscribed as canon 2, and represents the same situation as the preceding canon, namely that it is a repetition of canon 3 of the Council of Piacenza. For the contents cf. the Collection in Seven Books, n. 2, where the first seven canons of the Council of Piacenza are treated.

6) folio 29r pars 1, *de simonia,* cap. 17

Qui uero scienter . . . irritam esse censemus

Canon 4, Council of Rome, April 24-30, 1099, Mansi, XX, 961; this canon is the last half of c. 108, C. I, q. 1. This canon bears the number 3 in its inscription; it is also found as canon 4 of the Council of Piacenza. Cf. the Collection in Seven Books, n. 2, for the content of the *capitulum.*

7) folio 29r pars 1, *de simonia,* cap. 18

Nullus archiepiscopus . . . munus accipere presumat

This is a paraphrase of canon 4, Council of Rome, April 24-30, 1099, as found in Mansi, XX, 961. In the manuscript this canon is called *cap. XI.* The canon as reported in Mansi forbids simony in very general terms; in this collection some specific simoniacal gifts are singled out as forbidden. Actually the canon as found in this collection is textually not very close to that in Mansi.

8) folio 29r pars 1, *de simonia,* cap. 19

Quicumque adhuc pueri . . . uiuere potest

This canon is a paraphrase of canon 5, Council of Rome, Mansi, XX, 961; it is quite close in its ideas to c. 1, C. I, q. 5. Like canon 5 of Piacenza this canon states that, if the parents of a priest buy a church or benefice for their son, he may remain in orders, provided that he gives up the simonaically obtained charge. Cf. the information given about canon 5 of the Council of Piacenza in the Collection of Seven Books, n. 2.

9) folio 29r pars 1, *de simonia,* cap. 20

Illi vero qui . . . eos ministrare permittimus

This canon is inscribed as canon 6 of the Council of Rome; actually it is the first sentence of canon 6 as found in Mansi, XX, 961. As it is found here and in the Council of Piacenza, where the same canon was first promulgated, this canon forbids the clergy to buy ecclesiastical honors; violators of this norm had to surrender the honor or face deposition. It is part of c. 1, C. I, q. 5.

10) folio 29r-29v pars 1, *de simonia,* cap. 21

Si qui tamen . . . non patimur

Canon 7 of the Council of Rome according to both accounts of the council, Mansi, XX, 661 and 805. Since this canon was among those announced at the Council of Piacenza four years previously, further information about its contents may be obtained from the remarks made at the end of n. 2 of the Collection in Seven Books; n. 2 in its entirety deals with the first seven canons of Piacenza, which were verbally repeated in the Roman Synod of 1099.

11) folio 30r pars 1, *de simonia,* cap. 29

Ne aliquis laicus . . . ab omnibus fiat

Canon 31, Council of Clermont, Nov. 18-28, 1095, Mansi, XX, 818. Cf. c. 46, C. XII, q. 2, with the *notatio correctorum.* This canon is here ascribed to the third chapter of the Council of Clermont. Of special interest is the fact that the third word is *clericus* in all versions, except the present one; it has been made to refer to the laity. The canon forbids seizing the property of ecclesiastics. Cf. the Collection of Saint-Germain-des-Prés, n. 29.

12) folio 30v pars 1, *de simonia,* cap. 37

Ut ab excommunicatis . . . est precipua concedendum

JL 5393; this portion of the letter appears with great frequency in the collections after Urban II. Cf. the Collection in Two Books, n. 2, where the entire letter is identified.

13) folio 34v pars 2, *de episcopis,* cap. 23

Cenomanensem electum . . . periculo consulatur

JL 4610, a letter of Alexander II; this letter is inscribed to Urban II in Gratian (c. 13, D. LVI) and in the printed edition of the *Panormia.* It is not attributed to Urban in either of the two manuscripts of the *Panormia* examined, nor is mention of Urban II included in the present inscription. In fact here no sender is mentioned in the address. Cf. the *Panormia,* n. 3.

14) folio 38r pars 2, *de episcopis,* cap. 48

Si quis episcoporum . . . ab omnibus fiat

Canon 32, Council of Clermont, Nov. 18-28, 1095, Mansi, XX, 819. This canon was counted as n. 30 in the Collection of Saint-Germain-des-Prés; further information is obtainable in that place.

15) folio 39r-39v pars 2, *de episcopis,* cap. 60

Quia simpliciter . . . officio confirmamus

JL 5390; cf. the *Collectio Britannica,* n. 37.

16) folio 49r pars 2, *de episcopis,* cap. 101

Confirmitati tue . . . et dampnabilis

JL 5730; cf. the Collection of Turin in Seven Books, n. 1. A scribe's error has mixed the opening words. The usual version of this canon begins: *Compatimur infirmitati tue.*

17) folio 54v pars 2, *de episcopis,* cap. 132

Artaldus alanensis . . . sacerdotio me repellat

A historical note reported previously in the *Collectio Britannica,* n. 44.

18) folio 54v pars 2, *de episcopis,* cap. 134

Nullus in episcopatum . . . metropolitani licentia

Canon 1, Council of Benevento; cf. the Collection in Nine Books, n. 1.

19) folio 80r pars 3, *de clericis,* cap. 122

Presbiterorum filios . . . fuerint conuersari

Canon 14, Council of Melfi; cf. the recension "Bb" of the Collection of Anselm of Lucca, n. 1.

20) folio 80r pars 3, *de clericis,* cap. 123

Lugdunenis parrechie [parrochie ?] . . . canonum disciplina

JL 5723; cf. the *Tripartita,* n. 10.

21) folio 82r pars 3, *de clericis,* cap. 131

Ut nullus fiat . . . nisi leuita

First sentence of canon 3, Council of Clermont, Nov. 18-28, 1095, Mansi, XX, 817. Cf. the Collection of Saint-Germain-des-Prés, n. 9.

22) folio 82r pars 3, *de clericis,* cap. 133

Ne ulli filii . . . uel regulares fiant

Paraphrase of canon 11, Council of Clermont, Nov. 18-28, 1095, Mansi, XX, 817. Sons of concubines and clerics are forbidden to receive ordination or any ecclesiastical honor. This canon came into some consideration in the Collection of Saint-Germain-des-Prés, n. 13 (second sentence) and n. 14.

23) folio 82r pars 3, *de clericis,* cap. 135

Ut nullus deinceps . . . geminos habet

Canon 14, Council of Clermont, Nov. 18-28, 1095, Mansi, XX, 817. This canon was discussed in the Collection of Saint-Germain-des-Prés, n. 17.

24) folio 82v pars 3, *de clericis,* cap. 137

Ut omnis clericus . . . semper ordinetur

Canon 13, Council of Clermont, Mansi, XX, 817. This canon appears in the Collection of Saint-Germain-des-Prés, n. 16.

25) folio 82v pars 3, *de clericis,* cap. 138

Ne fiant ordinationes . . . ordinationes fieri

Canon 24, Council of Clermont, Mansi, XX, 818. This canon is to be found at n. 25 of the Collection of Saint-Germain-des-Prés.

26) folio 85r pars 3, *de clericis,* cap. 166

Eos qui post . . . interdictione mul(c)tentur

Canon 12, Council of Melfi, Sept. 10, 1089; cf. the Collection of *Codex Ms. Vaticanus Latinus 4977,* n. 2.

27) folio 85v pars 3, *de clericis,* cap. 168

Nullus sacerdos . . . a canonicatu arceatur

Canon 9 (actually inscribed canon 11), Council of Clermont, Mansi, XX, 817. This canon which reprobates all incontinence among major clerics and canons also forms the second part of n. 12 of the Collection of the Saint-Germain-des-Prés.

28) folio 86r pars 3, *de clericis,* cap. 173

Si quis amodo . . . ecclesiasticis habeat

JL 4477 (letter of Alexander II, here ascribed to *Urbanus II*), to the king and bishops of Dalmatia, (1061,) c. 16, D. LXXXI. Any cleric in major orders who cohabits with a woman is to cease from this or suffer the loss of his post; likewise such a one is neither to be permitted to sing the office in common, nor to be allowed to share in the choral distributions.

29) folio 86r pars 3, *de clericis,* cap. 174

Si quis presbiterorum . . . inuictus beneficium

JL 4612 (letter of Alexander II; here it follows the preceding canon inscribed to Urban II; the actual inscription of this canon is: *Idem clero mediolanensi*), to the clergy of Milan, 1066-1067, c. 17, D. LXXXI. Priests, deacons and subdeacons who desert their office and cohabit with a woman will suffer the loss of office and benefice.

30) folio 87r pars 3, *de clericis,* cap. 182

Ut nullus presbiter . . . episcopus sui

First sentence of canon 18, Council of Clermont, Nov. 18-28, 1095, Mansi, XX, 817. This canon has been considered in the Collection of Saint-Germain-des-Prés, n. 21.

31) folio 87r pars 3, *de clericis,* cap. 184

Ne episcopis vel . . . fidelitatem faciat

Canon 17, Council of Clermont, Mansi, XX, 817. This is the same as the canon treated in the Collection of Saint-Germain-des-Prés, n. 20.

32) folio 104r pars 4, *de monachis,* cap. 40

In ecclesiis ubi . . . conuersatio pendeat

This canon is not found included within the actual canons of Clermont, but it is found at the end of Lambert's account,

Mansi, XX, 819. The exact text, however, is found in c. 1, X, *de capellanis monachorum et aliorum religiosorum,* III, 37. For more details cf. the Collection of Saint-Germain-des-Prés, n. 3, where the same canon is found. Cf. canon 18, Council of Clermont, Mansi, XX, 817.

33) folio 112r pars 4, *de canonicis regularibus,* cap. 1

Postulationi tue libenter . . . sapienter administrentur

JL 5729, to Roger, the abbot of St. John of the Vines (Saint-Jean des Vignes), near Soissons, July 14, 1088-1099. Permission is given to fill the parishes attached to the monastery by investing the canons of the community for this parochial ministry.[57]

34) folio 112r pars 4, *de canonicis regularibus,* cap. 2

Mandamus et mandantes . . . in choro maneat

Although this canon is frequently found credited to Urban II in the collections of this period, it is not from his acts. It is found in c. 2, C. XIX, q. 3, under Urban's name; cf. the *Polycarpus,* n. 3.

35) folio 112r pars 4, *de canonicis regularibus,* cap. 3

Statuimus ne . . . cautione suscipiat

JL 5763; cf. the recension "Bb" of the Collection of Anselm of Lucca, n. 6.

36) folio 115v pars 5, *de baptismo,* cap. 10

Super quibus consuluit . . . compatres effecti sunt

JL 5741; cf. the *Tripartita* of Ivo, n. 5.

[57] On the use of the word "*ordinare*" in the sense of providing a cleric with a benefice or other means of support, cf. H. Feine, "Studien zum langobardisch-italischen Eigenkirchenrecht, III Teil," *Zeitschrift der Savigny-Stiftung für Rechtsgeschichte,* kanonistiche Abteilung, XXXII (1943), 70-71; C. Du Cange, *Glossarium mediae et infimae Latinitatis* (ed. of Niort, 1883-1887, photographically reproduced, 10 vols., Paris: Librairie des Sciences et des Artes, 1937), VI, 59, s. v. *ordinatio,* 4th meaning.

37) folio 115v pars 5, *de baptismo,* cap. 11

a. *Quod autem uxor . . . iniungi debet*

b. *Porro eos qui ecclesiam . . . canonum preiuditio*

JL 5742 and 5740 have here been consolidated into a single canon, just as they are found in the *Tripartita,* n. 6; the second canon of the pair is found alone in the Collection of *Codex Ms. Vaticanus Latinus 3829,* n. 3.

38) folio 120r-120v pars 5, *de baptismo,* cap. 52

Illud quoque precipimus . . . unquam exigatur

Canon 12, Council of Rome, April 24-30, 1099, Mansi, XX, 963. This canon is identical with canon 13 of the Council of Piacenza, March 1-7, 1095, Mansi, XX, 806, which may be found in the *Polycarpus,* n. 1.

39) folio 152r-152v pars 6, *de rebus ecclesiasticis,* cap. 94

Nullus laicus decimas . . . est offeratur

Canon 15, Council of Rome, April 24-30, 1099, Mansi, XX, 963-964. This canon is a repetition of canon 5 of the Council of Melfi, Sept. 10, 1089, Mansi, XX, 723. The offering of tithes to monasteries and houses of canons regular is to be made with the permission of the local ordinary or of the Roman Pontiff; if the bishop refuses his consent because of avarice, then the Pontiff is to be consulted.

40) folio 158r pars 6, *de rebus ecclesiasticis,* cap. 147

Ut nullus aliquem . . . laicorum accipiat

This canon is found as the first sentence of canon 15 of the Council of Clermont, Nov. 18-28, 1095, Mansi, XX, 817. It is found in the Collection of Saint-Germain-des-Prés, n. 18.

41) folio 158r pars 6, *de rebus ecclesiasticis,* cap. 148

Nullus abbas . . . concessione presumat

Canon 16, Council of Rome, April 24-30, 1099, Mansi, XX, 964. The same canon was first promulgated as canon 6, Council of Melfi, Sept. 10, 1089, Mansi, XX, 723. No abbot or rector of a church is to accept ecclesiastical goods from laymen without the permission of the bishop. This canon forbade the acceptance of tithes except by parish churches.

42) folio 158r pars 6, *de rebus ecclesiasticis,* cap. 149

Interdictum est ne . . . honoribus faciant

Canon 16, Council of Clermont, Nov. 18-28, 1095, Mansi, XX, 817. This canon was considered in the Collection of Saint-Germain-des-Prés, n. 19, where it also appears.

43) folio 166v pars 6, *de ieiunio,* cap. 2

Ut nullus christianus . . . carnem comedat

Canon 23, Council of Clermont, Mansi, XX, 817; also found in the Collection of Saint-Germain-des-Prés, n. 24, where it is examined.

44) folio 167r pars 6, *de ieiunio,* cap. 7

Primum quatuor . . . eiusdem excepta

This canon is not found anywhere in the acts of Urban II, except in the Collection of Saint-Germain-des-Prés, where it appears as the very first canon, and is called n. 1 in the present conspectus.

45) folio 167v pars 6, *de ieiunio,* cap. 9

Ut in sabbato . . . circa noctem

Canon 26, Council of Clermont, Nov. 18-28, 1095, Mansi, XX, 818. This canon has already been seen in the Collection of Saint-Germain-des-Prés, n. 26.

46) folio 178r pars 7, *de coniugiis,* cap. 31

Si uerum esse . . . in domino nubat

JL 5382; cf. the *Collectio Britannica,* n. 29.

47) folio 178r-178v pars 7, *de coniugiis,* cap. 32

De neptis tue . . . est etiam sentiendum

JL 5399; cf. the Collection of *Codex Ms. Vaticanus Latinus 4977,* n. 1.

48) folio 198v-199r pars 8, *de homicidiis,* cap. 13

Excommunicatorum interfectoribus . . . flagicio contraxerunt

JL 5536; cf. the First Collection of Prague, n. 2.

49) folio 207r pars 8, *de homicidiis,* cap. 75

Clerico quo iacente . . . et timore permaneat

JL 5474; cf. the *Panormia,* n. 9.

50) folio 212v-213r pars 8, *de incesta copulatione,* cap. 19

Notificamus tibi . . . aliquam iniungatur

JL 5388; cf. the *Collectio Britannica.* n. 35.

51) folio 213r pars 8, *de incesta copulatione,* cap. 23

Conuenit troie . . . non prohibeantur

Canon 1, Council of Troia; cf. the Collection of *Codex Ms. Vaticanus Latinus 3829,* n. 2.

52) folio 221v pars 9, *de excommunicatione,* cap. 38

Sanctis quippe . . . metus incutiatur

JL 5393; cf. the Collection in Two Books, n. 2, where the whole letter from which the present canon was extracted is found.

53) folio 222v pars 9, *de excommunicatione,* cap. 41

Iuratos wigoni milites . . . auctoritate persoluere

JL 5724; cf. the Collection in Nine Books, n. 12, together with the *Panormia,* n. 11, both of which give some idea of the contents of this canon.

54) folio 223v-224r pars 9, *de excommunicatione,* cap. 48

Sane quod super . . . moribus adiuuare

JL 5363; cf. the *Collectio Britannica,* n. 16.

55) folio 276r pars 12, *de penitentia,* cap. 2

Ne aliquis laicus . . . reuerti possint

Canons 21 and 22, Council of Clermont, Nov. 18-28, 1095, Mansi, XX, 818. This canon is found, just as it is here, in the Collection of Saint-Germain-des-Prés, n. 23.

The Collection of *Codex Ms. Vaticanus Latinus 1361*

Based on the order of the Collection of Anselm of Lucca, the present collection is dependent upon the *Panormia* of Ivo of Chartres. It is made up of 13 books, as is the work of Anselm. This collection was compiled in Italy between 1133 and 1137.[58]

1) folio 91v-93r lib. 3, cap. 94

Saluator predicit . . . coronam uite

JL 5743; cf. the recension "C" of the Collection of Anselm of Lucca, n. 1.

2) folio 103r lib. 4, cap. 43

Vendentes et ementes . . . habere permittas

JL 5381; cf. the *Collectio Britannica*, n. 26

3) folio 103r lib. 4, cap. 45

Hos qui post . . . interdictione mulctentur

Canon 12, Council of Melfi, Sept. 10, 1089; cf. the Collection of *Codex Ms. Vaticanus Latinus 4977*, n. 2. A rubricator erred in putting *Hos* for *Eos* in the opening word of the canon.

4) folio 103r-103v lib. 4, cap. 48

Statuimus ne . . . cautione suscipiat

JL 5763; cf. the recension "Bb" of the Collection of Anselm of Lucca, n. 6.

5) folio 103v-104r lib. 4, cap. 50

Que inquam leges . . . non estis sub lege

JL 5760; cf. the *Polycarpus*, n. 2. This canon usually begins with the words, *Due inquit leges*.

6) folio 104r lib. 4, cap. 51

Mandamus et mandantes . . . in choro maneat

This canon, inscribed *Idem*, after a canon of Urban II, is

[58] Fournier-Le Bras, *Histoire*, II, 225-226; Fournier, *Les Collections Canoniques*, pp. 144-147; Van Hove, *Prolegomena*, p. 329; Stickler, *Historia*, p. 187.

not Urban's, but has frequently been attributed to him in the collections of the pre-Gratian period. For more details, cf. the *Polycarpus,* n. 3.

7) folio 114v lib. 5, cap. 56

Quanto familiarius . . . tua episcopali iusticia

JL 5778, to Ingelram, bishop of Laon (actually this canon is inscribed: *Urbanus papa II.H. lugdunensi episcopo*), 1099. Urban orders that Ingelram restore to the monks of St. Remy of Reims the priory of St. Marculfus at Corbeny on the basis of the 30 years' peaceful possession enjoyed by monks of St. Remy.

8) folio 163r lib. 7, cap. 104

Presbiterorum filios . . . fuerint conuersari

Canon 14, Council of Melfi, Sept. 10, 1089; cf. the recension "Bb" of the Collection of Anselm of Lucca, n. 1.

9) folio 163r-163v lib. 7, cap. 105

Renomagensem electum . . . periculo assumatur

JL 4610, a letter of Alexander II, here inscribed *Idem* after a canon of Urban II. This canon is also ascribed to Urban in c. 13, D. LVI. Cf. the *Panormia,* n. 3. This letter is usually introduced with the word "*Cenomanensem,*" which the rubricator changed into "*Renomagensem;*" the final word is usually found to be *consulitur.* Perhaps the scribe became confused and put *assumatur* at the conclusion; the word *assumatur* actually occurs as the eighth word from the end. A distraction at the right moment may be the answer to the question of how *consulitur* became *assumatur.*

10) folio 163v lib. 7, cap. 106

Quia simpliciter . . . officio confirmamus

JL 5390; cf. the *Collectio Britannica,* n. 37.

11) folio 163v lib. 7, cap. 107

Daibertum a negzelone . . . nil dare potuit

JL 5383; cf. the *Collectio Britannica,* n. 30, where this canon also occurs.

12) folio 169v-170r lib. 8, cap. 32

Sane quia monachorum . . . iura seruentur

Canon 4 of the *Codex Cencii,* Council of Clermont, Nov. 18-28, 1095, Mansi, XX, 904; this canon forms the final pericope of canon 1, Council of Nîmes, July 8-12, 1096, Mansi, XX, 933, where part of what was legislated at Clermont was repeated. Cf. the recension " C " of the Collection of Anselm of Lucca, n. 2.

13) folio 170r lib. 8, cap. 33

Item placuit ut . . . periculo subiacebit

Following the previous canon, the present *capitulum* bears the inscription, *Idem,* and nothing more. This canon under Urban's name is incorporated in Gratian at c. 3, D. VI, *de poen.,* and also at c. 2, C. IX, q. 2. In footnote 14 at c. 2, C. IX, q. 2, Friedberg says that the present canon is found at the end of the eighth Book of the Collection of Anselm of Lucca, and is there inscribed *ex Hibernensi;* since a canon of Urban II was listed immediately before, Friedberg thinks that mistakenly the name of Urban was associated with both of these canons. The arrangement of the canons as suggested by Friedberg is borne out in *codex ms. Vaticanus latinus 4983,* folio 413v-414r, where the exact situation as explained by Friedberg may be found; cf. the recension " C " of the Collection of Anselm of Lucca, n. 2 and n. 27 of Appendix II of Part I.

14) folio 184r lib. 9, cap. 120

Super quibus consuluit . . . compatres effecti sunt

JL 5741; cf. the *Tripartita,* n. 5.

15) folio 184r-184v lib. 9, cap. 121

a. *Quod autem uxor . . . iungi debet*
b. *Porro eos qui ecclesiam . . . canonum preiudicio*

JL 5742 joined with JL 5740 to form a single canon, as in the *Tripartita,* n. 6; cf. also, the Collection of *Codex Ms. Vaticanus Latinus 3829,* n. 3, concerning JL 5740.

16) folio 196v lib. 10, cap. 53

Notificamus tibi . . . aliquam iniungatur

JL 5388; cf. n. 35 of the *Collectio Britannica.*

17) folio 196v-197r lib. 10, cap. 56

Conuenit troie . . . non prohibeantur

Canon 1, Council of Troia, March 11, 1093, Mansi, XX, 789; cf. the Collection of *Codex Ms. Vaticanus Latinus 3829,* n. 2.

18) folio 231r lib. 12, cap. 65

Predecessorum nostrorum . . . modis omnibus prohibemus

Canon from the Fifth Roman Synod of Gregory VII (here, however, the canon is inscribed *Urbanus II*), held Febr. 27-March 3, 1078.[59] This canon is found at c. 4, C. XV, q. 6, where it is attributed to Gregory VII. The canon removes the obligation of fealty when proffered to anyone who has become an excommunicated heretic.

19) folio 231r lib. 12, cap. 67

Excommunicatorum interfectoribus . . . flagicio contraxerunt

JL 5536; cf. the First Collection of Prague, n. 2.

20) folio 231r-231v lib. 12, cap. 68

Curatos guidoni milites . . . auctoritate persoluere

JL 5724; this is a rather poor version of the canon when compared with other variants of it. Cf. the Collection in Nine Books, n. 12. The opening words of this canon seem to have been subjected to errors made by the scribes and rubricators.

21) folio 245v-246r lib. 13, cap. 44

Questum est . . . habere soliti sunt

Canon 3 in the *Codex Cencii,* Council of Clermont, Nov. 18-28, 1095, Mansi, XX, 902. Canon 7 of Lambert's account is

[59] Canon found in P. Jaffé, *Monumenta Gregoriana* (Berlini: apud Weidmannos, 1865), p. 308. The canons are not numbered in this text.

related in content (cf. Mansi, XX, 817). This same canon was repeated in the Council of Nîmes, canon 1, July 8-12, 1096, Mansi, XX, 933, and is found in Gratian at c. 4, C. I, q. 3, where it is credited to the Council of Clermont. In content this canon contains the same provision as that which is reported in the Collection of Saint-Germain-des-Prés, n. 2.

The Collection in Thirteen Books

This collection exhibits no dependence upon the works of Ivo of Chartres. Some Gregorian texts are presented, but the rigor of the reform is lacking. The sources seem haphazardly selected and arbitrarily arranged. The author is unknown; he wrote probably in Poitiers, sometime in the last decade of the eleventh century.[60]

1) The only source of information concerning the canons of Urban II in this collection comes from the report of Fournier-Le Bras. Since the manuscript for this collection was not available, this report is the only source of knowledge to rely upon. Two canons are mentioned and both are fragments of JL 5393, the letter to Gebhard, bishop of Constance, which is reported in the Collection of Two Books, n. 2. There are several portions of this letter found among the canons of Urban; it is impossible to discover which of these are the two found in this collection.

The Collection in Ten Parts

Based largely upon the system and content of the *Panormia,* the Collection in Ten Parts was composed sometime after 1123 by an author whose identity, at least at the present time, is unknown. A substantial portion of the collection is made up of Reform materials written after the *Panormia.* The author composed an excellent supplement to Ivo's *Panormia.* There is a noticeable affinity between this collection and the Collection of Saint-Germain-des-Prés.[61]

[60] Fournier-Le Bras, *Histoire,* II, 251-259; Van Hove, *Prolegomena,* p. 331; Stickler, *Historia,* p. 187; Theiner, *Disquisitiones,* pp. 183-186.

[61] For this collection the following manuscript was consulted: *Vienna,*

1) folio 14r pars 1, tit. 9, cap. 9

Baptismus est si . . . trinitatis baptizaverit

JL 5741; this canon is actually an abridgment, after the fashion of an inscription, of the fragment identified in the *Tripartita,* n. 5.

2) folio 19r pars 1, tit. 33, cap. 5

Illud quoque precipimus . . . utique exigatur

Canon 12, Council of Rome, cf. The *Polycarpus,* n. 1, and the Second Collection of Châlons-sur-Marne, n. 38. The same canon was first given at Piacenza in 1095, and then repeated at the Council of Rome at Easter-time, 1099. Some versions of this canon forbid the accepting of money for confirmation, baptism and burial; others, such as the present version, have "*balsamo*" for "*baptismo.*" The penultimate word of the canon should be "*unquam.*"

3) folio 36v pars 2, tit. 32, cap. 1

Nullus laicus decimas . . . et anathemate feriatur

Canon 15, Council of Rome; cf. the Second Collection of Châlons-sur-Marne, n. 39, but with a different conclusion, which threatens a penalty for those who give their tithes to a monastery without the proper permission.

4) folio 48r pars 2, tit. 57, cap. 3

Ut nullus christianus . . . carnem comedat

Canon 23, Council of Clermont; cf. the Collection of Saint-Germain-des-Prés, n. 24.

5) folio 48v pars 2, tit. 57, cap. 8

Primum quatuor . . . eiusdem excepta

Canon 1, Council of Clermont, in the unique version of the acts of that Council found in the Collection of Saint-Germain-des-Prés, n. 1.

Österreichische Nationalbibliothek 2178 (*juris canonici 91*). Cf. Fournier-Le Bras, *Histoire,* II, 296-306; Fournier, *Les Collections Canoniques,* pp. 147-156; Van Hove, *Prolegomena,* p. 334; Stickler, *Historia,* p. 186.

6) folio 49v pars 2, tit. 58, cap. 3

Ut in sabbato . . . circa noctem

Canon 26, Council of Clermont; this canon was first reported in the Collection of Saint-Germain-des-Prés, n. 26.

7) folio 52r pars 3, tit. 2, cap. 6

Nullus in episcopatum . . . metropolitani licentia

Canon 1, Council of Benevento; cf. the Collection in Nine Books, n. 1.

8) folio 54r pars 3, tit. 7, cap. 4

Ut nullus aliquem . . . laicorum accipiat

First sentence of canon 15, Council of Clermont; the same sentence forms a separate canon in the Collection of Saint-Germain-des-Prés, n. 18, and in the Second Collection of Châlons-sur-Marne, n. 40.

9) folio 54r pars 3, tit. 7, cap. 5

Nullus abbas . . . concessione presumat

Canon 16, Council of Rome; found in the Second Collection of Châlons-sur-Marne, n. 41.

10) folio 54r pars 3, tit. 7, cap. 6

Interdictum est ne . . . honoribus ecclesiasticis faciant

Canon 16, Council of Clermont; cf. the Collection of Saint-Germain-des-Prés, n. 19.

11) folio 55v pars 3, tit. 11, cap. 3

Nemo preterea . . . uirginem uxorem habuerit

Canon 3, Council of Melfi; this canon is the same as the one found the Collection of *Codex Ms. Vaticanus Latinus 4977*, n. 4, and elsewhere, but here the first sentence is omitted: "*Ad sacros ordines non accedat nisi uirgo aut probate castitatis.*"

12) folio 56r pars 3, tit. 11, cap. 7

Ne fiant ordinationes . . . ordinationes fieri

Canon 24, Council of Clermont; this canon is found in the Collection of Saint-Germain-des-Prés, n. 25.

13) folio 56v pars 3, tit. 13, cap. 3

Ut omnis clericus . . . semper ordinetur

Canon 13, Council of Clermont; this canon is identified in the Collection of Saint-Germain-des-Prés, n. 16.

14) folio 59r pars 3, tit. 15, cap. 1

Ut nullus fiat . . . nisi leuita

First sentence of canon 3, Council of Clermont; this canon is included in the Collection of Saint-Germain-des-Prés, at n. 9.

15) folio 60r pars 3, tit. 18, cap. 1

Presbiterorum filios . . . fuerint conuersari

Canon 14, Council of Melfi, but here inscribed, "*ex decretis gregorii VI* (instead of *VII*) *et urbani II.*" Cf. the recension "Bb" of the Collection of Anselm of Lucca, n. 1.

16) folio 60r pars 3, tit. 18, cap. 2

Ne ulli filii . . . uel regulares fiant

Corresponds closely to canon 11, Council of Clermont; cf. the Second Collection of Châlons-sur-Marne, n. 22, and also the Collection of Saint-Germain-des-Prés, especially n. 14, and the second sentence of the canon treated under n. 13.

17) folio 60r pars 3, tit. 18, cap. 5

Cenomanensem electum . . . periculo consulatur

JL 4610, a letter of Alexander II, but here without any sender indicated; the addressee, Bartholomew, Archbishop of Tours, is here referred to as a bishop; the same inscription is found in this same canon in the Second Collection of Châlons-sur-Marne, n. 13, cf. also the *Panormia,* n. 3.

18) folio 60r-60v pars 3, tit. 18, cap. 6

Quia similiter . . . officio confirmamus

JL 5390; cf. the *Collectio Britannica,* n. 37. The word "*similiter*" is an error for "*suppliciter.*"

19) folio 61v pars 3, tit. 24, cap. 3

Nulli clerico . . . habere non possit

Canon 12, Council of Clermont; cf. the Collection of Saint-Germain-des-Prés, n. 15.

20) folio 62r pars 3, tit. 24, cap. 5

Ut nullus deinceps . . . geminos habere

Canon 14, Council of Clermont; cf. the Collection of Saint-Germain-des-Prés. n. 17.

21) folio 63v pars 3, tit. 26, cap. 6

Daiberto a gnezelone . . . nil dare potuit

JL 5383; cf. the *Collectio Britannica,* n. 30.

22) folio 65r pars 3, tit. 29, cap. 1

Eos qui post . . . interdictione mul(c)tentur

Canon 12, Council of Melfi; cf. the Collection of *Codex Ms. Vaticanus Latinus 4977,* n. 2.

23) folio 66v pars 3, tit. 34, cap. 6

Quicquid igitur . . . uires optinere censemus

Canon 2, Council of Rome; cf. the Second Collection of Châlons-sur-Marne, n. 4. The inscription is interesting: "*Ex concilio urbani pape habito rome in ecclesia beati petri anno christi MX.C.IX.VI kal. mai cap. I.*"

24) folio 66v-67r pars 3, tit. 34, cap. 7

Si qui tamen . . . conscientia commendat

Canon 3, Council of Rome; cf. the Second Collection of Châlons-sur-Marne, n. 5, and the Collection in Seven Books, n. 2.

25) folio 67r pars 3, tit. 34, cap. 8

Qui uero scienter . . . irritam esse censemus

Canon 4, Council of Rome; cf. the Second Collection of Châlons-sur-Marne, n. 6, together with the Collection in Seven Books, n. 2.

26) folio 67r pars 3, tit. 34, cap. 9

Vendentes et ementes . . . habere permittas

JL 5381; cf. the *Collectio Britannica,* n. 26.

27) folio 67r pars 3, tit. 35, cap. 1

Nullus archiepiscopus . . . munus accipere presumat

A paraphrase of canon 4, Council of Rome; this canon is identical with that of the Second Collection of Châlons-sur-Marne, n. 7.

28) folio 67r pars 3, tit. 35, cap. 2

Nullus abbas pretium . . . occasione presumat

Beginning of canon 17, Council of Rome, April 24-30, 1099, Mansi, XX, 964. This canon as it is found here was first promulgated in the Council of Melfi, canon 7, Sept. 10, 1089, Mansi, XX, 723. It was repeated in the Council of Rome, and more was added to the text there. It forbids an abbot from demanding anything from anyone making religious profession. This canon forms the very first sentence of c. 3, C. I, q. 2, and is there ascribed to the Council of Melfi.

29) folio 67r pars 3, tit. 35, cap. 3

Quicumque adhuc pueri . . . uiuere potest

A paraphrase of canon 5, Council of Rome; cf. the Second Collection of Châlons-sur-Marne, n. 8, along with the Collection of Seven Books, n. 2.

30) folio 67r pars 3, tit. 35, cap. 4

Illi uero qui . . . eos ministrare permittas

First part of canon 6, Council of Rome; cf. the Second Collection of Châlons-sur-Marne, n. 9.

31) folio 67r pars 3, tit. 35, cap. 5

Quos si alias . . . non accedant

The second sentence of canon 6, Council of Rome; April 24-30, 1099, Mansi, XX, 961; this canon was first promulgated at the Council of Piacenza, March 1-5, 1095, Mansi, XX,

805. It is therefore the continuation of the preceding canon, as Mansi has it. The previous canon demanded that those who bought ecclesiastical honors had both to tranfer to another church and to surrender the honor; the present canon demands that those who cannot effect a transfer, but who have reformed, may retain the exercise of their minor orders, but many not be advanced to major orders.

32) folio 67r pars 3, tit. 35, cap. 6

Si qui tamen . . . non patimur

Canon 7, Council of Rome; cf. the Second Collection of Châlons-sur-Marne, n. 10, and the Collection in Seven Books, n. 2.

33) folio 69r pars 3, tit. 41, cap. 6

Si quis amodo . . . ecclesiasticis habeat

JL 4477, a letter of Alexander II, here ascribed to Urban II. Cf. the Second Collection of Châlons-sur-Marne, n. 28.

34) folio 69r pars 3, tit. 41 cap. 7

Si quis presbiterorum . . . beneficium iudicamus

JL 4612 (another letter of Alexander II, here following upon a canon of the same Pope, and also wrongly ascribed to Urban), to the clergy of Milan, 1066-1067, c. 17, D. LXXXI. Major clerics who desert their canonical charge for sinful cohabitation are to be deprived of their benefices.

35) folio 69r pars 3, tit. 41, cap. 8

Eos etiam qui . . . esse adiudicamus

JL 4612; this fragment is from a portion of the same letter from which the previous canon is taken; cf. c. 18, D. LXXXI. Those clerics who desert their clerical duties for reasons of fornication are likewise to be declared deprived of their benefice. Note that the three previous canons are all falsely attributed to Urban II, and that these three canons are found in Gratian in a body at cc. 16-18, D. LXXXI, with the correct inscription.[62]

[62] For some discussion on this and the preceding canon, cf. D. Heintschel,

36) folio 71r pars 3, tit. 43, cap. 5
Clericum quo iacente . . . et timore permaneat
JL 5474; cf. the *Panormia,* n. 9.

37) folio 74r pars 3, tit. 54, cap. 5
In ecclesiis ubi . . . conuersatio pendeat
Canon 3, Council of Clermont, according to the version of the acts in the Collection of Saint-Germain-des-Prés, n. 3.

38) folio 82r pars 4, tit. 2, cap. 4
Postulatione tue libenter . . . sapienter administrentur
JL 5729; cf. the Second Collection of Châlons-sur-Marne, n. 33.

39) folio 82r pars 4, tit. 2, cap. 7
Statuimus ne . . . caucione suscipiat
JL 5763; cf. the recension "Bb" of the Collection of Anselm of Lucca, n. 6.

40) folio 85v pars 4, tit. 21, cap. 8
Ne aliquis laicus . . . reuerti possint
Canons 21 and 22, Council of Clermont; cf. the Collection of Saint-Germain-des-Prés, n. 23.

41) folio 87r pars 4, tit. 25, cap. 1
Ne episcopus uel . . . fidelitatem faciat
Canon 17, Council of Clermont; cf. the Collection of Saint-Germain-des-Prés, n. 20.

42) folio 87r pars 4, tit. 25, cap. 3
Ut nullus presbiter . . . episcopi sui
First sentence of canon 18, Council of Clermont; cf. the Collection of Saint-Germain-des-Prés, n. 21.

The Medieval Concept of an Ecclesiastical Office, The Catholic University of America Canon Law Studies, n. 363 (Washington, D. C.: The Catholic University of America Press, 1956), pp. 19-21.

43) folio 89r pars 4, tit. 28, cap. 8

Ne aliquis laicus . . . ab episcopis fiat

Canon 31, Council of Clermont; cf. the Collection of Saint-Germain-des-Prés, n. 29, and the Second Collection of Châlons-sur-Marne, n. 11.

44) folio 89v pars 4, tit. 30, cap. 3

Si quis episcoporum . . . ab omnibus fiat

Canon 32, Council of Clermont; cf. the Collection of Saint-Germain-des-Prés, n. 30.

45) folio 123v pars 6, tit. 13, cap. 14

Sanctis quippe . . . metus incutiatur

JL 5393; cf. the Collection in Two Books, n. 2, where the entire letter from which this fragment was taken is found.

46) folio 124r pars 6, tit. 15, cap. 2

Iuratos Wigoni milites . . . auctoritate persoluere

JL 5724; cf. the Collection in Nine Books, n. 12, and the *Panormia*, n. 11.

47) folio 125r-125v pars 6, tit. 18, cap. 2

Sane quod super . . . moribus adiuuare

JL 5363; cf. the *Collectio Britannica*, n. 16.

48) folio 134r-134v pars 7, tit. 15, cap. 3

De neptis tue . . . de uiro est sentiendum

JL 5399; cf. the Collection of *Codex Ms. Vaticanus Latinus 4977*, n. 1.

49) folio 136v pars 7, tit. 27, cap. 4

Videtur nobis ex . . . compatres effecti sunt

JL 5741; cf. the *Tripartita*, n. 5. This canon has a different beginning from the usual "*Super quibus consuluit*," but its identity with the latter cannot be called into question.

50) folio 136v pars 7, tit. 27, cap. 5

Quia piaculare flagitium . . . iniungi debet

JL 5742 (last sentence only); cf. the *Tripartita,* n. 6.

51) folio 147r pars 8, tit. 15, cap. 4

Notificamus tibi . . . aliquam iniungatur

JL 5388; cf. the *Collectio Britannica,* n. 35.

52) folio 150v pars 9, tit. 6, cap. 3

Non enim eos . . . trucidasse contigerit

JL 5536; cf. the *Panormia,* n. 16, and the First Collection of Prague, n. 2.

APPENDIX I

A Tabulation of Recurrent Canons and Their Interrelation in the Collections

This appendix has two objectives; the first is to present by chart the recurrence of the canons of Urban II in the collections; the second is to make some observations concerning the interrelation and the dependency of the collections, on the basis of the evidence given by the chart. For a helpful use of the chart several things are to be kept in mind. The chart lists every canon of Urban II, as found in the collections examined in Part I, and several other canons which are not Urban's, but which appear with some frequency under Urban's name in the collections. Unknown and dubious canons have not been given a place in the listing of the chart.

The remarks which follow the chart are derived from the evidence presented in the chart, but the chart alone does not indicate all of the relationships. It is impossible to indicate in the chart the fact that several canons are found in a cluster or in consecutive order, and this latter information is especially useful for determining the interrelation of several collections, when the only criterion available is the individual canons and their place in a collection.

This appendix does not attempt to arrive at wider conclusions than the premises allow. The premises in this case are quite limited, since almost everything depends upon the evidence from the canons of a single pope in collections which contain hundreds and even thousands of other texts. But the evidence from Urban's canons is valuable, even if it is limited in scope.

What follows is a series of observations and remarks concerning the interrelation between the various collections, based upon the evidence from recurrent canons. Before these specific remarks, several general observations should be made. Conciliar canons seem to appear with greater frequency than papal letters, if one omits consideration of the letters found in the *Collectio Britannica.* With every repetition taken into account, there are about twenty-five

	Collection of Vat. lat. 4977	Collection in 2 Books	Collectio Britannica	Collection of Turin in 7 Books	The Polycarpus	First Collection of Prague	Collection in 7 Books	Recension "Bb" of Anselm of Lucca	Recension "C" of Anselm of Lucca	Italian Collection in 3 Books	Collection in 9 Books	Collection of Vat. lat. 3829	Collection of Taurin. 903	The Tripartita	The Decretum	The Panormia	First Recension Caesaraugustana	Second Recension Caesaraugustana	Collection of St.-Germain-des-Prés	First Collection of Châlons-s-M.	Second Collection of Châlons-s-M.	Collection of Vat. lat. 1361	Collection in 13 Books	Collection in 10 Parts	Gratian
JL 5399	1	....	41	....	....	....	....	....	....	....	15	....	2	12	10	14	16	20	....	....	47	....	....	48	31.2.3
c. 12 Melfi	2	....	47	....	....	....	....	....	....	....	....	....	....	....	....	6	....	7	36	....	26	3	....	22	32.10
c. 3 Melfi	4	....	47	....	....	....	....	....	....	....	....	....	....	....	....	7	....	....	31	....	....	....	....	11	32.12
JL 5378	....	1	23	....	....	....	....	....	4	....	....	....	....	....	4										
JL 5393	....	2	38	....	....	....	....	....	3	....	....	1	....	1	3	10	2	2	....	3	12	....	1	45	9.1.4
														7	14						52				11.3.110
JL 5349	....	....	1																						
JL 5348	....	....	2																						
JL 5352	....	....	3																						
JL 5353	....	....	4																						
JL 5354	....	....	5																						
JL 5355	....	....	6																						
JL 5356	....	....	7																						
In adversa	....	....	8																						
JL 5357	....	....	9																						
JL 5358	....	....	10																						
Hoc tempore Anselmo	....	....	11																						
JL 5359	....	....	12																						
JL 5360	....	....	13																						
JL 5361	....	....	14																						
JL 5362	....	....	15																						
JL 5363	....	....	16	....	....	1	....	....	....	....	....	....	....	....	15	12	....	....	....	....	54	....	....	47	24.2.3
Hoc tempore	....	....	17																						
JL 5367	....	....	18																						
JL 5368	....	....	19																						
JL 5369	....	....	20																						
JL 5370	....	....	21																						
JL 5371	....	....	22																						
JL 5379	....	....	24																						
JL 5380	....	....	25																						
JL 5381	....	....	26	....	....	....	....	....	....	....	....	....	....	....	....	8	....	....	....	....	....	2	....	26	

Hainricus			28																						
JL 5382			29								16			11	9	13	17	21	34		46				31.2.1
JL 5383			30												5		6	6			3	11		21	1.7.24
JL 5384			31																						
JL 5385			32																						
JL 5386			33																						
JL 5387			34																						
JL 5388			35								17			13	11	15	18	22	35		50	16		51	35.6.3
JL 5389			36																						
JL 5390			37													4	15	17			15	10		18	56.14
JL 5396			39																						
JL 5397			40																						
JL 5404			42																						
JL 5405			43																						
Artaldus			44											4						5	17				8.3.2
JL 5407			45																						
JL 5408			46																						
Anno dominicae			47																						
c. 1 Melfi			47																						
c. 2 Melfi			47																31						
c. 4 Melfi			47																						
c. 5 Melfi			47																31		39			3	
c. 8 Melfi			47																						
c. 9 Melfi			47																						
c. 10 Melfi			47															19							
c. 11 Melfi			47																						
c. 13 Melfi			47																						
c. 14 Melfi			47					1		1	2			8	6	2	14	16			19	8		15	56.1
c. 15 Melfi			47																						
c. 16 Melfi			47															27							
JL 5730				1	4									3				25		4	16				35.2.11
c. 13 Piacenza					1					10	13						5	5	31		38			2	
JL 5760					2		3	4		2	3						11	13				5			19.2.2
Mandamus					3		1	5		3	4						12	14			34	6			19.3.2
c. 8 Piacenza					5		5			7									31						9.1.5
c. 9 Piacenza					5		5			7									31						9.1.5
c. 10 Piacenza					5		5			7									31						9.1.5
c. 11 Piacenza					5		5			7									31						9.1.5
c. 12 Piacenza					5		5			7							5	5	31						9.1.5
JL 5536						2								15	13	16	19	28			48	19		52	23.5.47
c. 1 Piacenza							2			5	7						5	5	31						1.3.5
c. 2 Piacenza							2			5	7						5	5	31		4			23	1.3.5

	Collection of Vat. lat. 4977	Collection in 2 Books	Collectio Britannica	Collection of Turin in 7 Books	The Polycarpus	First Collection of Prague	Collection in 7 Books	Recension "Bb" of Anselm of Lucca	Recension "C" of Anselm of Lucca	Italian Collection in 3 Books	Collection in 9 Books	Collection of Vat. lat. 3829	Collection of Taurin. 903	The Tripartita	The Decretum	The Panormia	First Recension Caesaraugustana	Second Recension Caesaraugustana	Collection of St.-Germain-des-Prés	First Collection of Châlons-s-M.	Second Collection of Châlons-s-M.	Collection of Vat. lat. 1361	Collection in 13 Books	Collection in 10 Parts	Gratian
c. 3 Piacenza							2			5	7						5	5	31		5			24	1.1.108
c. 4 Piacenza							2			5	7						5	5	31		6			25	1.1.108
c. 5 Piacenza							2			6	8						5	5	31		8			29	1.5.1
c. 6 Piacenza							2			6	8						5	5	31		9			30	1.5.1
																								31	
c. 7 Piacenza							2			6	8						5	5	31		10			32	1.5.1
c. 4 Benevento							4																		
JL 5759								2																	22.5.23
c. 4a Benevento								3																	
JL 5763								6			5			9	7		13	15	32		35	4		39	19.3.3
JL 5743									1	4	9											1			32.6
											11														1.3.8
																									1.3.12
c. 14 Piacenza										11	14														76.4
c. 1 Benevento											1				2	1	1	1	37	6	18			7	60.4
																		9							
c. 4 Clermont cc.									2		10							29				12			16.2.6
JL 5724											12					11	9	11			53	20		46	15.6.5
c. 1 Troia												2		14	12		8	23	33		51	17			35.6.4
JL 5740												3		6			4	4		2	2	15			1.5.2
																	7	24			37				
JL 4589														2			3	3			1				1.5.3
JL 5741														5			7	24		1	36			1	30.3.4
																								49	
JL 5742														6			7	24		2	2	15		50	30.4.6
																					37				
JL 5723														10	8						20				9.2.10
JL 5611															1										
JL 5722															5										
JL 4610																3					13	9		17	56.13
JL 5724																9		8			49			36	50.37

JL 5423																	10	12							
after c. 15 Piacenza																	5	5							
JL 5734																		18							
c. 1 Clermont w																			1		44			5	
c. 2 Clermont w																			2						
c. 3 Clermont w																			3		32			37	
c. 4 Clermont w																			4						
c. 5 Clermont w																			5						
c. 1 Clermont																			6						
																			7						
c. 2 Clermont																			8						
c. 3 Clermont																			9		21			14	60.1 (rel)
cc. 4, 5 Clermont																			10						
c. 6 Clermont																			11						
cc. 8, 9 Clermont																			12		27				
cc. 10, 11 Clermont																			13						
c. 14 Clermont w																			14		22			16	
c. 12 Clermont																			15					19	
c. 13 Clermont																			16		24			13	
c. 14 Clermont																			17		23			20	
c. 15 Clermont																			18		40			8	
c. 16 Clermont																			19		42			10	
c. 17 Clermont																			20		31			41	
c. 18 Clermont																			21		30			42	
cc. 19, 20 Clermont																			22						
cc. 21, 22 Clermont																			23	7	55			40	
c. 23 Clermont																			24		43			4	
c. 24 Clermont																			25		25			12	
c. 26 Clermont																			26		45			6	
c. 28 Clermont																			27						
cc. 29, 30 Clermont																			28						
c. 31 Clermont																			29		11			43	12.2.46 (rel)
c. 32 Clermont																			30		14			44	
JL 5471																			38						
JL 5794																			39						
c. 4 Rome sp																					7			27	
c. 5 Rome sp																					8				
JL 4477																					28			33	81.16
JL 4612																					29			34	81.17
																								35	81.18

	Collection of Vat. lat. 4977	Collection in 2 Books	Collectio Britannica	Collection of Turin in 7 Books	The Polycarpus	First Collection of Prague	Collection in 7 Books	Recension "Bb" of Anselm of Lucca	Recension "C" of Anselm of Lucca	Italian Collection in 3 Books	Collection in 9 Books	Collection of Vat. lat. 3829	Collection of Taurin. 903	The Tripartita	The Decretum	The Panormia	First Recension Caesaraugustana	Second Recension Caesaraugustana	Collection of St.-Germain-des-Prés	First Collection of Châlons-s-M.	Second Collection of Châlons-s-M.	Collection of Vat. lat. 1361	Collection in 13 Books	Collection in 10 Parts	Gratian
JL 5729																					33			38	
c. 16 Rome																			31		41			9	
JL 5778																						7			
c. 3 Clermont cc.																						21			1.3.4
c. 17 Rome																			31					28	1.2.3
c. 18 Rome																			31						

EXPLANATION

1) The numbers in the chart refer to the numbers used in Part I of this study.
2) Numbers which are omitted reflect canons which are not Urban's or whose origin is unknown.
3) When two numbers are in one block, this indicates that the text, or parts of it, are repeated in that collection.
4) Canons are indicated for the councils. Jaffé numbers for the letters, and the opening word or words for historical notices.
5) References to Gratian's *Decretum* are indicated with a listing of the larger divisions first; thus 31.2.3 means c. 3, C. XXXI, q. 2.
6) Abbreviations: sp = special version of a canon, having a noticeably different wording.
   cc = found in the *Codex Cencii*.
   w = peculiar to the Wolfenbüttel manuscript, i.e., the Collection of Saint-Germain-des-Prés.
   rel = related to the passage cited in Gratian.
7) The canons of the Council of Rome are not found on the chart (except for several canons that are textually close to the more common version). Since the canons from this council were first promulgated at Piacenza (cc. 1-13) and at Melfi (cc. 1-3, 5-7), to find a canon from this Council of Rome, it is necessary to look to the Council of Piacenza or of Melfi. Generally the canons of the Council of Rome are found in the more recent collections (which are found to the right hand side of the page in the chart); thus, when a canon is from either Piacenza or Melfi and is found in one of the last six collections, it is very probably from the Council of Rome.

more texts from letters than there are from conciliar canons. In general the recurrence, then, is about evenly distributed among the canons and the letters. Since many of the canons from the councils appear together in a single canon, there is a greater number of individual canons taken from the letters than from the councils. But, if those letters which appear only once (in the *Collectio Britannica*) were disregarded, the balance would be rather evenly distributed between the conciliar canons and the papal letters.

Regarding the more specific relations among the collections, a very striking similarity can be noted between the first several folios of the Collection of *Codex Ms. Vaticanus Latinus 4977* and D. XXXII of Gratian's *Decretum*. Folio 5r and 5v of this collection contains cc. 8, 9, 10, 11, 12, 13, 15 and 16 of D. XXXII, together with the same sequence and even the same errors in attribution. The relationship found here seems to be attributable to more than mere coincidence; a definite dependence upon the texts found in these folios by Gratian seems clear. Whether he used this collection or another from the same tradition, no one can say for certain. For further information the reader is directed to the section concerning the Collection of *Codex Ms. Vaticanus Latinus 4977,* n. 4, in Part I of this study.

Most of the texts of the *Collectio Britannica* are found nowhere else; but those which do appear in the other collections frequently turn up in the following collections: the Collection in Nine Books, the three works by Ivo of Chartres, the two recensions of the *Collectio Caesaraugustana,* the second Collection of Châlons-sur-Marne, the Collection of *Codex Ms. Vaticanus Latinus 1361* and the Collection in Ten Parts. The pattern among these collections themselves, however, in relation to the texts from the *Britannica* is not uniform. The indications from the *Collectio Britannica* and its recurrent canons seems to back up the allegation that the collectors before Gratian did not know of the *Britannica* in the form in which it is known today.[1] Apparently most of the texts of the *Britannica* never became very widely diffused among the collections.

There is a pair of canons which is found again and again in the

[1] Reference to the *Britannica* in a different form is made by Fournier-Le Bras, *Histoire,* II, 282-283.

collections. These canons are JL 5760 (*Due inquit leges sunt . . .*) and *Mandamus et mandantes.* This pair is almost always found together and in that order. What is even more remarkable is the fact that the second canon is not Urban's at all, but in every place where it is found in the collections it is ascribed to Urban II. The pair is found in the *Polycarpus,* nn. 2 and 3, the recension "Bb" of the Collection of Anselm of Lucca, nn. 4 and 5, the Italian Collection in Three Books, nn. 2 and 3, the Collection in Nine Books, nn. 3 and 4, the first recension of the *Collectio Caesaraugustana,* nn. 11 and 12, the second recension of the *Collectio Caesaraugustana,* nn. 13 and 14, and the Collection of *Codex Ms. Vaticanus Latinus 1361,* nn. 5 and 6. This combination is lacking in the Collection in Seven Books, nn. 3 and 1, and in the second Collection of Châlons-sur-Marne, n. 34, where only the second member of the pair is found. These two canons are found in Gratian, and although they are not too distant, the pattern found in the pre-Gratian collections is lacking (the two are in c. 2, C. XIX, q. 2, and c. 2, C. XIX, q. 3, respectively). The mistake in inscription found in the collections has passed into Gratian. The dependence exhibited by this pair of texts seems sufficiently established, especially since the error in ascription is so consistent. In general it can be said that the various collections where this pair of canons appears show dependence; each collection was made shortly after the one preceding; usually the later collection resembles those that precede it, but each successive collection has more canons than those which went before it. There are two exceptions to this pattern of growth; the recension "Bb" of the Collection of Anselm of Lucca and the Collection of *Codex Ms. Vaticanus Latinus 3829* lack many of the canons found in prior collections.

Fragments of JL 5378 and JL 5393 are in juxtaposition in the Collection in Two Books, nn. 1 and 2, in recension "C" of the Collection of Anselm of Lucca, nn. 4 and 3, and in the *Decretum* of Ivo, nn. 4 and 3. While this proximity does not prove a great deal, it could be an indication of dependence. Since Ivo's *Decretum* was such an extensive collection, it is not surprising that these two canons should be found there. It should be mentioned that fragments of JL 5393 are found more than any other canon of Urban's in the collections.

JL 5399 (*De neptis tuae . . .*) and JL 5382 (*Si verum esse . . .*) are found in juxtaposition in the Collection in Nine Books, nn. 15 and 16, in the *Tripartita,* nn. 12 and 11, in the *Decretum* of Ivo, nn. 10 and 9, and in the *Panormia,* nn. 14 and 13. JL 5388 (*Notificamus tibi . . .*) is found in close conjunction with these two canons, but it is never found juxtaposed. All three of these canons are found frequently throughout the collections. In spite of the indication given by these canons, Ivo's works do not show very much affinity with the Collection in Nine books, so far as the canons of Urban show.

JL 5740, 5741 and 5742 are often seen in proximity in the collections. All three of these fragments, indeed, are addressed to Vitalis of Brescia, and one could expect them to appear in close conjunction throughout the collections. These three canons are found sometimes joined to form a single canon; at other times JL 5742 and JL 5740 are united and, JL 5741 is found separate; In every case the three are in proximity. Cf. the *Tripartita,* nn. 5 and 6, the first recension of the *Collectio Caesaraugustana,* n. 7, the second recension of the *Collectio Caesaraugustana,* n. 24, the first Collection of Châlons-sur-Marne, nn. 1 and 2, the second Collection of Châlons-sur-Marne, nn. 36 and 37, the Collection of *Codex Ms. Vaticanus Latinus 1361,* n. 15, and the Collection in Ten Parts, nn. 49 and 50.

JL 5763 and canon 14 of the Council of Melfi appear in nn. 6 and 7 of the *Decretum* of Ivo, in nn. 8 and 9 of the *Tripartita,* in nn. 13 and 14 in the first recension of the *Collectio Caesaraugustana,* and in nn. 15 and 16 of the second recension of the *Collectio Caesaraugustana.* In the two recensions of the *Caesaraugustana* the canons are not consecutive. From the canons of Urban II as found in these collections, there does not seem to be any very close affinity between either recension of the *Caesaraugustana* and any of the works of Ivo of Chartres, except for fragments which recur rather consistently. For this reason it is difficult to come to any conclusion from Urban's canons alone. It should be remembered, however, that the *Caesaraugustana* is considered to be based largely on the *Decretum* and the *Tripartita* of Ivo, especially the first recension.[2]

[2] Cf. Van Hove, *Prolegomena,* p. 333; Stickler, *Historia,* p. 184.

In indication of a further relationship between the *Tripartita* and the two recensions of the *Collectio Caesaraugustana*, it should also be noted that JL 4589, a letter of Alexander II erroneously ascribed to Urban II, is consecutive with JL 5393 in these collections. Cf. the *Tripartia,* nn. 1 and 2, and the first and second recensions of the *Collectio Caesaraugustana,* nn. 2 and 3. JL 4589 is also in the second Collection of Châlons-sur-Marne, n. 1, and there it is also ascribed to Urban II. This same fragment from Alexander II appears closely linked with JL 5740 in the two recensions of the *Caesaraugustana,* nn. 3 and 4, in the second Collection of Châlons-sur-Marne, nn. 1 and 2, and in Gratian at c. 3, C. I, q. 5, and at c. 2, C. I, q. 5. The close connection between these two last-mentioned fragments, especially since one is falsely ascribed to Urban, may be accepted as a good indication of probable dependence.

Although it may be unnecessary to mention it, there is a very close relation between the two recensions of the *Caesaraugustana.* The second recension has many more canons of Urban, but every canon of his in the first recension is also in the second.

JL 5390 and canon 14 of the Council of Melfi are found together in the first recension of the *Collectio Caesaraugustana,* nn. 15 and 14, in the second recension of the same collection, nn. 17 and 16, in the second Collection of Châlons-sur-Marne, nn. 15 and 19, in the Collection of *Codex Ms. Vaticanus Latinus 1361,* nn. 10 and 8, and in the Collection in Ten Parts, nn. 18 and 15.

There is a quite evident relation between the Collection of Saint-Germain-des-Prés, the second Collection of Châlons-sur-Marne and the Collection in Ten Parts. These three collections contain all of the canons from the Council of Clermont, with the exception of the two canons from the *Codex Cencii* of the same council, which are found in the Collection of *Codex Ms. Vaticanus Latinus 1361,* nn. 12 and 21. This situation is noteworthy for it indicates that the *Codex Cencii* passed into a different tradition from the series of canons of Lambert of Arras. The collections which give a complete coverage for the Council of Clermont do not have any of the canons from the *Codex Cencii.* In the three prior collections the arrangement is not very close, although the content is very similar. A mere glance at the chart is enough to show how predominant this affinity is.

JL 5382 and JL 5388, first found in the *Collectio Britannica,* nn. 29 and 35, appear in close conjunction very regularly throughout the collections. These two are found in the Collection in Nine Books, nn. 16 and 17, in the *Tripartita,* nn. 11 and 13, in the *Decretum* of Ivo, nn. 9 and 11, in the *Panormia,* nn. 13 and 15, in the first recension of the *Collectio Caesaraugustana,* nn. 17 and 18, in the second recension of the *Collectio Caesaraugustana,* nn. 21 and 22, in the Collection of Saint-Germain-des-Prés, nn. 34 and 35, and in the second Collection of Châlons-sur-Marne, nn. 46 and 50. In these same collections JL 5399 often appears along with the mentioned pair of texts. All of the collections cited in this connection appear to have some interrelation with one another but there is really not sufficient consistency among the other canons of these collections to come to a more definite conclusion regarding the dependency.

Two more canons which as a pair reveal themselves in a regular pattern are canon 1 of the Council of Troia and JL 5388. The pattern is evident in the *Tripartita,* nn. 13 and 14, in the *Decret*um, nn. 11 and 13, in the second recension of the *Collectio Caesaraugustana,* nn. 22 and 23, in the Collection of Saint-Germain-des-Prés, nn. 35 and 33, in the second Collection of Châlons-sur-Marne, nn. 50 and 51, in the Collection of *Codex Ms. Vaticanus Latinus 1361,* nn. 16 and 17, and in the *Decretum Gratiani* at c. 3, C. XXXV, q. 6, and at c. 4, C. XXXV, q. 6. The consistent arrangement of this pair speaks of some interdependence among the collections. In the series of collections given above, the only one which, perhaps, one would except not to receive mention is the Collection of *Codex Ms. Vaticanus Latinus 1361.* This collection, although it shows many similarities with the other collections, seems to come from a different tradition than most of the others. Of all the collections examined, the Collection of *Codex Ms. Vaticanus Latinus 1361* exhibits a rather close similarity with the three collections of Ivo of Chartres. There are some indications that Ivo's collections depend not upon any one or two collections, but upon many.

There is enough evidence, even solely from the canons of Urban II, to link the *Polycarpus,* the Collection in Seven Books, the Italian Collection in Three Books, and the Collection in Nine

Books into a framework of interrelation. From Urban's sources alone the dependence exhibited by these collections could not be called close. But with sources from only one Pope as the criterion, there are very few examples of really outstanding dependence.[3]

The relation which exists between the *Panormia* and the Collection in Ten Parts is fairly evident from an examination of the chart, except for the canons from the Council of Piacenza; this council was probably held after the completion of the *Panormia.*[4]

Several parallels exist between the *Tripartita* of Ivo and the first Collection of Châlons-sur-Marne, but since the later collection has only seven canons from Urban, the relationship mentioned by Fournier-Le Bras is not proved apodictically.[5]

[3] Fournier-Le Bras, *Histoire,* II, 179-180, 189.

[4] Fournier-Le Bras, *Histoire,* II, 298.

[5] *Histoire,* II, 309.

APPENDIX II

Canons Included in the *Decretum Gratiani* Which are Ascribed to Urban II

All the canonical collections of the past reached their culmination about the year 1140 when the Camaldolese monk Gratian finished his monumental *Concordia Discordantium Canonum.* Never an official collection, the *Decretum,* as it came to be known, did become a recognized part of the *Corpus Iuris Canonici*—the complete and systematic collection of the law of the Church. This is not the place to elaborate upon the magnificent service rendered to Canon Law by Magister Gratianus, but the importance of his well-known work explains the reason for the inclusion of this appendix.

Because of the unique place accorded to Gratian's *Decretum,* it is evident that in any such study as this one could not omit consideration of those canons of Urban II which were eventually to find a place in the *Concordia Discordantium Canonum.* What may be of even greater interest is the fact that there is a substantial number of canons which erroneously bear the name of Urban in Gratian's collection.

This appendix has as its principal purpose the separation of the canons falsely ascribed to Urban from those that are genuine. Some fragments appear in Gratian under the general title, *Urbanus papa,* with no further indications of the first or second Pope who bore that name; there are canons belonging to Urban which carry a completely erroneous inscription. Still other canons having Urban's name attached to them cannot be identified with certainty. Finally several texts which bear the correct inscription in the *Decretum* did appear erroneously under the name of Urban II in some of the earlier collections examined by the present writer.[1]

[1] No attempt has been made to include these last-named fragments in the present appendix. Three of the fragments are from Alexander II: c. 16, D. LXXXI (JL 4477) is found under the name of Urban in the second Collection of Châlons-sur-Marne, n. 28, and in the Collection in Ten Parts, n. 33; c. 17, D. LXXXI (JL 4612) is ascribed to Urban in the second

This appendix will strive to indicate as much evidence as possible in order to determine whether or not Urban was the true author of the canons which bear his name, and to indicate the texts properly belonging to Urban, but wrongly ascribed to another source.

Every canon from Gratian will be identified by way of a cross-reference to the place where the canon can be found in the various pre-Gratian collections, as examined in Part I of this dissertation. Only the first collection in which the canon occurs will be given. To discover in what other collections a given canon is also found, the reader can readily consult the chart found in Appendix I.

1) c. 6, D. XXXII *circa med.* Berardi, *Canones,* II, 2, 358

Inscribed: *Urbanus in epist. destinata preposito S. Vincentii.*

This canon is the last portion of JL 5743; cf. the recension "C" of the Collection of Anselm of Lucca, n. 1. Other parts of the same letter are found at cc. 8 and 12, C. I, q. 3. *S. Vincentii* of the inscription should be *S. Iuventii,* but the former reading appears in some of the pre-Gratian collections.

2) c. 10 D. XXXII Berardi, *Canones,* I, 436

Inscribed: *Item Urbanus II in Sinodo apud Melfiam* [cap. 12].

This text is canon 12, Council of Melfi, Mansi, XX, 724; cf. the Collection of *Codex Ms. Vaticanus Latinus 4977,* n. 2.

3) c. 11, D. XXXII Berardi, *Canones,* II, 2, 361-362

Inscribed: *Item* (i. e. *Urbanus II*) *Dominico Gradensi Patriarchae.*

This canon is from JL 4575, a letter of Alexander II; cf. the Collection of *Codex Ms. Vaticanus Latinus 4977,* n. 3, where this fragment also appears under Urban's name. Berardi (1719-1768) noted that in a manuscript of Ivo's

Collection of Châlons-sur-Marne, n. 29, and the Collection in Ten Parts, n. 34; c. 18, D. LXXXI (also JL 4612) appears in the Collection in Ten Parts, n. 35, with Urban as its source. There is also a single canon from Paschal II, reproduced in the *Decretum* of Gratian at c. 5, C. XXX, q. 3 (JL 6436), which in the Italian Collection in Three Books, n. 12, carries the inscription of Urban II.

Panormia from Turin, Book III, chapter 102, the present canon is found without any sender's name; but the preceding chapter 101, in this manuscript of Turin is from Urban II (canon 12, Council of Melfi). Therefore, Berardi reasoned, this arrangement of the canons led Gratian to presume that the present fragment was also from Urban II. While this argument is a possibility, it should be noted that in the printed edition of the *Panormia* in Migne (*PL,* CLXI, 1153) and in two manuscripts of the *Panormia,* examined by the present writer (*Munich, Bayerische Staatsbibliothek lateinische 4545,* folio 57r and *Douai, Bibliothèque municipale 584,* folio 62v), the canon under discussion is also found without any sender indicated. In all three of these versions of the *Panormia,* however, something else of note was found: between the present canon (chapter 102) and the canon of Urban (chapter 101) an additional canon from the *sexta syndous* had been inserted (this "extra" canon is also found at c. 7, D. XXXII). This additional canon makes the numbering of the chapters different in the manuscript of Turin, as mentioned by Berardi, and what is found in Migne and in the other manuscripts examined by the writer. While the evidence from the manuscripts when examined tends to weaken somewhat Berardi's conjecture, this evidence by no means renders the conjecture inadmissible. Deserving of mention is the fact that Innocent III attributed this passage to Urban II in c. 9, X, *de aetate et qualitate et ordine praeficiendorum,* I, 14.

4) c. 12, D. XXXII Berardi, *Canones,* I, 436-437

Inscribed: *Idem* (i. e. *Urbanus II*) *Meldensi Sinodo presidens ait* [cap. 3].

The erroneous form, *Meldensi,* appears also in the *Panormia,* Book III, chapter 104 (*PL,* CLXI, 1152; *Munich, Bayerische Staatsbibliothek lateinische 4545,* folio 57v, and *Douai, Bibliothèque municipale 584,* folio 62v). This *capitulum* is from canon 3, Council of Melfi, Mansi, XX, 723; cf. the Collection of *Codex Ms. Vaticanus Latinus 4977,* n. 4. This canon is repeated by Innocent III at c. 9, X, *de aetate et qualitate et ordine praeficiendorum,* I, 14; cf. the preceding number 3) of this appendix.

5) c. 37, D. L. Berardi, *Canones,* II, 2, 363

Inscribed: *Unde Urbanus II scribit Guarnerio Merseburgensi Episcopo.*

This canon is from JL 5474; cf. the *Panormia,* n. 9.

6) c. 1, D. LVI Berardi, *Canones,* II, 2, 370-371

Inscribed: *Unde Urbanus Papa II ait.*

This *capitulum* is from canon 14, Council of Melfi, Mansi, XX, 724; cf. the recension "Bb" of the Collection of Anselm of Lucca, n. 1. Practically the same content and wording appear in JL 5409, to Pibo, bishop of Toul; this letter was written very shortly before or after the Council of Melfi. The closing phrase of the present canon is repeated at c. 11, D. LVI.

7) c. 11, D. LVI Berardi, *Canones,* II, 2, 370-371

Inscribed: *Unde Urbanus in fine superioris capituli distinguendo subiunxit.*

This fragment is a phrase from the canon considered in the preceding number 6) of this appendix; it is from canon 14 of the Council of Melfi.

8) c. 13, D. LVI Berardi, *Canones,* II, 2, 360-361

Inscribed: *Unde Urbanus* [Papa II] *scribit Bartholomeo Thuron. Archiepiscopo.*

This canon is from JL 4610, a letter of Alexander II; cf. the *Panormia,* n. 3. This canon appears in the *Panormia* of Ivo at Book III, chapter 53. The inscription of this canon as found in the *Panormia* varies according to manuscripts. Two manuscripts examined by the writer (*Munich, Bayerische Staatsbibliothek lateinische 4545,* folio 52v, and *Douai, Bibliothèque municipale 584,* folio 56v) give this canon with only the following inscriptions: *Bartholomeo turonen. archiepiscopo;* no sender is indicated. In the printed text of the *Panormia* (*PL,* CLXI, 1142), however, the present canon is ascribed to Urban. The same canon is found in several of the pre-Gratian collections, but in these too the inscription is not always consistent. In the Collection of *Codex Ms. Vaticanus Latinus 1361*, n. 9, this canon is ascribed to Urban II; in the second Collection of Châlons-sur-Marne, n. 13, and in the Collection in Ten Parts, n. 17, no sender is indicated. Thus from the various inscriptions found no certain argument may be deduced. The internal arrangement of the canons in the *Panormia* gave Berardi the occasion for a hypothesis which Friedberg apparently endorsed (in footnote 116). Chapter 52 of the *Panormia*, which precedes the canon under discussion in that collection, is from the *Liber Pontificalis* and consists of examples of Popes whose fathers had themselves been in sacred orders; chapter 52 was given in contradistinction to chapter 51, which is canon 14 of the Council of Melfi, held by Urban II in 1089, and forbade the sons of priests to be advanced to holy orders. From this order of canons in the *Panormia* Berardi offered the opinion that, when Gratian took chapter 53 from Ivo's work, the *magister* attributed the canon to Urban who was the last pontiff mentioned. Neither the evidence from the various inscriptions of this canon nor the hypothesis of Berardi completely answers the question of how this canon came to be attributed to Urban II. Berardi's theory, while not approaching certainty, does not lack probability. In the face of the evidence at hand it is difficult to decide who was the first to link the present text with the name of Urban II. Was it Ivo of Chartres, was it Gratian, or was it some compiler who labored between these two outstanding canonists? Berardi favored Gratian; but at least one pre-Gratian collection (that of *Codex Ms. Vaticanus Latinus 1361*, n. 9) had already passed the canon on to posterity under the authorship of Urban. It seems rather unlikely that Ivo, a contemporary of Urban, would have made a mistake in attribution. Therefore the present writer favors the opinion that some canonist, or even, perhaps, a scribe, erroneously connected the name of Urban II with the present canon sometime within the fifty odd years between Ivo's *Panormia* and Gratian's *Decretum*.

9) c. 14, D. LVI Berardi, *Canones,* II, 2, 366

Inscribed: *Similiter et illud Urbani intelligendum est, quod ipse scribit Patrono Legionensi Episcopo.*

This canon is from JL 5390; cf. the *Collectio Britannica,* n. 37; the addressee should be *Petro.* In footnote 128 Friedberg (1837-1910) gave a reference to the first edition of Jaffé's *Regesta* as 4381; this number is a printer's error; it should read 4301.

10) c. 1, D. LX Berardi, *Canones,* I, 440-441

Inscribed: *De his ita statutum est in Concilio Urbani Papae, celebrato Aluerniae.*

This *capitulum* is from canon 2, Council of Clermont, according to the *Codex Cencii,* Mansi, XX, 901-902; this *capitulum* does not appear verbatim in any of the pre-Gratian collections examined by the writer, but the canon found in the Collection of Saint-Germain-des-Prés, n. 9, is very similar to the present one.

11) c. 4, D. LX Berardi, *Canones,* I, 438

Inscribed: . . . *iuxta illud Urbani Papae.*

Canon 1, Council of Benevento, Mansi, XX, 737; cf. the Collection in Nine Books, n. 1. Berardi observed that the "*veteres*" had considered this canon to be from Urban I, until Baluze (1630-1718) edited a *codex* of Anagni, which had the correct inscription. Cf. the *notationes Correctorum* also. The error mentioned by Berardi and the *Correctores* explains why Innocent III incorrectly ascribed this canon to Urban I in c. 9, X, *de aetate et qualitate et ordine praeficiendorum,* I, 14.[2]

12) c. 6, D. LXVIII Berardi, *Canones,* II, 2, 371

Inscribed: *Item Urbanus* [Papa II].

It is doubtful whether this canon comes from Urban II; cf. the Italian Collection in Three Books, n. 9. The *Correctores*

[2] Concerning the Anagni *codex,* mentioned by Baluze, cf. his note in the work of Petrus de Marca, *De Concordia Sacerdotii et Imperii,* III, 479-482, at the close of chapter XIII of Book VIII of the treatise.

Romani attributed this canon to Urban II. Berardi asserted that the canon could belong to either Urban or Paschal II, but he preferred the latter pontiff. Friedberg was content to call it a "*caput incertum*" in footnote 77. Theiner (1804-1874), in the appendix to his *Disquisitiones Criticae*, p. 127, s. v. *Quorum vices*, attributed this canon to Urban II. The quotation from St. Augustine is from his commentary on Psalm 44. In conclusion it can be said that, since the evidence is by no means strong, the canon may be considered as doubtfully belonging to Urban II.

13) c. 2, D. LXX Berardi, *Canones*, I, 438-439

Inscribed: *Item ex sinodo Urbani* [II] *habita Placentiae* [c. 15].

This canon is taken verbatim from canon 15, Council of Piacenza, Mansi, XX, 806; this canon is not found in any of the collections examined in Part I of this study.

14) c. 4, D. LXXVI Berardi, *Canones*, I, 439

Inscribed: *Contra Urbanus* [II in Concilio Placentino, c. 14].

Canon 14, Council of Piacenza, Mansi, XX, 806; cf. the Italian Collection in Three Books, n. 11.

15) c. 108, C. I, q. 1 Berardi, *Canones*, I, 439

Inscribed: *De quibus Urbanus Papa* [II in Concilio Placentino, cap. 3 et 4] *ait*.

This capitulum is from canons 3 and 4, Council of Piacenza, Mansi, XX, 805; the same canons are also in the Council of Rome, Mansi, XX, 961; cf. the Collection in Seven Books, n. 2.

16) c. 3, C. I, q. 2 *palea* Berardi, *Canones*, I, 437

Inscribed: [Unde Urbanus Papa in Concilio apud Melfiam, c. 12.]

The first sentence of this passage is found in canon 7 of the Council of Melfi, Mansi, XX, 723; this same extract is repeated in canon 17 of the Council of Rome, Mansi, XX,

964; cf. the Collection in Ten Parts, n. 28. What follows the text from Melfi is not from Urban II, but from a Roman synod of Gregory the Great, Mansi, IX, 1217.

17) c. 4, C. I, q. 3 Berardi, *Canones,* I, 441

Inscribed: *Item ex Concilio Urbani Papae II habito Aluerniae.*

Canon 3, Council of Clermont, according to the *Codex Cencii,* Mansi, XX, 902; this canon was repeated in canon 1 of the Council of Nîmes, July 8-12, 1096, Mansi, XX, 933; cf. the Collection of *Codex Ms. Vaticanus Latinus 1361,* n. 21.

18) c. 5, C. I, q. 3 Berardi, *Canones,* I, 439

Inscribed: *Idem* [in Concilio Placentino, c. 1 et 2].

Canons 1 and 2, Council of Piacenza, Mansi, XX, 805; the canons are repeated in canons 1 and 2 of the Council of Rome, Mansi, XX, 961; cf. the Collection in Seven Books, n. 2. Before the emendation of the *Correctores,* this canon was inscribed, *Item Gregorius.*

19) cc. 8 and 12, C. I, q. 3 Berardi, *Canones,* II, 2, 358

c. 8 inscribed: *Item Urbanus* [II] *Episcopus, seruus seruorum Dei, dilecto filio L. Preposito ecclesiae sancti Vincentii apud Ticinum, salutem et apostolicam benedictionem.*

c. 12 inscribed: . . . *docens sanctus Urbanus ait.*

Both of these *capitula* are from JL 5743; cf. the recension "C" of the Collection of Anselm of Lucca, n. 1. C. 12 is also included in the much longer c. 8; the inscription on c. 12 is clearly false in that it ascribes the *capitulum* to Saint Urban I. The fragment of c. 12 may be found in the Italian Collection in Three Books, n. 4. The inscription to c. 12 is a *dictum Gratiani* according to the *Correctores,* but their conjecture seems to collapse when one recalls that what they call a *dictum* is found in a collection which was finished some forty years before Gratian's *Decretum.* Another portion of this same letter was mentioned above in number 1) of this appendix. What was said in that place concerning the word *Vincentii* holds for c. 8 in this place: the correct reading is *Iuventii.*

20) c. 1, C. I, q. 5 Berardi, *Canones,* I, 439

Inscribed: . . . *auctoritate diffinitur Urbani, qui scribens de symoniacis ait inter cetera* [in Concilio Placentino, c. 5 et sequentibus, itemque in Concilio Romano].

Canons 5, 6 and 7, Council of Piacenza, Mansi, XX, 805; these were repeated in canons 5, 6 and 7 of the Council of Rome, Mansi, XX, 961; cf. the Collection in Seven Books, n. 2.

21) c. 2, C. I, q. 5 Berardi, *Canones,* II, 2, 367-368

Inscribed: . . . *ex epistola eiusdem* (i.e. Urban II) *colligitur, missa Vitali Presbitero in hec uerba.*

This canon is a fragment from the letter, JL 5740; cf. the Collection of *Codex Ms. Vaticanus Latinus 3829,* n. 3.

22) c. 3, C. I, q. 5 Berardi, *Canones,* II, 2, 363-364

Inscribed: *Urbanus II scribit Alberto Metensi Episcopo.*

This letter is from Alexander II, JL 4589, and is falsely credited to Urban II here; cf. the *Tripartita,* n. 2, the first and second recensions of the *Collectio Caesaraugustana,* n. 3, and the second Collection of Châlons-sur-Marne, n. 1: in each of these collections the canon is also ascribed to Urban II. In the first edition of the *Regesta,* Jaffé also listed this canon under the name of Urban II (at number 4091). In footnote 20 Friedberg pointed out that, if the present canon is to be attributed to Urban II, then the address must be wrong. In the second edition of the *Regesta,* Loewenfeld placed this canon among the letters of Alexander II; for evidence to back this change he cited letter n. 70 of the letters of Alexander II in the *Collectio Britannica.* Berardi favored Urban as the author, but noted that the inscription presented a problem, since Herimannus and Poppo were bishops of Metz during Urban's pontificate.

23) c. 24, C. I, q. 7 Berardi, *Canones,* II, 2, 358-359

Inscribed: *Unde Urbanus II scribit Petro Pistoriensi Episcopo et Rustico Abbati Vallis umbrosae.*

This canon is a fragment of JL 5385; cf. the *Collectio Britannica,* n. 30.

24) c. 2, C. VIII, q. 3 Berardi, *Canones,* II, 2, 369-370

Inscribed: *De secundo uero casu in gestis Urbani II legitur.*

The exact source of this fragment is unknown, as Ewald admitted in his study of the *Collectio Britannica* (p. 365); cf. the *Collectio Britannica,* n. 44. In the course of the years there has been a great deal of confusion about the name of the diocese in this fragment. *The Correctores Romani* indicated that Gratian's original reading of Arles should be corrected into Aleth. But actually the place referred to was Elne, which in Urban's time was a suffragan of Narbonne, as the fragment explains.

25) c. 4, C. IX, q. 1 Berardi, *Canones,* II, 2, 355

Inscribed: *Unde Urbanus II scribit dicens.*

A fragment from JL 5393; cf. the Collection in Two Books, n. 2. This portion of the letter is very similar to that written to Pibo, bishop of Toul, some six months later (JL 5409).

26) c. 5, C. IX, q. 1 Berardi, *Canones,* I, 440

Inscribed: *Unde idem Urbanus ait* [in Sinodo Placentina, cap. 9 et sequentibus].

Canons 8-12, Council of Piacenza, Mansi, XX, 806; these canons were repeated in canons 8-11 of the Council of Rome, Mansi, XX, 963; cf. the *Polycarpus,* n. 5.

27) c. 2, C. IX, q. 2 *palea* Berardi, *Canones,* II, 2, 371-373

Inscribed: [Unde Urbanus Papa.]

It is unlikely that this canon belongs to Urban II, although it is found under his name the Collection of *Codex Ms. Vaticanus Latinus 1361,* n. 13. In note 14 Friedberg mentioned that this canon is found in the Collection of

Anselm of Lucca at the end of Book VIII. Although Thaner (1839-1915) did not make any mention of this canon at the place indicated in his edition of Anselm's work,[3] several points should be indicated here. First of all, the manuscript of Anselm's collection, which Friedberg and many others used, is perhaps the worst existing copy of Anselm's work; it is a seventeenth century copy of a copy, and is not a representative edition of Anselm's work.[4] But in spite of his dependency on this poor manuscript, Friedberg's contention that the present canon is found at the end of Book VIII in Anselm's collection is borne out in the study of the Naples' manuscript of the recension " A " of Anselm's collection.[5] In the place indicated Fournier (1855-1935) clearly explained that at the close of Book VIII in the Naples' manuscript a pair of canons is found. The first of these is Urban's canon, *Sane quia monachorum,* which is from canon 4, Council of Clermont (*Codex Cencii*), Mansi, XX, 902, found at c. 6, C. XVI, q. 2. This canon of Clermont, according to the report of Fournier, is followed by a canon inscribed: *ex concilio Hiberniensi,* which begins with the words *Item placuit ut deinceps nulli sacerdotum liceat quemlibet commissum alteri. . . .* This last canon mentioned by Fournier is surely the present canon found in Gratian. Therefore what Friedberg stated in footnote 14 has been borne out. And the latter's suggestion that some compiler, perhaps Gratian, confused the inscription found with the canon, *Sane quia monachorum,* and erroneously linked that inscription with the next canon, *Item placuit ut,* seems admissible. In this manner the latter canon could

[3] F. Thaner, ed., *Anselmi Episcopi Luccensis Collectio Canonum una cum Collectione Minore* (2 vols. in 1; Oeniponte: Librariae Academicae Wagnerianae, 1906-1915), pp. 446-456; this edition is unfinished and ends with c. 15 of Book XI.

[4] P. Fournier, "Observations sur diverses recensions de la collection canonique d'Anselm de Lucques," *Annales de l'Université de Grenoble,* XIII (1901), 455-456.

[5] *Ibid.,* p. 436. This arrangement is found in *codex ms. Vaticanus latinus 4983,* folio 413v-414-r; cf. the recension " C " of the Collection of Anselm of Lucca, n. 2.

have come to be identified with Urban II. This is a conjecture based upon reasonable grounds and indications. It is the best conclusion which can be reached on the basis of the proofs at hand. This same canon is repeated at c. 3, D. VI, *de poen,* and is inscribed in that place: *Unde Urbanus II.*

28) c. 10, C. IX, q. 2 Berardi, *Canones,* II, 2, 355-358

Inscribed: *De his ita scribit Urbanus Papa Hugoni Lugdunensi Archiepiscopo.*

This canon is from JL 5723; cf. the *Tripartita,* n. 10.

29) c. 110, C. XI, q. 3 Berardi, *Canones,* II, 2, 354

Inscribed: *Unde Urbanus II Genebaldo Constantiensi Episc.*

Another fragment from JL 5393; cf. the Collection of Two Books, n. 2. The name of the addressee is generally given as *Gebhardus;* for variants of this name cf. Friedberg's footnote 1192.

30) c. 37, C. XII, q. 2 Berardi, *Canones,* I, 444, and II, 2, 373

Inscribed: *Item Urbanus Papa.*

The text of this canon is actually identical with canon 22 of the First General Council of the Lateran (1123), held by Callistus II, Mansi, XXI, 286, except that all of the proper names have been removed. These names were those of the schismatical successors of the antipope Guibert (Clement III) in the see of Ravenna, viz. Otto, Guido, Jerome and Philip. The *Correctores* noted that an old manuscript ascribed this canon to Urban II. This canon is not found in the pre-Gratian collections under Urban's name.

31) c. 46, C. XII, q. 2 Berardi, *Canones,* I, 441

Inscribed: *Item ex Concilio Urbani Papae Aluerniae habito.*

Canon 1 of the Council of Clemont according to the *Codex Cencii,* Mansi, XX, 901; canon 31 of the same council according to the account of Lambert of Arras gives the same sense, as the *Correctores* noted, Mansi, XX, 818; cf. the Collection of Saint-Germain-des-Prés, n. 29.

32) c. 5, C. XV, q. 6 Berardi, *Canones,* II, 2, 364-365
Inscribed: *Item Urbanus II Episcopo Vapicensi.*
This canon is from JL 5724; cf. the *Panormia,* n. 11, and the Collection in Nine Books, n. 12; in these pre-Gratian collections the letter is directed also to the bishop of Embrun and Die, as well as to the bishop of Gap.

33) c. 24, C. XVI, q. 1 Berardi, *Canones,* II, 2, 140-141
Inscribed: *Idem* (after a canon of Gregory the Great).
This text is quoted in canon 3, Council of Nîmes, Mansi, XX, 934-935. Although Friedberg stated that this fragment seems to come from canon 3 of the Council of Nîmes (footnote 163 at c. 24, C. XVI, q. 1), cf. the next entry for further information about this canon.

34) c. 25, C. XVI, q. 1 Berardi, *Canones,* II, 2, 149-152
Inscribed: *Item ex decreto Bonifatii Papae.*
Berardi claimed that this passage was drawn from canon 2, Council of Nîmes, Mansi, XX, 934. While it is true that the present canon as well as the previous one treated in number 33) of this appendix are both quoted in the Council of Nîmes, these texts did not originate with that council. J. J. Ryan has indicated that both of these spurious canons existed prior to the Council of Nîmes, since they were used by Saint Peter Damian.[6]

35) c. 2, C. XVI, q. 2 *palea* Berardi, *Canones,* II, 2, 373-374
Inscribed: *Sed uidetur contraire Urbanus Papa II, dicens.*
This canon is from the Council of Mainz, held in 813, canon

[6] "Official use was made of these texts [i. e. those here under discussion] before the end of the eleventh century at the Council of Nîmes, in 1096, where they are again seen in sequence. The *Decretum Bonifacii* supplied canon 2, and canon 3 is clearly dependent on the spurious Gregorian canon [Mansi, XX, 934]."—J. J. Ryan, *Saint Peter Damiani and his Canonical Sources,* the Pontifical Institute of Mediaeval Studies, Studies and Texts, n. 2 (Toronto: the Pontifical Institute of Mediaeval Studies, 1956), p. 58.

38. The error in the inscription seems to have occurred when canons 2, 3, 4 and 5 (all *paleae*) were inserted between canon 1 and canon 6. Canon 6 is from Urban II, but lacks any inscription. Therefore in all probability the inscription now found with canon 2 originally introduced canon 6.

36) c. 6, C. XVI, q. 2 Berardi, *Canones,* I, 441-442

This canon lacks an inscription; cf. the preceding entry. Found in the Collection in Nine Books, n. 10, the present canon is canon 4, Council of Clermont, according to the *Codex Cencii,* Mansi, XX, 902; this canon is again seen in canon 1 of the Council of Nîmes, Mansi, XX, 933.

37) c. 7, C. XVI, q. 2 Berardi, *Canones,* I, 440

Inscribed: *Item ex Concilio apud Flauentiam habito.*

Generally the reading *Flauentiam* was taken as a mistake for *Placentiam,* but the fragment is not found among the acts of that council. Berardi saw in the canon a very possible relation to Urban II, especially with canon 6 of the Council of Melfi (Mansi, XX, 723) and canon 7 of the Council of Clermont (Mansi, XX, 817). But several very interesting points have been brought to the attention of the present writer.[7] There is a Florentine *abbreviatio* of the *Decretum* of Gratian, which could well represent the work of the *magister* in a more pure form. In that manuscript the present *questio II* of *Causa XVI* is found with only two canons: the first is the canon now found at *capitulum* 1, the second is the canon of Urban found at *capitulum* 6. In the Florentine manuscript chapters 2, 3, 4, 5 and 7 are not found. This omission offers rather strong arguments in

[7] The information concerning the *abbreviatio* of Gratian's *Decretum* comes from an oral report of Dr. Stephan Kuttner concerning the research of W. Holtzmann. "In the field of Gratian MSS, P. Huizing at the suggestion of W. Holtzmann has undertaken the full analysis of a MS from Camaldoli (Florence, Bibl. Naz. Conv. soppr. A. 1.402), which was thus far considered an *Abbreviatio* but may turn out to be of especial value for tracing the stages of revision of the Decretum itself."—Stephan Kuttner, "Bulletin for 1957 of the Institute of Research and Study in Medieval Canon Law," *Traditio,* XIII (1957), 466.

favor of the conclusion that the canon here under discussion is not Urban's at all. It has very likely been inserted by some later collector. This last contention is strengthened by the fact that the *dictum* found at the close of the present chapter is clearly a reference to *capitulum* 6 (which comes from Urban II), but contains nothing whatsoever to link it with chapter 7. Gratian's *dictum* reads thus:

> *Ecce Urbanus Papa prohibet inuestituras parrochialium ecclesiarum per monachos fieri, quas Iohannes Papa eis concessit. Sed illud Iohannis Papae intelligendum est de illis capellis, que cum omni iure suo ab episcopis monachis conceduntur. Istud autem Urbani intelligendum est de illis, quas abbates in propriis prediis edificant in uillis uel in castellis suis.*

This *dictum* clearly mentions chapter 1, of Pope John, and the chapter of Urban II, which is chapter 6. The wording implies that only these two canons were originally placed in the present *questio*. The opening words of the *dictum* also imply that the preceding canon is from Urban, but as the text continues it is clear that reference is made to chapter 6, not 7. The only reasonable conclusion is that in all probability the present canon is not from Urban II, and that it is unlikely that the canon was found in the original *Decretum*.

38) c. 1, C. XVI q. 4 Berardi, *Canones,* II, 2, 374-375

Inscribed: . . . *Quod Urbanus II prohibuit, dicens.*

This canon is not from Urban II; it is canon 17 of the First General Council of the Lateran (1123), convoked by Callistus II, Mansi, XXI, 304. This canon forbade parochial functions to monks; Urban however, favored an extending of the parochial ministry to these religious (cf. canons 2 and 3 of the Council of Nîmes, Mansi, XX, 934-935). The present canon, therefore, does not seem to belong to Urban II.

39) c. 2, XVI, q. 7 *palea* Berardi, *Canones,* II, 2, 375-376

Inscribed: [Unde Urbanus II.]

Ascribed to Urban II and linked with the Council of Clermont, this canon is not found in the acts of that council. Friedberg called it (in footnote 12) a "*caput incertum, scriptum post annum 1095 quo habitum est Concilium Claromontanum.*" Berardi considered the canon as a paraphrase of canon 6, Council of Clermont, Mansi, XX, 817: "*. . . non verba Concilii, sed potius sententiam . . .*" (p. 375). The *Correctores* noted that this canon was attributed to Urban in the *Compilatio Prima* of Bernard of Pavia (c. 1, *de capellanis monachorum et aliorum religiosorum,* III, 32). No certain conclusion is possible about this canon; it can be placed among the canons doubtfully attributable to Urban.

40) c. 39, C. XVI, q. 7 Berardi, *Canones,* II, 2, 362

Inscribed: *Unde Urbanus II.*

This canon cannot be identified with certainty. Friedberg thought (in footnote 366) that this canon might be a résumé of canons 5 and 6 of the Council of Melfi, Mansi, XX, 723. Berardi had mentioned the same possibility and had added that the text might be drawn from JL 5431, a letter to Hugh, bishop of Grenoble. No definite conclusion is possible concerning this canon.

41) c. 31, C. XVIII, q. 2 Berardi, *Canones,* III, 456

Inscribed: *Item Urbanus II.*

Falsely ascribed to Urban II, this fragment is from canon 19, First General Council of the Lateran, held in 1123 by Callistus II, Mansi, XXI, 285-286. Schroeder (1875-1942) maintained, "It is this rule of Gregory [VII, in 1078] that the council here confirms."[8] No certain conclusion is possible. Not all of Urban's acts have survived, nor have the authentic acts of the First General Council of the Lateran (1123). The question remains doubtful. The present canon

[8] H. J. Schroeder, *Disciplinary Decrees of the General Councils* (St. Louis: B. Herder Book Co., 1937), p. 192.

definitely seems to be at odds with canon 3, Council of Nîmes, Mansi, XX, 902; the two are practically contradictory. The Lateran canon forbids monks to acquire ecclesiastical property by way of a thirty years' prescription; canon 3 of Nîmes explicitly granted this concession to the monks.

42) c. 2, C. XIX, q. 2 Berardi, *Canones,* II, 2, 368-369

Inscribed: *Unde Urbanus Papa* [II] *in capitulo sancti Rufi.*

JL 5760; cf. the *Polycarpus,* n. 2. The authenticity of this canon was questioned by Berardi, but by no one else. He claimed that this canon is contrary to what Urban is credited with saying in cc. 2 and 3, C. XIX, q. 3, and that the entire text is a monastic forgery. For proof Berardi cited the fact that Ivo of Chartres, a contemporary of Urban II, never adverted to the existence of this canon. Berardi was of the opinion that Ivo would never have omitted such an important canon, if he knew of it. The entire text appears to be a paraphrase of another text. Even the opening words are not in the usual form of a decretal: *Duae inquit leges sunt. . . .*

43) c. 2, C. XIX, q. 3 Berardi, *Canones,* II, 2, 376

Inscribed: *Item Urbanus Papa II.*

This canon is not Urban's; cf. the *Polycarpus,* n. 3. This canon is found nine times in the pre-Gratian collections examined by the writer and is ascribed to Urban in every place; in six of the nine collections it is found in conjunction with the canon treated in the previous entry, number 42 of this appendix. This canon is from chapter 25 of the work of Anselm of Havelberg, *Liber de Ordine Canonicorum Regularium, PL,* CLXXXVIII, 1109.

44) c. 3, C. XIX, q. 3 Berardi, *Canones,* II, 2, 359-360

Inscribed: *Unde Urbanus II scribit Abbati sancti Rufi.*

This canon is found in JL 5763; cf. the recension "Bb" of the Collection of Anselm of Lucca, n. 6. Friedberg pointed out (in footnote 13) that this canon was incorporated in the first edition of Jaffé's *Regesta,* at n. 4313. This is an error, because n. 4313 is JL 5760 in the second edition of the *Regesta.* Loewenfeld added to the confusion at JL 5763, where he noted that this excerpt may be found at c. 2, C. XIX, q. 3, instead of c. 3.

45) c. 23, c. XXII, q. 5 Berardi, *Canones,* II, 2, 376

Inscribed: [Unde Urbanus II ait.]

This canon is from JL 5759; cf. the recension "Bb" of the Collection of Anselm of Lucca, n. 2. This canon is found at c. 5, X, *de iureiurando,* II, 24.

46) c. 47, C. XXIII, q. 5 Berardi, *Canones,* II, 2, 365-366

Inscribed: *Item Urbanus II Godifredo, Lucano Episcopo.*

A fragment from JL 5536; cf. the first Collection of Prague, n. 2.

47) c. 22, C. XXIII, q. 8 Berardi, *Canones,* II, 2, 376-377

Inscribed: *Item Urbanus Papa.*

There is no trace of this canon or of one resembling it among the writings of Urban II. Berardi favored the view that this text was drawn from one of several letters of Urban which have been lost. No very definite conclusion is possible with such scanty evidence.

48) c. 3, C. XXIV, q. 2 Berardi, *Canones,* II, 2, 365

Inscribed: *Item Urbanus* [II] *Vilimundo Episcopo.*

This text can be found in JL 5363; cf. the *Collectio Britannica,* n. 16.

49) c. 24, C. XXIV, q. 3 Berardi, *Canones,* II, 2, 377

Inscribed: *Item Urbanus.*

This canon is not from the acts of Urban II; it may be found in canon 20, First General Council of the Lateran (1123), Mansi, XXI, 286.

50) c. 32, C. XXIV, q. 3 Berardi, *Canones,* III, 457

Inscribed: *Item Urbanus Papa.*

No source for this canon can be given with certainty. Friedberg called it uncertain. Berardi claimed that it cannot belong to Urban I and that the canon should be ascribed to Urban II, because the content agrees with the historical context of the latter pontiff. There is a similarity between the present canon and the text found in canon 13 of the Council of Toulouse, held in 1056 under Victor II, as well as with parts of JL 5393. This fragment is found in the Italian Collection in Three Books, n. 8. Theiner, in the appendix to his *Disquisitiones Criticae* (p. 117, s. v. *Qui aliorum*) credited this canon to Urban I. This canon should be placed among the canons doubtfully attributable to Urban II.

51) c. 37, C. XXIV, q. 3 Berardi, *Canones,* II, 2, 377-378

Inscribed: *Item ex epistola Urbani Papae.*

The exact source of this canon is unknown. Berardi surmised that the canon had its origin around the time of Urban II, and that the text might be Urban's. Friedberg (in footnote 425) noted that the origin is uncertain. Nothing further can be said on the basis of such little proof.

52) c. 6, C. XXV, q. 1 Berardi, *Canones,* II, 2, 378

Inscribed: *Item Urbanus Papa.*

This canon is not found among the letters or acts either of Urban I or Urban II. Berardi admitted that it is difficult to come to a decision, but saw some parallel in JL 5743; cf. the recension "C" of the Collection of Anselm of Lucca, n. 1.

53) c. 4, C. XXX, q. 3 Berardi, *Canones,* II, 2, 367-368

Inscribed: *Unde Urbanus II scribit Vitali Presbitero Brisciensi, dicens.*

This fragment is from JL 5741; cf. the *Tripartita,* n. 5. This canon was at one time considered a part of the *dictum Gratiani* at the end of c. 3, C. XXX, q. 3.

54) c. 6, C. XXX, q. 4 Berardi, *Canones,* II, 2, 367-368
Inscribed: *De his ita scribit Urbanus II Vitali, Presbytero Brixiensi.*
JL 5742; cf. the *Tripartita,* n. 6.

55) c. 1, C. XXXI, q. 2 Berardi, *Canones,* II, 2, 378-379
Inscribed: *Item Iudicium Urbani Papae.*
JL 5382; cf. the *Collectio Britannica,* n. 29.

56) c. 3, C. XXXI, q. 2 Berardi, *Canones,* II, 2, 367
Inscribed: *Item Sanctio, Regi Aragonum.*
This canon is from JL 5399; cf. the Collection of *Codex Ms. Vaticanus Latinus 4977,* n. 1.

57) c. 3, D. VI, *de poen.* Berardi, *Canones,* II, 2, 371-373
Inscribed: *Unde Urbanus II.*
This canon has already been considered above in number 27) of the present appendix.

58) c. 11, C. XXXV, q. 2 Berardi, *Canones,* II, 2, 362-363
Inscribed: *Ait enim Urbanus II Hugoni, Gratianopolitano Episcopo.*
JL 5730; cf. the Collection of Turin in Seven Books, n. 1.

59) c. 3, C. XXXV, q. 6 Berardi, *Canones,* II, 2, 366-367
Inscribed: *Item Urbanus Richario Genuensi Episcopo.*
JL 5388; cf. the *Collectio Britannica,* n. 35. The addressee should probably read *Cyriaco* instead of *Richario.*

60) c. 4, C. XXXV, q. 6 Berardi, *Canones,* I, 437-438
Inscribed: *Item ex Concilio Urbani Papae habito in Apulia.*
This canon is identical with canon 1, Council of Troia, Mansi, XX, 789; cf. the Collection of *Codex Ms. Vaticanus Latinus 3829,* n. 2.

CANONS OF URBAN II AS FOUND IN THE *DECRETUM* OF GRATIAN

	Genuine	False	Doubtfully Attributable	Unknown
1) c. 6, D. XXXII	x			
2) c. 10, D. XXXII	x			
3) c. 11, D. XXXII		x (Alexander II)		
4) c. 12, D. XXXII	x			
5) c. 37, D. L	x			
6) c. 1, D. LVI	x			
7) c. 11, D. LVI	x			
8) c. 13, D. LVI		x (Alexander II)		
9) c. 14, D. LVI	x			
10) c. 1, D. LX	x			
11) c. 4, D. LX	x			
12) c. 6, D. LXVIII			x	
13) c. 2, D. LXX	x			
14) c. 4, D. LXXVI	x			
15) c. 108, C. I, q. 1	x			
16) c. 3, C. I, q. 2	x			
17) c. 4, C. I, q. 3	x			
18) c. 5, C. I, q. 3	x			
19) cc. 8 and 12, C. I, q. 3	x			
20) c. 1, C. I, q. 5	x			
21) c. 2, C. I, q. 5	x			
22) c. 3, C. I, q. 5		x (Alexander II)		
23) c. 24, C. I, q. 7	x			
24) c. 2, C. VIII, q. 3				x
25) c. 4, C. IX, q. 1	x			
26) c. 5, C. IX, q. 1	x			
27) c. 2, C. IX, q. 2 *palea*		x (cf. text)		
28) c. 10, C. IX, q. 2	x			
29) c. 110, C. XI, q. 3	x			
30) c. 37, C. XII, q. 2			x	
31) c. 46, C. XII, q. 2	x			
32) c. 5, C. XV, q. 6	x			
33) c. 24, C. XVI, q. 1			x (cf. text)	
34) c. 25, C. XVI, q. 1			x (cf. text)	
35) c. 2, C. XVI, q. 2 *palea*		x		
36) c. 6, C. XVI, q. 2	x			
37) c. 7, C. XVI, q. 2				x
38) c. 1, C. XVI, q. 4		x		
39) c. 2, C. XVI, q. 7 *palea*			x	
40) c. 39, C. XVI, q. 7			x	
41) c. 31, C. XVIII, q. 2			x	
42) c. 2, C. XIX, q. 2	x (cf. text)			
43) c. 2, C. XIX, q. 3		x		
44) c. 3, C. XIX, q. 3	x			
45) c. 23, C. XXII, q. 5	x			
46) c. 47, C. XXIII, q. 5	x			
47) c. 22, C. XXIII, q. 8			x	
48) c. 3, C. XXIV, q. 2	x			
49) c. 24, C. XXIV, q. 3		x		
50) c. 32, C. XXIV, q. 3			x	
51) c. 37, C. XXIV, q. 3				x
52) c. 6, C. XXV, q. 1			x	
53) c. 4, C. XXX, q. 3	x			
54) c. 6, C. XXX, q. 4	x			
55) c. 1, C. XXXI, q. 2	x			
56) c. 3, C. XXXI, q. 2	x			
57) c. 3, D. VI, *de poen.*		x (cf. text)		
58) c. 11, C. XXXV, q. 2	x			
59) c. 3, C. XXXV, q. 6	x			
60) c. 4, C. XXXV, q. 6	x			

PART II

A COMPENDIUM OF THE CANONICAL THOUGHT OF POPE URBAN II

PART II

A COMPENDIUM OF THE CANONICAL THOUGHT OF POPE URBAN II

The second part of this study will strive to present in orderly form the substance of the canonical thought of Urban II. Here will be combined the legislation which was incorporated in the canonical collections along with the texts which never found their way into any of the collections up to and including the *Decretum Gratiani.* In this way all of the acts of Urban, bearing on matters of Canon Law, will be put into a single body. The advantage of this arrangement is that the reader can see at a glance exactly whether and what Urban decided, taught and legislated on a given subject.

As an aid in differentiating from the other enactments, which were never incorporated in any of the collections, the documents which became part of the canonical tradition, two kinds of type have been used. The larger type designates decrees, canons and letters found in one or more of the canonical collections. The smaller type represents the papal acts and conciliar canons which were never absorbed into any of the collections.

The canons from the collections are identified by means of a cross-reference to the various collections examined in Part I of this study. In all cases references to the *Decretum* of Gratian have been indicated. The other texts from outside these collections will be identified in their proper place.

As for the sequence of topics, the general arrangement of the medieval books of decretals, first suggested by Bernard of Pavia, has been followed. There has been made some modification in line with what the matter itself demanded. A special section on the Roman Pontiff has been placed at the very beginning of the compendium. No special section has been devoted to judicial procedure, since Urban taught almost nothing concerning such matters. Likewise matrimony has not been given a separate treatment here, but it has been included in the section dealing with sacramental discipline, because Urban's canonical treatment is not of sufficient detail or length to demand a separate chapter. Accordingly there are three chapters dealing with persons, things and penalties.

The method of arrangement that has been adopted has its limitations. It is frequently no easy task to fit specific enactments into pre-arranged categories. And it should be kept in mind that even the entire body of Urban's canonical thought does not form a systematic and comprehensive *summa* of the Canon Law of his day. Urban frequently attempted to overcome the abuses of his time by way of direct legislative interference. Such a procedure inevitably involved the stressing of certain matters at the expense of neglecting others. The result may not be a very representative cross-section of the whole of Canon Law at the close of the eleventh century, but this method perhaps better brings into perspective the gradual development of the legal system of the Church.

CHAPTER I

The Law of Persons

Article I. The Roman Pontiff

The reign of Urban II took its course in an environment of opposition. Throughout his pontificate Urban had to contend with an anti-pope and an imperial schism. It is not surprising that the Pope showed a vigorous determination to fight the enemy and that a very important phase of this battle was fought by means of legislation. In the face of opposition to the very office which was his, Urban steadfastly adhered to the rights and powers which belonged to the Roman Pontiff.

On the day after his election to that high post, in the proclamation of his election, Urban courageously asserted that it was his studied intention to follow in the path of Gregory VII.[1] Urban had assumed the task of leading the Church, and this he did ever keeping it in mind that his power was supreme. He called to task kings[2] and prelates for interfering in the work and management of ecclesiastical affairs.[3]

Outside of the pre-Gratian collections there are instances of rebukes given by Urban to members of the hierarchy.[4]

The collections of the period before Gratian offer abundant evidence of Urban's attempt to centralize the power of the papacy,

[1] JL 5348 and 5349: the *Collectio Britannica,* nn. 1 and 2. These two fragments are not in Gratian. The numbers used in the designation of the various collections refer to the enumeration followed in Part I of this study.

[2] JL 5397: the *Collectio Britannica* n. 40; not in Gratian.

[3] JL 5385: the *Collectio Britannica,* n. 32; not in Gratian.

[4] JL 5484, ca. May, 1092, *Atrebatenses clerici,* to Rainaldus, archbishop of Reims; JL 5522, May 13, 1094, *Fraternitati vestrae,* given at the Lateran, to Rainaldus of Reims and his suffragan bishops; JL 5525, May 20, 1094, *Quam grave sit,* given at Rome to Godinus, bishop of Brindisi; JL 5653, July 15, 1096, *Postquam apud,* given at Nîmes in the monastery of St. Giles, to the church and bishop of Burgos; JL 5678, Jan. 9-March 4, ca. 1097, *Quod de Guapicensi,* to Hugh, archbishop of Lyons and papal legate.

especially in the matter of dioceses and their incumbents. The papacy had the final say in the appointment of bishops. The Pope could uphold a bishop whose election had not been canonical.[5] It was within the prerogatives of the papacy to chose candidates for the episcopate when local disputes arose,[6] and to rebuke the faithful of a diocese who accepted an invader for their shepherd.[7] Likewise the Pope enjoyed the ultimate decision in the matter of the division of dioceses and provinces.[8]

The material outside of the collections presents abundant evidence of this centralization of the authority of the Holy See in the selection of bishops and the determination of dioceses.[9]

The Pope, as final judge in all ecclesiastical matters, at times demanded that controversies be settled by himself at the papal court. There is an example of this papal reservation of a dispute in the *Collectio Britannica*.[10] The Pope in one case reversed the decision of a metropolitan.[11]

[5] JL 5354, 5355 and 5356: the *Collectio Britannica*, nn. 5, 6 and 7 respectively; JL 5380: the *Collectio Britannica*, n. 25. (Not in Gratian.)

[6] JL 5794: the Collection of Saint-Germain-des-Prés, n. 39 (this fragment is not in Gratian); cf. Sdralek, pp. 40-41. Cf. the historical note in the *Collectio Britannica*, n. 44, in the *Tripartita*, n. 4, in the first Collection of Châlons-sur-Marne, n. 5, and in the second Collection of Châlons-sur-Marne, n. 17; this fragment is found in Gratian at c. 2, C. VIII, q. 3.

[7] JL 5367 and 5370: the *Collectio Britannica*, nn. 17, 18 and 21; none of these canons is found in Gratian. Cf. Fliche, *Histoire*, VIII, 230-231.

[8] JL 5357, 5358, 5361 and 5362: the *Collectio Britannica*, nn. 8, 9, 10, 14 and 15; none of these is in Gratian. Cf. Fliche, *Histoire*, VIII, 222 and 235.

[9] Concerning consecration of a bishop: JL 5473, undated, *Noverit tua fraternitas*, to Rainaldus, archbishop of Reims, and JL 5472, Dec. 2, 1092, *Atrebatensis ecclesia*, given at Castraneto, to the clergy and people of Arras; cf. Fliche, *Histoire*, VIII, 221-222. For papal decisions concerning the erection, translation and division of dioceses: JL 5413, Oct. 11, 1089, *Quia nobis*, given at Trani, to Godinus, bishop of Oria; JL 5568, May 26, 1095, *Quoniam frater*, given at Milan, to the clergy and laity of the town of Sermorens, France; JL 5595, Nov. 29, 1095, *Querelam venerabiles*, given at Clermont, to Guigo, count, and to the clergy and people of Grenoble; JL 5717, Dec. 25, 1098, *Quamvis clericorum*, given at Rome, to Manasses, archbishop of Reims; cf. Fliche, *Histoire*, VIII, 327.

[10] JL 5389: the *Collectio Britannica*, n. 36; this fragment is not in Gratian.

[11] Historical note in the *Collectio Britannica*, n. 44, in the *Tripartita*,

The Pope's power as judge is even more abundantly documented from sources outside of the pre-Gratian collections. At times Urban settled a controversy by constituting a tribunal having delegated papal power.[12] At times it was necessary to call the aggrieved parties to Rome, or to the location of the papal court.[13] Disputes between abbots [14] and even between a bishop and a civil prince were brought to a happy outcome through papal intervention.[15] In two cases Urban removed dioceses from the jurisdiction of their metropolitans and subjected them immediately to the Holy See in an effort to stem the tide of local disputes and controversies.[16]

What remains of the register of Urban II is literally filled with concessions of privileges to various monastic communities. Although none

---

n. 4, in the first Collection of Châlons-sur-Marne, n. 5, and in the second Collection of Châlons-sur-Marne, n. 17, and at c. 2, C. VIII, q. 3.

[12] P. Kehr, *Papsturkunden in Spanien in Abhandlungen der Gesellschaft der Wissenschaften zu Göttingen*, philologisch-historische Klasse (Vol. I, *Katalanien*, pt. I, Archivberichte, pt. II, Urkunden und Regesten, Neue Folge, 1926, Band XVIII, n. 2; Vol. II, *Navarra und Aragon*, pt. I, Archiveberichte, pt. II, Urkunden und Regesten, Neue Folge, 1928, Band XXII, n. 1), I, pt. II, p. 282, letter n. 19, 1091, *Tanto iam tempore*, to Frotardus, abbot of Thomières concerning the monastery of San Cugat, Barcelona; the archbishop of Bordeaux and the bishop of Grenoble were to act as judges. Cf. *ibid.*, p. 283, letter n. 20, 1091, *Inter venerabiles*, to Amatus, archbishop of Bordeaux; *ibid.*, pp. 278-279, letter n. 17, Nov. 17, 1089, *Quia religionis tuae*, to the same Frotardus; JL 5523, May 16, 1094, *Sollicitudinis nostrae*, given at Rome, to Hugh, archbishop of Lyons and legate of the Holy See.

[13] H. Wiederhold, *Papsturkunden in Frankreich* in *Nachrichten von der königl. Gesellschaft der Wissenschaften zu Göttingen*, philologisch-historische Klasse, Beiheft, 1907, p. 59, letter n. 4, undated, *Quantum Dei*, to Veranus invader; JL 5773, April 4, 1097-1099, *Beati Aegidii monasterium*, given at the Lateran, to Raymond, bishop of Nîmes.

[14] JL 5633, March 30, 1096, *Querelam die*, given at Poitiers concerning the dispute between the monastery at Cormery-sur-Indre and the canons of St. Martin's of Tours; JL 5721, ca. 1098, *Petitiones religionis*, to Odilo, abbot of St. Giles, Nîmes, concerning a dispute with the abbot of Cluny.

[15] Jaffé, *Regesta Pontificum Romanorum*, I, 670 (after JL 5466), August, 1092, in the archiepiscopal palace at Salerno a dispute between the archbishop of Salerno, Alphanus II, and Roger, duke of Apulia (1085-1111), son of Robert Guiscard. Cf. also Pflugk-Harttung, *Acta inedita*, II, 149.

[16] JL 5446, April 1, 1091, *Sacrorum canonum*, given at Benevento, to the bishop of Monopoli; JL 5653, July 15, 1096, *Postquam apud*, given in the monastery of St. Giles, Nîmes, to the church of Burgos.

of these grants has been incorporated in any of the collections made during or after the pontificate of Urban at least some allusion to this practice should be made here.[17] Monasteries were not the sole benefactors of papal bounty. The Holy See granted special privileges to dioceses and important churches. Thus the bishop of Santiago de Compostela enjoyed the privilege of being consecrated by the Roman Pontiff himself.[18]

It is interesting that, although none of the numerous concessions of Urban II to monastic groups have been incorporated in any of the collections before Gratian, yet there are two fragments in the *Collectio Britannica* which clearly define that the privileges extended to monastic properties were not to interfere with the acquired rights of the local ordinary.[19] The custom existed in the time of Urban for the Pope to grant favors only to those who personally, or through an agent, presented themselves before the pontifical throne.[20]

Both within and without the collections there are references to Urban's use of his supreme power for the granting of sanations and dispensations. Within the collections one finds an account of a general sanation granted to all the clergy of Milan who had been

[17] For example, JL 5372, Nov. 1, 1088, *Cum omnibus sanctae,* given at Rome, to Hugh, abbot of Cluny; JL 5376, Nov. 14, 1088, *Cum omnibus sanctae,* given at Rome, to the monastery at Châteauroux, France; JL 5402, July 4, 1089, *Potestatem ligandi,* given at Rome, to the monastery of Sts. Anianus and Lawrence at Nevers, France; JL 5457, Jan. 1096, *Iustis votum assensum,* given at Anagni, to the monastery of the Holy Savior at Schaffhausen; JL 5461, March 14, 1092, *Potestatem ligandi,* given at Anagni, to the monastery of St. Sophia in Benevento; JL 5483, April 20, 1093, *Piae voluntas affectus,* given on Mt. Gargano, to the monastery of St. Mary at Zwiefalten, Linz, Austria; JL 5539, Feb. 1, 1095, *Desiderium quod ad,* given at Florence, to the monastery of St. Peter at Puzzuoli; JL 5634, March 30, 1096, *Beatum confessorem,* given at Poitiers, to the archbishops and bishops of France; JL 5728, 1088-1099, *Piae postulatio voluntatis,* to the monastery at Lagny-sur-Marne, France.

[18] JL 5601, undated, *Veterum synodalium,* given at Privas, France, to the church of St. James at Compostela.

[19] JL 5371 (which does, however, contain a passing reference to privileges already granted to Cluny) and JL 5384; the *Collectio Britannica,* nn. 22 and 31; these texts are not in Gratian.

[20] JL 5352 and 5379: the *Collectio Britannica,* nn. 3 and 24; these canons are not in the *Decretum* of Gratian.

ordained by the schismatic bishop Theobald, the predecessor of Anselm. When Anselm was reconciled, Urban put all in order for the rest of the clergy.[21] This sanation seems to have been of a different nature from the customary reconciliation of clerics ordained *extra ecclesiam*.[22] Need for a papal dispensation was indicated when a subdeacon was to be chosen a bishop.[23] Urban dispensed from the need of legitimacy demanded of candidates for the episcopacy.[24]

Outside of the collections other instances of the granting of dispensations are found. The dispensation from illegitimacy on the part of candidates to be appointed as bishops is found elsewhere.[25] Likewise Urban rescinded the profession of an abbot forcibly made to a bishop.[26] The Pope voided an unjust decision of a metropolitan and his suffragans [27] and commuted the vow of an archbishop to go to the Holy Land.[28]

Among the many prerogatives which belonged to the Roman Pontiff, the sources outside of the collections, present some examples. Although canonization was still far from becoming an exclusively papal prerogative, Urban exercised his right in this regard.[29] In order to keep in close

---

[21] JL 5359, 5360 and 5386: the *Collectio Britannica*, nn. 11, 12, 13 and 33 (none of these canons are in Gratian). Cf. Fliche, *Histoire*, VIII, 213.

[22] Cf. *infra*, pp. 159-162.

[23] Canon 1, Council of Benevento: the Collection in Nine Books, n. 1, and c. 4, D. LX.

[24] JL 5390: the *Collectio Britannica*, n. 37, the *Panormia*, n. 4, the first recension of the *Collectio Caesaraugustana*, n. 15, the second recension of the *Collectio Caesaraugustana*, n. 17, the second Collection of Châlons-sur-Marne, n. 15, the Collection of *Codex Ms. Vaticanus Latinus 1361*, n. 10, the Collection in Ten Parts, n. 18, and c. 14, D. LVI.

[25] Canon 15, Council of Clermont, according to the compendium of Ordericus Vitalis, Nov. 18-28, 1095, Mansi, XX, 885, and canon 19 of the same council in the version of William of Malmesbury, Mansi, XX, 905. This canon resembles the canon above from the Council of Benevento.

[26] JL 5499, Nov. 24, 1093, *Relatum nobis*, given at Rome, to the congregation of the Holy Trinity at Vendôme.

[27] JL 5522, May 13, 1094, *Fraternitati vestrae*, given at the Lateran, to Rainaldus, archbishop of Reims and his suffragans.

[28] JL 5674, Dec. 25, 1096, given at Rome, to Bernard, archbishop of Toledo and primate of Spain.

[29] JL 5677, Jan. 9-March 4, 1097, *Cum largiente domino*, to the clergy,

touch with local problems and attempts at reform, he made regional and diocesan synods subject to confirmation by the Pope.[30] One papal prerogative exercised with regularity by Urban was the Pope's right to convoke synods.[31]

Only six of these councils received mention in the collections. These are the councils of Melfi,[32] Benevento,[33] Troia,[34] Piacenza,[35]

nobility and people of Trani; JL 5762, 1088-1099, *Ex consideratione,* to Otto, bishop of Strasbourg.

[30] JL 5549, March 15, 1095, *Claruisse plurimos,* given at Piacenza, to the church of Burgos.

[31] Urban convoked eleven councils in all: at Rome in 1089 (only references to this council exist), Hefele-Leclercq, *Conciles,* V, I, 343-344 and Fliche, *Histoire,* VIII, 207 and note 2; at Melfi, Sept. 10, 1089, Jaffé, *Regesta Pontificum Romanorum,* I, 664; at Benevento, March 28, 1091, *ibid.,* I, 667-668; at Troia, March 11, 1093, *ibid.,* I, 671; at Piacenza, March 1-7, 1095, *ibid.,* I, 677; at Clermont, Nov. 18-28, 1095, *ibid.,* I, 681-682; at Tours, March 16-22, 1096, *ibid.,* I, 685; at Nîmes, *ibid.,* I, 688; at Bari, Oct. 3-5, 1098, *ibid.,* I 694; at the Lateran (called by some the second Roman synod), 1097-1099 (Hefele-Leclercq date this council in Jan. 1097—*Conciles,* V, I, 453); at Rome (called the third Roman synod), April 24-30, 1099, *ibid.,* I, 700.

[32] Historical note in *Collectio Britannica,* n. 47, where twelve canons of this council are given; canon 14 is found in Gratian at c. 1, D. LVI; canon 12 at c. 10, D. XXXII; and canon 3 at c. 10, D. XXXII.

[33] Canon 1 of this council appears with frequency: in the Collection of Nine Books, n. 1, in the *Decretum,* n. 2, in the *Panormia,* n. 1, in the first recension of the *Collectio Caesaraugustana,* n. 1, in the second recension of the *Collectio Caesaraugustana,* nn. 1 and 9, in the Collection of Saint-Germain-des-Prés, n. 37, in the first Collection of Châlons-sur-Marne, n. 6, in the second Collection of Châlons-sur-Marne, n. 18, in the Collection in Ten Parts, n. 7, and in Gratian at c. 4, D. LX. Canon 4 of the Council of Benevento is found only once: in Collection of Seven Books, n. 4, and another canon in the second section of this same canon 4 is found once only in the recension "Bb" of the Collection of Anselm of Lucca, n. 3. Neither of these last two canons is found in Gratian.

[34] Canon 1 is found in the Collection of *Codex Ms. Vaticanus Latinus 3829,* n. 2, and in c. 4, C. XXXV, q. 6; for the other places where this canon is found among the pre-Gratian collections the reader is directed to the chart in Appendix I of Part I.

[35] The majority of the canons of this council are found in the *Polycarpus,* n. 5, in the Collection in Seven Books, n. 2, and in c. 5, C. IX, q. 1; c. 1, C. I, q. 108; c. 5, C. I, q. 3, and c. 1, C. I, q. 5. For parallel places in the collections see the chart in Appendix I.

Clermont,[36] and of Rome (1099).[37] No references are found to the other five councils of Urban within the collections.

History remembers Urban II for restoring prestige to the papacy through his ability to compromise to the advantage of the Church.[38] It is not easy, however, to find this temporary policy of compromise put into words; the twelfth canon of the Council of Piacenza perhaps best approaches a statement of Urban's position.[39]

The notions and examples cited above given only a partial picture of the rôle of the Roman Pontiff in Urban's time. They are sufficient, however, to indicate the contribution of Urban II toward the centralization of ecclesiastical authority in the papacy.

Article II. Cardinals, Legates, Primates and Metropolitans

This section will begin with the few ideas concerning ecclesiastical elections that could be gleaned from Urban's sources. The collections give some consideration to this subject. The normal procedure in episcopal elections was for the clergy and the people (usually certain nobles) to make their choice.[40] If, in the choice

[36] The canons from the Council of Clermont appear frequently in the Collection of Saint-Germain-des-Prés, in the second Collection of Châlons-sur-Marne, and in the Collection in Ten Parts; canons are found in Gratian at c. 1, D. LX; c. 4, C. I, q. 3, and c. 46, C. XII, q. 2. See the chart for the complete listing of canons from Clermont (Appendix I, Part I).

[37] Most of the canons from this council were previously enacted at the Councils of Piacenza and Melfi. In the three collections referred to in the previous footnote, the canons from this third Council of Rome are found in abundance, but in the chart in Appendix I these have been placed with the canons from Melfi and Piacenza, with which they textually agree.

[38] Cf. Fliche, *Histoire*, VIII, 201; Setton-Baldwin, *A History of the Crusades*, I, 222-229, *passim*.

[39] "Quamvis autem misericordiae intuitu, magnoque necessitate cogente, hanc . . . dispensationem constituerimus, nullum tamen praeiudicium sacris canonibus fieri volumus; sed obtineant proprium robur. Et cessante necessitate, illud quoque cesset quod factum est pro necessitate."—Mansi, XX, 806; this canon is found in the *Polycarpus*, n. 5, in the Collection in Seven Books, n. 5, in the Italian Collection in Three Books, n. 7, in the first and second recension of the *Collectio Caesaraugustana*, n. 5, in the Collection of Saint-Germain-des-Prés, n. 31, and in c. 5, C. IX, q. 1.

[40] JL 5354, 5355, 5356 and 5380: the *Collectio Britannica*, nn. 5, 6, 7 and 25 respectively. These texts are not in Gratian.

of a candidate, a division arose, the final decision was left for the Pope.[41]

The sources outside of the collection testify to the same procedure.[42] The law stated that the election should be held within three months of the vacancy.[43] The letters of Urban reveal little actual detail of the procedure in the election; brief reference was made to the election of a provost and of an abbot.[44]

In all there are very few details concerning cardinals, and their rights and privileges. There is one letter in the collections which indicates that the cardinals were permitted to bestow the pallium upon an archbishop *sede Romana vacante;* such a grant, however, had to be confirmed upon the election of the new Pope.[45]

The rest of the information comes from outside the collections. There are a few examples of special privileges granted to some of the cardinals: no priest could celebrate Mass in the presence of a cardinal without the permission of the Pope; no priest was permitted to bless the baptismal font on the eve of Easter and Pentecost, except with the approval of the Holy Father or of the nearest cardinal.[46] The clergy, if attached to a diaconal church held by a cardinal-deacon as his

---

[41] JL 5794: the Collection of Saint-Germain-des-Prés, n. 39 (not in Gratian); historical note in the *Collectio Britannica*, n. 44, the *Tripartita*, n. 4, the first collection of Châlons-sur-Marne, n. 5, the second Collection of Châlons-sur-Marne, n. 17, and c. 2, C. VIII, q. 3.

[42] JL 5350, March-April, 1088, *Nolumus latere*, given at Terracina, to the bishops Valence, Geneva, Maurienne, Grenoble, Die, Vivrais, and to the clergy and people of Vienne; JL 5442, Feb. 10, 1090, *Gaudemus filii*, given at Benevento, to Lanzo and Rudolph, abbots, Adalbero, *primicerius*, to the archdeacons and all the clergy and people of Metz.

[43] JL 5350, as in the previous footnote.

[44] P. Kehr, *Italia Pontificia*, VI, pt. I, p. 319, letter n. 271, Oct. 6, 1096, given at Cremona, to Andericus, priest, and his brothers at Brescia; J. Ramackers, *Papsturkunden in Frankreich* in *Abhandlungen der Gesellschaft der Wissenschaften zu Göttingen*, philologisch-historische Klasse, 1940, Dritte Folge, n. 23, pp. 38-41, letter n. 5, May 17, 1099, *Petis a me*, given at Rome, to Bernold, provost of the church of St. Mary, Watten, France.

[45] JL 5385: the *Collectio Britannica*, n. 32; not in Gratian.

[46] JL 5737, 1088-1099, to the clergy of the church of the Holy Savior, within the parish of St. Chrysogonus, Rome; also called Felix Aquila; cf. JL 6901.

titular church, were exempted from the usual service at baptisms, scrutinies, processions and other functions.[47] During the pontificate of Urban II the college of cardinals assumed a more vital rôle as counsellors to the Holy Father than previously. This process of the evolution of the role of the cardinals as the chief administrative body of the Church continued into the twelfth century.[48]

Gregory VII had used permanent papal legates to strengthen his control throughout the Church; at the start of his pontificate Urban had followed Gregory's example, but when the allegiance of several of the legates became doubtful, Urban resorted to the temporary legation. The collections furnish only one instance of the appointment of a legate.[49]

Letters not incorporated into the pre-Gratian collections offer several other examples.[50] Urban had served as special legate of Gregory VII and from personal experience was acquainted with the potentialities of such a program. Primates were often chosen as legates.[51] One duty of the legate, besides that of supervision and representation in the name of the Pope, was to preside over councils.[52] At times a legate enjoyed special authority from the Holy See to the extent that his

---

[47] P. Kehr, *Nachträge zu den Papsturkunden Italiens* in *Nachrichten von der königl. Gesellschaft der Wissenschaften zu Göttingen*, philologisch-historische Klasse, 1908, pp. 228-229, letter, n. 3, to cardinal-priests; cf. P. Kehr, *Italia Pontificia*, I, 7, letter n. 282, 1088-1099.

[48] Fliche, *Histoire*, VIII, 208-209; JL 5411, Sept. 21, 1089, *Cum universis sancte*, given at Venosa, to the monastery of La Cava; JL 5449, June 28, 1091, *Cum omnes*, given at Benevento; JL 5505, Feb. 6, 1094, *Qualiter in*, given at Rome, to the archbishop of Magdeburg, the bishop of Verdun, and the other bishops and the abbots of Saxony; JL 5506, Feb. 6, 1094, *Qualiter in*, given at Rome, to all the faithful of Saxony.

[49] JL 5389: the *Collectio Britannica*, n. 36 (not in Gratian).

[50] JL 5643, April 25, 1095, *Ex ipsis redemptionis*, given at the monastery of Terramaggiore at Samnio, Italy, to the clergy and people of Spain and the province of Narbonne; JL 5706, July 5, 1098, *Quia propter prudentiam*, given at Salerno, to Roger, count of Calabria and Sicily; concerning the later effects of this letter, cf. Mourret, *History*, IV, 270; Fliche, *Histoire*, VIII, 209-212, gives the background and indicates exactly what the legations accomplished.

[51] JL 5415, Dec. 25, 1089, *Potestatem ligandi*, given at Rome, to Rainaldus, archbishop of Reims.

[52] JL 5549, March 14, 1095, *Claruisse plurimas*, given at Piacenza, to Gomesanus, bishop of Burgos.

judgment was looked upon as deriving from the Pope himself; sometimes all appeal was precluded from the decision of a legate.[53] The legate was expected to practice vigilance; interest in local disputes was looked upon as part of his duty.[54] To the legate was due the same unhesitating obedience and respect that was to be given to the Roman Pontiff himself.[55]

Urban restored to the archbishop of Toledo the title of primate of all of Spain; this recognition was granted as an expression of papal approval of the work of restoration and reform going on in that peninsula.[56]

The bestowal of primacy upon Bernard, archbishop of Toledo, is given even more extensive coverage within the *Collectio Britannica*.[57] Even before restoring to Bernard the title of primate Urban had granted him the pallium personally when the archbishop had been in Rome.[58] Upon his return to unity with the Holy See, Anselm, archbishop of Milan, was also granted the pallium by Urban.[59]

Sources found outside of the collections made before Gratian have some information about the pallium and its use by archbishops.[60] The

---

[53] JL 5469, Oct. 27, 1092, *Si sacerdotale quod*, given to Rainaldus, archbishop of Reims.

[54] JL 5417, 1089, *Quantum de tua religione*, to Ranierus, cardinal-priest and apostolic legate; JL 5523, May 16, 1094, *Sollicitudinis nostrae*, given at Rome, to Hugh, archbishop of Lyons and legate of the Holy See.

[55] P. Kehr, *Papsturkenden in Spanien*, I, pt. II, p. 281, letter, p. 18, 1088-1099, *Veniente nuper*, to the abbot of Thomières.

[56] JL 5366, Oct. 15, 1088, *Cunctis sanctorum*, given at Anagni, to Bernard, archbishop of Toledo. For another example of this privilege, cf. JL 5707, June 20, 1098, *Singulare semper*, given at Salerno, to Alphanus II, archbishop of Salerno.

[57] JL 5367, 5370 and 5371: the *Collectio Britannica*, nn. 17, 18, 21 and 22 (none of these canons is in Gratian); cf. Fliche, *Histoire*, VIII, 230-231.

[58] Reference to this concession is made in JL 5367; and in the *Collectio Britannica*, n. 18. Cf. Fliche, *Histoire*, VIII, 230.

[59] JL 5359, 5360 and 5386: the *Collectio Britannica*, nn. 11, 12, 13 and 33 (not in Gratian).

[60] JL 5415, Dec. 25, 1089, *Potestatem ligandi*, given at Rome, to Rainaldus, archbishop of Reims; JL 5548, March 12, 1095, *Necessitate et utilitate*, given at Piacenza, to Guido, archbishop of Vienne; H. Wiederhold, *Papsturkunden in Frankreich*, Beiheft, 1913, pp. 39-40, letter, n. 6, Oct.

metropolitan archbishop exercised an important function within the network of ecclesiastical control and supervision. To his superiors he owed obedience; to his subjects vigilance.[61] To the Holy See belonged the right to establish and confirm the appointment of metropolitans.[62]

Urban's decision in the dispute between Naples and Capua, reported in the *Collectio Britannica,* illustrates the authority which the Roman Pontiff exercised over the metropolitans of his era.[63]

Article III. Bishops

The episcopate was the principal means of exercising a close control and of effecting the needed reforms on a local level within the Church. The network of bishops offered an excellent potential for supervision throughout the whole of Christendom; it is in no way surprising that Urban II took every possible advantage of this framework in his efforts to reform and to centralize papal authority. Nothing could be more beneficial to the papal program than to ally to it the episcopate.

It is of interest that most of Urban's attempts to win over the bishops are recorded in sources outside of the canonical collections. The appeals were generally made in letters to individual persons; these overtures were not absorbed into the collections. But the particular program to be undertaken, once the bishop had allied himself to the Pope, was spelled out in conciliar decrees for the most part, and these decrees are usually incorporated in the collections. It is for this reason that the specific attempts to win adherents to the papal side are recorded outside the collections, while the plan to be followed by the same adherents is encom-

28, 1097, *Potestatem ligandi*, given at the Lateran, to Raymond, archbishop of Auch.

[61] JL 5509, Feb. 24, 1094, *Multa et gravia*, given at Rome, to Fulconus, bishop of Beauvais; JL 5619, March 4, 1096, *Scripsimus nuper*, given at Tours, to Hugh, bishop of Soissons, to Lambert, bishop of Arras, to Philip, bishop of Châlons-sur-Marne, to Gerard, bishop of Thérouanne, and to all the suffragan bishops of the archdiocese of Reims.

[62] JL 5568, May 26, 1095, *Quoniam frater*, given at Milan, to all the clergy and faithful of Sermorens, France; JL 5758, 1088-1099, to the church at Otranto, Italy.

[63] JL 5357, 5358, 5361 and 5362: the *Collectio Britannica*, nn. 8, 9, 10, 14 and 15; not in Gratian.

passed within the matters treated in the collections. In accordance with this general division, what follows is mostly from outside the collections.

The desperate need for bishops to be allied to the papal cause is recognized by all historians.[64] Urban's correspondence is replete with admonitions and encouragement to members of the episcopate. The bishop was the shepherd of his flock in the fullest sense.[65] The bishop was the protector and peace-maker for his diocese.[66] Loyalty and respect toward the Pope[67] and the metropolitan was expected from every bishop.[68] The faithful, on their part, owed to their bishop true obedience.[69]

But for the bishop who had forsaken his pastoral trust, Urban had only rebuke and penalties. Excommunication and the withdrawal of

---

[64] For example, when Urban was elected, ". . . only five German bishops recognized the new pope."—Setton-Baldwin, *A History of the Crusades*, I, 225.

[65] H. Wiederhold, *Papsturkunden in Frankreich*, Beiheft, 1913, pp. 39-40, letter n. 6, Oct. 28, 1097, *Potestatem ligandi*, given at the Lateran, to Raymond, archbishop of Auch, France.

[66] JL 5409, ca. Sept., 1089, *Super quaestionibus*, to Pibo, bishop of Toul; JL 5458, Jan. 28, 1092, *Venerunt ad*, given at Anagni, to the bishop of Constance; JL 5617, Dec. 31, 1095, *Pervenit ad nos*, given at Limoges, to the bishops of Cahors, Rodez, Auvergne and Limoges; JL 5615, Feb. 6, 1096, *Omnipotenti Deo*, given at Angers to Manasses, archbishop of Reims; JL 5646, May 7, 1096, *Fraternitatem vestram*, given at Toulouse, to Isnardus, bishop of Toulouse, to Simon, bishop of Agen, to Gerard, bishop of Cahors, and to Raymond, bishop of Lectoure; JL 5665, August 7, 1096, *Inter Scafusensium*, given at Forcalquier, France, to Gebhard, bishop of Constance; JL 5731, 1088-1099, *Misimus dilectioni tuae*. to Hugh, bishop of Grenoble; P. Kehr, *Italia Pontificia*, III, 390, letter, n. '410-note, 1088-1099.

[67] JL 5500, Dec. 25, 1093, *Decuerat fraternitatis*, given at Rome, to Rainaldus, archbishop of Reims; JL 5509, Feb. 24, 1094, *Multa et gravia*, given at Rome, to Fulconus, bishop of Beauvais.

[68] JL 5619, March 4, 1096, *Scripsimus nuper*, given at Tours, to Hugh, bishop of Soissons, to Lambert, bishop of Arras, to Philip, bishop of Châlons-sur-Marne, and to Gerard, bishop of Thérouanne.

[69] JL 5615, Feb. 6, 1096, *Affectionis quidem*, given at Angers, to the clergy, soldiers and faithful of Reims.

[70] JL 5595, Nov. 29, 1095, *Querelam venerabiles*, given at Clermont, to Guigo, count, and to the clergy and people of Grenoble; JL 5619, 1095, *Adversus apostolicam sedem*, to Guido, archbishop of Vienne.

obedience and tribute were threatened.[70] Suspension was likewise a possible penalty.[71]

The pre-Gratian collections present a very good résumé of the bishop and his place in the Church. He is to be a shepherd,[72] worthy of obedience from his flock;[73] if he neglects his sacred task, let him be punished.[74]

The sources outside of the collections mention that among the functions reserved solely for bishops were the administration of the sacraments of confirmation and orders, the consecration of holy oils, of chalices, of patens and of churches.[75]

The two ranking prelates immediately beneath the bishop were the archdeacon and the archpriest, in that order.[76] Urban's sources offer few details about these two dignitaries. From the texts which were included in the pre-Gratian collections one sees that to serve as archdeacon it was necessary for a cleric to have been previously ordained a deacon.[77] The archpriest had to be an ordained priest.[78]

The sources outside of the collections permit the archdeacon to appoint chaplains for lay princes.[79]

---

[71] JL 5525, May 20, 1094, *Quam gravis sit*, given at Rome, to Godinus, bishop of Brindisi; JL 5685, June 4, 1097, *Quam arroganter*, given at the Lateran, to Hugh, archbishop of Lyons; JL 5712, ca. Nov. 1098, *Dolemus pro vobis*, to the clergy and people of Liége.

[72] JL 5724: the *Panormia*, n. 9, the second recension of the *Collectio Caesaraugustana*, n. 8, the second Collection of Châlons-sur-Marne, n. 49, the Collection in Ten Parts, n. 36, and c. 37, D. L.

[73] JL 5408: the *Collectio Britannica*, n. 46 (not in Gratian).

[74] JL 5611: the *Decretum* of Ivo of Chartres, n. 1; this fragment is not in Gratian.

[75] J. Ramackers, *Papsturkunden in Frankreich*, 1940, Dritte Folge, n. 23, pp. 38-41, letter, n. 5, May 17, 1099, *Petis a me*, given at Rome, to Bernold, provost of the church of St. Mary, Watten, France.

[76] Cf. D. Heintschel, *The Medieval Concept of an Ecclesiastical Office*, pp. 62-66.

[77] Canon 3, Council of Clermont, Mansi, XX, 817: the Collection of Saint-Germain-des-Prés, n. 9, the second Collection of Châlons-sur-Marne, n. 21, the Collection in Ten Parts, n. 14; this canon is related in content to c. 1, D. LX.

[78] Canon 3, Council of Clermont; cf. the previous footnote.

[79] Canon 18, second sentence, Council of Clermont, Mansi, XX, 817;

But to ascertain the further norms that affected chaplains it is necessary to return to the collections. Although the archdeacon had power in this regard, the collections mention the permission of the bishop.[80] In monastic churches the bishop and the abbot were to select jointly a chaplain who was to serve the pastoral needs of the people; this vicar was responsible to the ordinary for his pastoral ministry, and to the abbot for the temporal administration.[81]

Article IV. Ordination and Episcopal Consecration

Since there was much abuse and controversy concerning the sacrament of orders, there is abundant legislation both outside and within the pre-Gratian collections. In an attempt to stem the tide against schism, simony, lay investiture and clerical incontinency, Pope Urban adopted some very specific measures. A considerable number of these became incorporated in the canonical collections of that period.

From the collections it was clear that sacred orders were differentiated from the other orders. Sacred orders included the diaconate and the priesthood.[82] To be elected to the episcopacy the candidate had to be at least a deacon, or, with the special permission of the metropolitan or the Pope himself, a subdeacon.[83] The

although the first section of this canon appears within the pre-Gratian collections, the present regulation does not.

[80] Canon 18, first sentence, Council of Clermont, Mansi, XX, 817: the Collection of Saint-Germain-des-Prés, n. 21, the second Collection of Châlons-sur-Marne, n. 30, and the Collection in Ten Parts, n. 42; this canon is not in Gratian.

[81] Canon 3 in the special version of the acts of the Council of Clermont as found in the Collection of Saint-Germain-des-Prés, n. 3; this canon is repeated in the second Collection of Châlons-sur-Marne, n. 32, and in the Collection in Ten Parts, n. 37. It is not found in Gratian, but does occur in c. 1, X, *de capellanis monachorum et aliorum religiosorum*, III, 37.

[82] Canon 1, Council of Benevento, Mansi, XX, 737: the Collection in Nine Books, n. 1, the *Decretum* of Ivo, n. 2, the *Panormia*, n. 1, the first recension of the *Collectio Caesaraugustana*, n. 1, the second recension of the *Collectio Caesaraugustana*, nn. 1 and 9, the Collection of Saint-Germain-des-Prés, n. 37, the first Collection of Châlons-sur-Marne, n. 6, the second Collection of Châlons-sur-Marne, n. 18, the Collection in Ten Parts, n. 7, and c. 4, D. LX.

[83] Cf. the previous footnote and canon 5, Council of Clermont, Mansi,

legitimacy which was demanded of the candidate for the episcopate could be dispensed with by the Roman Pontiff.[84]

Outside of the collections there was specific demand for the "*dignitas natalium*" for every bishop, although the possiblity of an exception stood available.[85] These few regulations were apparently all which Urban enacted concerning episcopal consecration. Much greater detail was accorded to ordination to the priesthood.

The canonical collections made at the end of the eleventh and in the first half of the twelfth centuries include many regulations concerning candidates for sacred orders, especially the priesthood. A proper canonical age was determined for priests as well as for deacons and even subdeacons; the age established was thirty, twenty-four, and fourteen respectively.[86] Because of the contemporary problem of clerical celibacy, aspirants to sacred orders were required to be virgins, or of proven chastity before advancement; married men were not barred, provided that they had been married but once and to a virgin.[87] Those in "servile condition" could not be promoted to the ranks of the clergy.[88]

A title was demanded of everyone promoted to major orders;

XX, 817, and canon 4 of the same council as found in the special account of Clermont in the Collection of Saint-Germain-des-Prés; both of these canons are found in that collection at nn. 10 and 4 respectively. These texts are not in Gratian.

[84] JL 5390: the *Collectio Britannica*, n. 37, the *Panormia*, n. 4, the first recension of the *Collectio Caesaraugustana*, n. 15, the second recension of the *Collectio Caesaraugustana*, n. 17, the second Collection of Châlons-sur-Marne, n. 15, the Collection of *Codex Ms. Vaticanus Latinus 1361*, the Collection in Ten Parts, n. 18, and c. 14, D. LVI.

[85] Canon 15, Council of Clermont, in the compendium of Ordericus Vitalis, Mansi, XX, 885; canon 19 of the same council according to William of Malmesbury, Mansi, XX, 905.

[86] Canon 4, Council of Melfi: the *Collectio Britannica*, n. 47; not in Gratian.

[87] Canon 3, Council of Melfi, Mansi, XX, 723: the Collection of *Codex Ms. Vaticanus Latinus 4977*, n. 4, the *Collectio Britannica*, n. 47, the *Panormia*, n. 7; repeated as canon 14, Council of Rome, Mansi, XX, 963: the Collection of Saint-Germain-des-Prés, n. 31, and the Collection in Ten Parts, n. 11; in Gratian at c. 12, D. XXXII.

[88] Canon 11, Council of Melfi, Mansi, XX, 723-724: the *Collectio Britannica*, n. 47; not in Gratian.

this title was customarily the specific church at which the cleric was to serve abidingly.[89] "*Clerici acephali*" could not be tolerated, especially in episcopal curias, which appear to have been a gathering place for such unattached clerics. This prohibition was in its application directed especially at the "*monachi vagantes.*"[90] Each of the orders was to be received according to the usual pattern: first the minor orders and then the major; it was forbidden to by-pass any intervening order.[91]

To the proper bishop of each candidate belonged the right to ordain his own cleric; ordination by any other prelate without the consent of the candidate's own ordinary was uncanonical, but could be tolerated, if the character of the candidate was upright.[92] Urban permitted an abbot to ordain his own religious to minor orders for service in the parochial churches served by the monastery.[93] The approved times for ordinations were the Ember Saturdays and the Saturday in mid-Lent.[94]

The sources which come from outside the collections serve to supplement the norms which are found in the canonical collections of that period. Generally monks were directed to receive orders from the local episcopal ordinary; this decision had been reached as the outcome of bitter disputes in the tenth and the eleventh century. But by exceptional privilege the Pope permitted some monks to seek ordination from any bishop in good standing within the Church.[95] It was

---

[89] Canon 13, Council of Clermont, Mansi, XX, 817: the Collection of Saint-Germain-des-Prés, n. 16, the second Collection of Châlons-sur-Marne, n. 24, and the Collection in Ten Parts, n. 13; not in Gratian.

[90] Canon 9, Council of Melfi, Mansi, XX, 723: the *Collectio Britannica*, n. 47; canon 10 of the same council is in the *Britannica* and also in the second recension of the *Collectio Caesaraugustana*, n. 19; not in Gratian.

[91] JL 5734: the second recension of the *Collectio Caesaraugustana*, n. 18; not in Gratian.

[92] JL 5723: the *Tripartita*, n. 10, the *Decretum*, n. 8, the second Collection of Châlons-sur-Marne, n. 20, and c. 10, C. IX, q. 2.

[93] JL 5729: the second Collection of Châlons-sur-Marne, n. 33, and the Collection in Ten Parts, n. 38; not in Gratian.

[94] Canon 24, Council of Clermont, Mansi, XX, 818: the Collection of Saint-Germain-des-Prés, n. 25, the second Collection of Châlons-sur-Marne, n. 25, and the Collection in Ten Parts, n. 12; not in Gratian.

[95] JL 5454, Nov., 1091, *Noverit nos vestrae*, to the monks of the congregation of St. Giles at Nîmes.

frequently the practice that, if a bishop had fallen into schism or heresy, those monks who normally depended upon that prelate for orders were expected to seek ordination from other bishops.[96] Ordination either outside one's own diocese, or by someone other than by one's own proper bishop, was strictly forbidden, except with proper dimissorial letters—"*formata epistola.*"[97] The need for a title was indicated also in the sources outside of the collections.[98] As a general rule a cleric was expected to serve in the church where he was titled originally, except in a case of necessity wherein a single priest was given the care of two separate churches. Even in this exceptional case the cleric still retained only his original title.[99] Because of the lack of clerics in some regions, the bishops were given discretionary powers to accept or reject those who had received ordination without a canonical title.[100] In a somewhat similar manner, abbots were at times allowed to accept clerics without the usual testimonial letters from the proper bishops of the latter.[101]

The ordinary time for sacred ordination was the four Ember Saturdays along with the Saturday in "*mediana quadragesimae.*"[102] This legislation was a repetition of the regulations which were first enacted by Gelasius I in the year 494.[103] It is interesting

[96] P. Kehr, *Italia Pontificia*, VI, pt. I, p. 319, letter n. 271, Oct. 16, 1096, *Piae postulatio*, given at Cremona, to Andericus, priest, and his brothers at Brescia.

[97] Canon 3, Council of Benevento, March 28, 1091, Mansi, XX, 739.

[98] JL 5409, ca. Sept., 1089, *Super quaestionibus*, to Pibo, bishop of Toul; canon 15, Council of Piacenza, March 1-7, 1095, Mansi, XX, 806-807; this is the only canon of the Council of Piacenza which does not appear in any of the collections.

[99] Canon 15, Council of Piacenza, Mansi, XX, 806-807.

[100] JL 5409, ca. Sept., 1089, *Super quaestionibus*, given to Pibo, bishop of Toul.

[101] JL 5768, 1088-1099, *Religionis vestrae petitionis*, to Gualcelinus, abbot.

[102] Canon 24, Council of Clermont, Mansi, XX, 818: the Collection of Saint-Germain-des-Prés, n. 25, the second Collection of Châlons-sur-Marne, n. 25 and the Collection in Ten Parts, n. 12; not in Gratian.

[103] JL 636; c. 7, D. LXXV. Cf. J. Reiss, *The Time and Place of Sacred Ordination*, The Catholic University of America Canon Law Studies, n. 343 (Washington, D. C.: The Catholic University of America Press, 1953), pp. 8-12; the relation between sacred ordination and the Ember Days is traced.

to note that the time of the rite of ordination determined how long the Ember fast was to last for that day.[104]

The sources from outside the collections furnish the same norms regarding the times for sacred ordination. The usual times for ordinations to the sacred orders were the Ember Saturdays and the Saturday in mid-Lent; the connection between the fast and the time for ordination was noted too.[105] These same sources also add a note not found inside the collections: two sacred orders could not be received on one and the same day.[106]

Urban did much to temper the strict doctrines of Gregory VII concerning the sons of priests and their reception of sacred orders. Following the general rule established in the Ninth Council of Toledo (657), Gregory had disqualified the sons of priests and of other major clerics from the reception of holy orders. In a canon which was included in almost every major collection of that period, Urban mitigated this serverity by demanding that such candidates could serve at the altar, provided that they made profession in a religious community,[107] or if they at least had lived a commendable life in accord with the sacred canons and had never accepted

[104] Canon 24, Council of Clermont, Mansi, XX, 818; the Collection of Saint-Germain-des-Prés, n. 25, the second Collection of Châlons-sur-Marne, n. 25 and the Collection in Ten Parts, n. 12; this canon is not in Gratian.

[105] Canon 8, Council of Clermont, according to the compendium of canons by Ordericus Vitalis, Mansi, XX, 885; canon 11 of the same council in the enumeration of William of Malmesbury, Mansi, XX, 904.

[106] P. Kehr, *Italia Pontificia*, VII, pt. II, p. 59, letter n. 177, August 31, ca. 1093, *De Torcellensis*, given at Telese, to the patriarch of Grado. This letter also warned against false dimissorial letters.

[107] Canon 14, Council of Melfi, Mansi, XX, 724: the *Collectio Britannica*, n. 47, the recension "Bb" of the Collection of Anselm of Lucca, n. 1, the Italian Collection in Three Books, n. 1, the Collection in Nine Books, n. 2, the *Tripartita*, n. 8, the *Decretum*, n. 6, the *Panormia*, n. 2, the first recension of the *Collectio Caesaraugustana*, n. 14, the second recension of the *Collectio Caesaraugustana*, n. 16, the second Collection of Châlons-sur-Marne, n. 19, the Collection of *Codex Ms. Vaticanus Latinus 1361*, n. 8, the Collection in Ten Parts, n. 15; this canon is found in Gratian at c. 1, D. LVI. Regarding the prohibition of ordination for the sons of clerics who were living in concubinage, cf. canons 10, 11 and 14, Council of Clermont, Mansi, XX, 817: the Collection of Saint-Germain-des-Prés, nn. 13 and 14, the second Collection of Châlons-sur-Marne, n. 22, and the Collection in Ten Parts, n. 16; none of these canons is in Gratian.

investiture of any kind from the hand of a layman.[108] Gratian added a clarifying note to this rule by observing that the prohibition was leveled against only those sons who persisted in the evil ways of their fathers.[109]

A more intricate problem, treated with considerable detail in the various collections, concerned the ordination conferred by heretical and simoniacal bishops who had been excommunicated because of their crimes,[110] and the ordinations performed in connection with a simoniacal agreement.[111] Urban eventually led the attack against the existing abuses at the Council of Piacenza in 1095; the decrees of this council were repeated at his last council, held at St. Peter's in Rome in 1099. In general, Urban's solution distinguished between deliberate and unintentional transgressions of the canons. Those who unwittingly received ordination *intra ecclesiam* at the hands of a simoniac were mercifully permitted to retain their grade, provided that no simony was involved in the conferral, and the life

[108] JL 5585: the *Collectio Britannica*, n. 32; not in Gratian.

[109] *Casus ad* c. 1, D. LVI; *dictum Gratiani post* c. 1, D. LVI.

[110] There are several pertinent passages about such ordinations in the long letter, JL 5743, which has been transcribed in its entirety in the recension "C" of the Collection of Anselm of Lucca, n. 1, in the Collection in Nine Books, n. 11, and in the Collection of *Codex Ms. Vaticanus Latinus 1361*, n. 1; c. 6, D. XXXII, is also from this letter. Other portions of this letter are found in the pre-Gratian collections and in Gratian, but these passages concern simony more directly.

[111] Actually Urban left the final decision on this last question for the Council of Piacenza; these ideas will be considered presently; for Urban's earlier notions on this subject of simoniacal ordination, cf. JL 5393: the Collection in Two Books, n. 2, the *Collectio Britannica*, n. 38, the recension "C" of the Collection of Anselm of Lucca, n. 3, the Collection of *Codex Ms. Vaticanus Latinus 3829*, n. 1, the *Tripartita*, nn. 1 and 7, the *Decretum* of Ivo of Chartres, nn. 3 and 14, the *Panormia*, n. 10, the first and second recension of the *Collectio Caesaraugustana*, n. 2, the first Collection of Châlons-sur-Marne, n. 3, the second Collection of Châlons-sur-Marne nn. 12 and 52, the Collection in Thirteen Books, n. 1, and the Collection in Ten Parts, n. 45; excerpts from this letter are found at c. 110, C. XI, q. 3, and c. 4, C. IX, q. 1. The entire question of the attitude of Urban II toward orders conferred *extra ecclesiam* is by no means clear or certain. All agree that Urban made a valuable contribution toward the eventual solution, but there seems to be no unanimity concerning his actual practice in every case. Cf. Hefele-Leclercq, *Conciles*, V, I, 341-344, especially p. 343, note 1.

of the candidate was otherwise commendable. But orders knowingly sought from a simoniacal prelate were declared to be without effect ("... *omnino irritam esse decernimus.*").[112] With equal severity Urban condemned those who received orders knowingly from heretics and other prelates excommunicated by name. The antipope, Guibert (Clement III), was mentioned explicitly in this connection.[113]

Ordinations by schismatics who sided with the antipope and the imperial faction of Henry IV were ratified by special concession, upon the return of the candidate to unity.[114] If, however, the ordinand culpably requested the sacred rite from a schismatic, the special concession was forfeited.[115] It should be observed that Pope Urban insisted throughout that his norms were a definite departure from the common teaching and that he invoked these measures in order to cope with a temporary situation of abuse.[116] In a letter to

[112] Canons 3 and 4, Council of Piacenza, Mansi, XX, 805: the Collection in Seven Books, n. 2, the Italian Collection in Three Books, n. 5, the Collection in Nine Books, n. 7, the first and second recension of the *Collectio Caesaraugustana*, n. 5. These norms were repeated in canons 3 and 4 of the Council of Rome, Mansi, XX, 961: the Collection of Saint-Germain-des-Prés, n. 31, the second Collection of Châlons-sur-Marne, nn. 5 and 6, and the Collection in Ten Parts, nn. 24 and 25. These canons are found in Gratian at c. 108, C. I, q. 1.

[113] Canons 8 and 9, Council of Piacenza, Mansi, XX, 806: the *Polycarpus*, n. 5, the Collection in Seven Books, n. 5, the Italian Collection in Three Books, n. 7; this legislation was repeated in canons 8 and 9 of the Council of Rome, Mansi, XX, 963: the Collection of Saint-Germain-des-Prés, n. 31; in Gratian at c. 5, C. IX, q. 1.

[114] Canon 10, Council of Piacenza, Mansi, XX, 806: the *Polycarpus*, n. 5, the Collection in Seven Books, n. 5, the Italian Collection in Three Books, n. 7; repeated as canon 10, Council of Rome, Mansi, XX, 963: the Collection of Saint-Germain-des-Prés, n. 31; c. 5, C. IX, q. 1.

[115] Canon 11, Council of Piacenza, Mansi, XX, 806: the *Polycarpus*, n. 5, the Collection in Seven Books, n. 5, the Italian Collection in Three Books, n. 7; repeated as canon 11, Council of Rome, Mansi, XX, 963: the Collection of Saint-Germain-des-Prés, n. 31; in Gratian at c. 5, C. IX, q. 1.

[116] Canon 12, Council of Piacenza, Mansi, XX, 806: the *Polycarpus*, n. 5, the Collection in Seven Books, n. 5, the Italian Collection in Three Books, n. 7, the first and second recension of the *Collectio Caesaraugustana*, n. 5; repeated as canon 11 of the Council of Rome, Mansi, XX, 963: the Collection of Saint-Germain-des-Prés, n. 31; c. 5, C. IX, q. 1.

Anselm, archbishop of Milan, Urban specified how priests ordained *extra ecclesiam* should be reconciled with a repetition of the entire ordination ceremony except the anointing.[117] Urban admitted the validity of orders received in the Church by one who later defected from the Church.[118] Among the canons which were included in the collections, there is only one which some theologians offer as a case of reordination. But the circumstances surrounding this case are not of sufficient weight to induce any apodictic conclusion. In the text itself Urban explicitly denied that he was reordaining; but by repeating the ceremony he gave very strong indications that he considered the first ordination of Daimbert, a deacon, as null.[119]

[117] JL 5378: the Collection in Two Books, n. 1, the *Collectio Britannica*, n. 23, the recension " C " of the Collection of Anselm of Lucca, n. 4, and the *Decretum* of Ivo, n. 4; not in Gratian. This fragment actually serves to introduce the entire controversy of reordination. The actual problem here revolves around the exact nature of the imposition of hands, which Urban had ordered. Some maintain that this ceremony was the sacrament of penance, by which reconciliation was effected; others insist that this ceremony was a supplying of everything, except what was regarded as the essential rite of ordination. Saltet (1870-1952) claimed that the fragment under consideration and the *dictum Gratiani* before c. 24, C. I, q. 7, offer clear proof that the Pope and his allies considered the anointing as the essential rite of ordination, and that the ordination of deacons *extra ecclesiam* was treated differently from that of priests and bishops, precisely because there was no unction in the rite of ordination to the diaconate. Cf. L. Saltet, *Les Réordinations* (Paris: J. Gabalda et Cie., 1907), pp. 218-257, especially pp. 232-234 and 243-244: see also S. Many, *De Sacra Ordinatione* (Parisiis: apud Letouzey et Ané, Editores, 1905), pp. 74-75; A. Schebler, *Die Reordinationen in der " altkatholischen " Kirche unter besonderer Berücksichtigung der Anschauungen Rudolph Sohms*, Kanonistische Studien und Texte herausgegeben von Dr. Albert M. Koeniger, Band 10 (Bonn: Ludwig Röhrscheid Verlag, 1936), pp. 269-271 (hereafter cited Schebler, *Die Reordinationen*); E. Amman, " Réordinations," *Dictionnaire de Théologie Catholique* (Paris: Librairie Letouzey et Ané, 1903-), XIII, 2416-2421; M. Rosati, *La Teologia Sacramentaria nella lotta contro la Simonia e l'Invesitura laica del Secolo XI*, Dissertatio ad Lauream in Faculatate Theologica Pontificiae Universitatis Gregorianae (Tolentino: Tipografia S. Nicola, 1951), pp. 54-58 (hereafter cited Rosati, *La Teologia Sacramentaria*).

[118] JL 5387: the *Collectio Britannica*, n. 34; not in Gratian. Cf. Saltet, *Les Réordinations*, pp. 224-226.

[119] JL 5383: the *Collectio Britannica*, n. 30, the *Panormia*, n. 5, the first and second recension of the *Collectio Caesaraugustana*, n. 6, the second

Another point as found in the collections, forbade a bishop to ordain or consecrate any abbot who had received lay investiture.[120] Clerics whose ordination had not been canonical were sometimes barred from further advancement after their reconciliation and return to unity.[121]

The sources from outside the pre-Gratian collections add very little to the extensive coverage already given to the problems connected with sacred ordination in that period. The exclusion of the offspring of clerics in concubinage was repeated in the sources outside of the collections.[122] There are a few additional sources for the problem of ordination *extra ecclesiam*.[123]

Collection of Châlons-sur-Marne, n. 3, the Collection of *Codex Ms. Vaticanus Latinus 1361*, n. 11, and the Collection in Ten Parts, n. 21; in the *Decretum Gratiani* at c. 24, C. I, q. 7. Many scholars affirm that this case concerned the repetition of an ordination which was invalid, because it was performed by a heretical and excommunicated bishop: cf. Saltet, *Les Réordinations*, pp. 241-244; Amman, "Réordinations," *Dictionnaire de Théologie Catholique*, XIII, 2416-2421. There are others who maintain that Daimbert's case is not so certain: cf. Rosati, *La Teologia Sacramentaria*, pp. 56-58, quoting P. Fournier, "Bonizon de Sutri, Urbain II et la comtesse Mathilde," in *Bibliothéque de l'École des Chartes*, LXXVI (1915), 286; Fliche, *Histoire*, VIII, 215-218 and 266. See also the preceding footnote concerning the difference between the diaconate and the other two sacred orders. Saltet maintained that Urban had a different theological explanation for the diaconate administered *extra ecclesiam* than from the priesthood and the episcopate administered *extra ecclesiam;* the basis for this distinction was the unction. This explanation is particularly relevant in Daimbert's case, since he was a deacon. Cf. Saltet, *Les Réordinations*, pp. 242-243.

[120] Canon 17, Council of Rome, Mansi, XX, 964: the Collection of Saint-Germain-des-Prés, n. 31 (not in Gratian).

[121] Fragment of JL 5393: the Collection of Two Books, n. 2, the *Collectio Britannica*, n. 38, the recension "C" of the Collection of Anselm of Lucca, n. 3, the Collection of *Codex Ms. Vaticanus Latinus 3829*, n. 1, the *Tripartita*, nn. 1 and 7, the *Decretum*, n. 3, the first and second recension of the *Collectio Caesaraugustana*, n. 2, the first Collection of Châlons-sur-Marne, n. 3, the second Collection of Châlons-sur-Marne, n. 12, the Collection in Thirteen Books, n. 1, and c. 4, C. IX, q. 1.

[122] Canon 16 Council of Clermont (Ordericus Vitalis' version), Mansi, XX, 885, and canon 20 of the same council according to William of Malmesbury, Mansi, XX, 905.

[123] JL 5409, ca. Sept., 1089, *Super quaestionibus*, to Pibo, bishop of Toul; JL 5694, April 17, 1097-1098, *De ordinationibus*, given at the Lateran, to

In conclusion, all that can be expressed is doubt and uncertainty. Exactly what did Urban mean by the word, "*irrita?*" Most of the modern theologians and scholars think that by *irrita* Urban intended to express the fact that such orders were not given the full acknowledgment of the Church. The same problem was taken up and finally resolved by the canonists of the twelfth century.[124]

Article V. The Laity

Unfortunately most of the legislation concerning the laity is negative in scope. But in a period when the papacy sought to wrest its rights from those who had usurped ecclesiastical rights, it is not surprising that the laity was responsible for many abuses. The existence of an imperial schism at the time tended to increase the

Bernard, bishop of Bologna; P. Kehr, *Italia Pontificia*, VII, pt. II, p. 59, letter n. 177, August 31, ca. 1093, *De Torcellensis*, given at Telese, to Peter, the patriarch of Grado.

[124] For the details from later canonists, cf. Saltet, *Les Réordinations*, pp. 289-308. There is one very good indication of the position of Urban which Schebler mentions in his *Die Ordinationen*, pp. 273-274. The argument runs along these lines: canon 15 of Piacenza calls ordination without a title "*irrita.*" Canonists are generally of the opinion that, in the context of canon 15, *irrita* does not mean invalid; therefore the same word does not have to be taken in the strict sense of invalid in the other canons of Piacenza. This argument does not lack relevance, but it should be mentioned that at least R. Sohm (1841-1917) and C. Mirbt (1860-1929) have taken the opposite position and claim that, if *irrita* means invalid in the other canons of Piacenza, then in canon 15 an ordination that is conferred without title is also to be regarded as invalid. The view of Sohm and Mirbt has been considered as untenable by V. Fuchs, *Der Ordinationstitel von seiner Entstehung bis auf Innozenz III*, Kanonistische Studien und Texte herausgegeben von Dr. Albert M. Koeniger, Band 4 (Bonn: Kurt Schroeder Verlag, 1930), pp. 249-250; Fuchs cites G. Phillips (1804-1872) and Saltet as opposing the view of Mirbt and Sohm. For others who with Fuchs hold the same views concerning ordination and Urban II, cf. H. Lennerz, *De Sacramentis Novae Legis in Genere* (3. ed., Romae: apud Aedes Universitatis Gregorianae, 1950), p. 143, together with the whole line of argumentation, pp. 107-151; F. Cappello, *Tractatus Canonico-Moralis de Sacramentis*, Vol. IV, *De Sacra Ordinatione* (3. ed., Taurini: Marietti, 1951), pp. 188-189; C. Journet, *The Church of the Word Incarnate*, Vol. I, *The Apostolic Hierarchy* (New York and London: Sheed and Ward, 1955), pp. 110-113.

opposition to Church policies by laymen, since the latter were encouraged in their opposition by the existing political situation.

A substantial amount of the legal thought concerned with the overcoming of lay interference in ecclesiastical matters is found in the canonical collections of the period before Gratian. The general principle of Urban's policy was that the laity was to have no power over the clergy.[125] Specifically the clergy was absolutely forbidden to take any oaths, in court or elsewhere, to a layman.[126] In a similar manner the retention and administration of ecclesiastical property was restricted to the clergy; laymen were prohibited from retaining tithes and churches, and from granting ecclesiastical benefices.[127] It was considered completely contrary to the law for a layman to have any control or voice in the bestowal of churches; frequent threats were leveled against members of the laity who were guilty of seizing a church or a monastery, or who had interfered in its government.[128] Some insight into the problems of that time may be gained when it is noted that the Pope found it necessary to condemn laymen who seized the personal property of others, especially that of bishops and other clerics.[129] Finally the law explicitly

[125] JL 5722: the *Decretum* of Ivo, n. 5. Canon 11, Council of Melfi, Mansi, XX, 723: the *Collectio Britannica*, n. 47. Neither text is in Gratian.

[126] JL 5759: the recension "Bb" of the Collection of Anselm of Lucca, n. 2; c. 23, C. XXII, q. 5. Canon 17, Council of Clermont, Mansi, XX, 817: the Collection of Saint-Germain-des-Prés, n. 20, the second Collection of Châlons-sur-Marne, n. 31, and the Collection in Ten Parts, n. 41; not in Gratian.

[127] Canon 15, Council of Clermont, Mansi, XX, 817: the Collection of Saint-Germain-des-Prés, n. 18, the second Collection of Châlons-sur-Marne, n. 40 and the Collection in Ten Parts n. 8; canons 19 and 20 of the same council, Mansi, XX, 818: the Collection of Saint-Germain-des-Prés, n. 22. None of these canons is found in Gratian.

[128] JL 5397: the *Collectio Britannica*, n. 40; JL 5471: the Collection of Saint-Germain-des-Prés, n. 38; canon 16, Council of Rome, Mansi, XX, 964 (this decree was first promulgated at the Council of Melfi, canon 6): the Collection of Saint-Germain-des-Prés, n. 31, the second Collection of Châlons-sur-Marne, n. 41, and the Collection in Ten Parts, n. 9. None of these texts is in Gratian.

[129] Canons 21 and 22, Council of Clermont, Mansi, XX, 818: the Collection of Saint-Germain-des-Prés, n. 23, the first Collection of Châlons-sur-Marne, n. 7, the second Collection of Châlons-sur-Marne, n. 55, and the Collection in Ten Parts, n. 40; not in Gratian. Canon 31, Council

forbade a cleric from receiving investiture or even patronage from a layman, especially the emperor or the king.[130]

The notions found outside the collections are generally quite similar to those already considered in the collections. Thus, the absolute denial of any voice in the disposition or bestowal of church property and benefices was repeated.[131] Several provisions of the Council of Nîmes in 1096 dealt with some abuses among the laity. The proscription against lay investiture was renewed.[132] In the same council laymen were absolutely denied any control in the matter of ecclesiastical burial, of the tithes, or of any other offering made to the Church.[133]

In spite of the denial of all lay rights over the clergy, Urban did grant to the secular rules of Sicily the privilege of approving the papal choice for the apostolic legate to that country.[134] Furthermore, Urban was not unwilling to ask for lay assistance in the protection of the Church from its enemies.[135]

---

of Clermont, Mansi, XX, 818: the Collection of Saint-Germain-des-Prés, n. 29, the second Collection of Châlons-sur-Marne, n. 11, and the Collection in Ten Parts, n. 43; related to this last canon is c. 46, C. XII, q. 2.

130 The canon following canon 15 of the Council of Piacenza, Mansi, XX, 807: the first and second recension of the *Collectio Caesaraugustana*, n. 5; not in Gratian.

131 JL 5516, March 31, 1094, *Saepe tuam indolem*, given at Rome, to William, count of Poitiers; JL 5584, Nov., 1095, *Venerabilem fratrem*, to Guarnerius, son of Pontio; JL 5585, Nov., 1095, *Audivimus Guarnerium*, given to Richerius, archbishop of Sens; JL 5704, May-June, 1098, given at the Lateran, to William II, King of England; JL 5739, 1088-1099, *Lanzonem presbyterum*, to the clergy and people of Salerno; JL 5804, May 6, 1099, *Et persona tua*, given at Rome, to Gontrardus, bishop of Valence.

132 Canon 8, Council of Nîmes, July 8-12, 1096, Mansi, XX, 936.

133 Canon 6, Council of Nîmes, Mansi, XX, 935.

134 JL 5706, July 5, 1098, *Quia prudentiam*, given at Salerno, to Roger, count of Calabria and Sicily; cf. Fliche, *Histoire*, VIII, 320-322, for some of the difficulties caused by this grant. See also Cantor, *England*, pp. 117-118.

135 JL 5458, Jan. 22, 1092, *Venerunt ad*, given at Anagni, to Gebhard, bishop of Constance, and several civil rulers; JL 5546, March 11, 1095, *Pro carissimo fratre*, given at Piacenza, to Robert, count of Flanders; Jaffé, *Regesta Pontificum Romanorum*, I, 679 (after JL 5560) concerning the oath of Conrad, son of Henry IV, to Urban; JL 5662, July 27, 1096, *Audientes magnificentiam*, to Colomannus, King of Hungary; JL 5705, ca. June, 1098, *Quam cito has*, given at Benevento, to Lanuinus.

CHAPTER II

The Law of Things

Article I. The Obligations of the Clergy

There can be no question that there were three great evils infecting the clergy during the time of Urban II: simony, lay investiture and incontinence. In this particular article, however, the accent will be more upon the prescriptions governing the clergy in matters other than the three mentioned above. Investiture will be taken up in the following article, and the other two crimes will be considered *in extenso* in the third chapter, where there is the question of ecclesiastical crimes and penalties. General norms, however, will be given here concerning these three.

The norms which aimed at reforming the ranks of the clergy appear both within and outside of the canonical collections. There was a very evident need for reform within the clerical ranks, especially if there was going to be any real reform in the Church at large. Urban realized this, and was not slow to begin his offensive.

Of the canons incorporated in the canonical collections, there are several concerning clerical conduct. Clerics who habitually devoted themselves to work and business not ecclesiastical in nature or purpose were rebuked.[1] The clergy were expressly forbidden to bear arms[2] and to wear pompous clothing.[3] They were to avoid anything which even suggested *cohabitatio suspiciosa*.[4]

Every diocesan cleric was expected to render strict obedience to his bishop.[5] In accord with the proscription of the laity's exercise

[1] Canon 9, Council of Melfi, Mansi, XX, 723: the *Collectio Britannica*, n. 47; not in Gratian.

[2] Canon 4, Council of Clermont, Mansi, XX, 817: the Collection of Saint-Germain-des-Prés, n. 10; not in Gratian.

[3] Canon 13, Council of Melfi, Mansi, XX, 724: the *Collectio Britannica*, n. 47; not found in Gratian.

[4] Canon 10, Council of Clermont, Mansi, XX, 817: the Collection of Saint-Germain-des-Prés, n. 13; not in Gratian.

[5] JL 5407 and 5408: the *Collectio Britannica*, nn. 45 and 46; not in Gratian.

of power over the clergy, clerics were forbidden to take an oath administered to them by a layman; only the bishop had the right to demand such a guarantee from his clergy, and then only concerning ecclesiastical administration.[6] The fear expressed by this prohibition was no doubt based upon the danger of lay investiture and other rights which the laity exercised over the clergy.[7]

Every cleric, from the reception of the subdiaconate, was expected to practice clerical celibacy.[8] The problem of clerical incontinence should be looked at in the context of simony and lay investiture; like every temporal benefice, their ecclesiastical benefice was by many of the clergy regarded as a hereditary possession. Many of the clergy had gone so far as to marry or to live in open concubinage. In addition to reiterating the strict obligation of celibacy upon all major clerics, Urban theatened the penalties of degradation and loss of office. Incontinent clerics were forbidden to celebrate Holy Mass.[9]

[6] JL 5759: the recension "Bb" of the Collection of Anselm of Lucca, n. 2; c. 23, C. XXII, q. 5.

[7] The unnumbered canon found after canon 15, Council of Piacenza, Mansi, XX, 807: the first and second recension of the *Collectio Caesaraugustana*, n. 5; canon 17, Council of Clermont, Mansi, XX, 817: the Collection of Saint-Germain-des-Prés, n. 20, the second Collection of Châlons-sur-Marne, n. 31, and the Collection in Ten Parts, n. 41; neither of these canons is found in Gratian.

[8] Canon 12, Council of Melfi, Mansi, XX, 723: the Collection of *Codex Ms. Vaticanus Latinus 4977*, n. 2, the *Collectio Britannica*, n. 47, the *Panormia*, n. 6, the second recension of the *Collectio Caesaraugustana*, n. 7, the Collection of Saint-Germain-des-Prés, n. 36, the second Collection of Châlons-sur-Marne, n. 26, the Collection of *Codex Ms. Vaticanus Latinus 1361*, n. 3, and the Collection in Ten Parts, n. 22; c. 10, D. XXXII.

[9] Canon 2, Council of Melfi, Mansi, XX, 723: the *Collectio Britannica*, n. 47, and the Collection of Saint-Germain-des-Prés, n. 31, where the canon is from the Council of Rome, canon 13, Mansi, XX, 963; this canon is not in Gratian. Canon 12, Council of Melfi, Mansi, XX, 724: the Collection of *Codex Ms. Vaticanus Latinus 4977*, n. 2, the *Collectio Britannica*, n. 47, the *Panormia*, n. 6, the second recension of the *Collectio Caesaraugustana*, n. 7, the Collection of Saint-Germain-des-Prés, n. 36, the second Collection of Châlons-sur-Marne, n. 26, the Collection of *Codex Ms. Vaticanus Latinus 1361*, n. 3, and the Collection in Ten Parts, n. 22; in Gratian at c. 10, D. XXXII. Canon 9, Council of Clermont, Mansi, XX, 817: the Collection of Saint-Germain-des-Prés, n. 12, and the second Collection of Châlons-sur-

The sources found outside of the collections substantiate the legislation incorporated in the canonical compilations; furthermore several new ideas are presented. Among the proscriptions found outside of the collections, there was one rebuke directed toward those clerics who deserted their ecclesiastical charge in order to obtain a more lucrative position.[10] Clerics and monks both enjoyed the *privilegium fori*[11] and the *privilegium canonis.*[12]

Article II. Ecclesiastical Benefices and Church Property

The Gregorian period was fraught with abuses in the distribution, retention and administration of church benefices. These abuses existed at every level, diocesan, parochial, and even monastic. Pope Urban continued the fight begun by Gregory VII to secure for the Church the effective control of every ecclesiastical benefice. The basic evil was that of lay investiture. The secular rulers attempted to control not only the ecclesiastical beneficiaries, but also the very benefices themselves. While it is true that the secular powers looked upon this papal offensive as an attempt of the spiritual realm to swallow up the temporal order, the primary objective of the reform movement was the restoration of the proper balance and perspective to the spiritual powers and rights of the Church. The evils which the reformers fought against had been of long-standing duration. Therefore to the majority of the laity, as well as to many of the clergy, the "abuses" had come to be regarded as the ordinary state of things. The Popes were looked upon as favoring a revolution—a revolution which, in the estimation of those likely to be most affected, would permanently remove much temporal prestige, political power and material wealth.

Marne, n. 27; not in Gratian. JL 5381: the *Collectio Britannica*, n. 26, the *Panormia*, n. 8, the Collection of *Codex Ms. Vaticanus Latinus 1361*, n. 2, and the Collection in Ten Parts, n. 26; not in Gratian.

[10] Canon 9, Council of Nîmes, Mansi, XX, 936.

[11] P. Kehr, *Italia Pontificia*, VI, pt. I, p. 319, letter n. 271, Oct. 16, 1096, *Piae postulatio*, given at Cremona, to Andericus, priest; canon 14, Council of Nîmes, Mansi, XX, 936.

[12] Canon 12, Council of Clermont, according to the account of Ordericus Vitalis Mansi, XX, 885: this canon also includes "*sanctimoniales*" as sharing in the privilege; canon 16 of William of Malmesbury's compendium of the acts of the same council, Mansi, XX, 905.

Hence the opposition to the reform program from both the clergy and the laity was understandable.

Even in the face of almost universal opposition, Urban continued the offensive. The root of the problem, lay investiture, was proscribed by Urban: no cleric was to receive investiture of an ecclesiastical office or benefice at the hands of a secular prince. The sources from outside of the canonical collections contain such prohibitions.[13] The appointment to and investiture of every monastery, diocese and church belonged properly to the legitimate power of the Church and to its ecclesiastical ministers.[14]

The proscriptions against lay investiture, which became incorporated in the collections, are not so numerous as one might suppose. Perhaps Urban felt it superfluous to repeat every condemnation of his predecessors. In addition to the specific rebukes, two are found in connection with the councils.[15]

Throughout the entire dispute the Pope continued to assert the doctrine based upon the supreme and absolute right of the Church in the matter of bishoprics and their incumbents.[16] The bishop, as the

---

[13] Canon 8, Council of Nîmes, Mansi, XX, 936; P. Kehr, *Papsturkunden in Spanien*, I, pt. II, pp. 278-279, letter n. 17, Nov. 17, ca. 1089, *Quia religionis tuae*, to Frotardus, abbot of Thomières.

[14] P. Kehr, *Italia Pontificia*, IV, 301, letter n. 280, note, 1097, *Monasterium s. Clementis de Piscaria*, given at Chieti, to Grimoaldus, abbot of the monastery of St. Clement, Pescara; *ibid.*, VIII, 449, letter n. 595, July, 1088, to John, archbishop of Naples; JL 5731, 1088-1099, *Misimus dilectioni tuae*, given to Hugh, archbishop of Grenoble.

[15] Canon 8, Council of Melfi, Mansi, XX, 723: the *Collectio Britannica*, n. 47; canon 16, Council of Clermont, Mansi, XX, 817: the Collection of Saint-Germain-des-Prés, n. 19, the second Collection of Châlons-sur-Marne, n. 42, and the Collection in Ten Parts, n. 10; neither of these canons is in Gratian.

[16] This has been considered *supra*, pp. 141-142; cf. in addition, JL 5525, May 20, 1094, *Quam grave sit*, given at Rome, to Godinus, bishop of Brindisi; JL 5549, March 14, 1095, *Claruisse plurimas*, given at Piacenza, to the church of Burgos; JL 5568, May 26, 1095, *Quoniam frater*, given at Milan, to the clergy and faithful of Sermorens; JL 5574, to the clergy and faithful of Cambrai; JL 5598, Nov. 30, 1095, *In concilio apud*, given at Clermont, to the clergy and people of Cambrai; JL 5610, Dec. 5, 1095, *Veterum synodalium*, given at Privas, to the church of Santiago de Compostela; JL 5653, July 15, 1096, *Postquam apud*, given at Nîmes, in

pastor of his diocese, was responsible for the *cura animarum.* The care of souls was his to guard and to apportion to the various parishes and churches.[17]

Monks were more and more becoming engaged in the direct pastoral ministry. When monks were active in the *cura animarum,* they were subject to the local ordinary regarding their ministry.[18] The ideal in this co-operative effort of the secular and the religious clergy was for the abbot and the bishop to reach some agreement concerning their common pastoral endeavor.[19] But in his conviction that monks were better able to fulfil the pastoral ministry than the secular clergy, Urban was very definitely adding his voice to a new idea, and one which was later responsible for some misunderstanding.[20]

The collections before Gratian do not give very extensive coverage to the matter just considered. The rights of the bishop to distribute benefices were upheld in several of the texts.[21]

Some of the prescriptions concerning ecclesiastical benefices have already been alluded to previously in other connections; but in the present context, with a view to the inclusion of all Urban's rulings

the monastery of St. Giles, to the church of Burgos; JL 5683, April 18, 1097, *Sicut iniusta poscentium,* given at the Lateran, to the church at Auvergne; JL 5685, June 4, 1097, *Quam arroganter,* given at the Lateran, to Hugh, archbishop of Lyons.

[17] JL 5780, Jan. 10, 1099, *Religiosis desideriis dignum,* given at the Lateran, to the bishop of Autun; JL 5804, May 6, 1099, *Et persona tua,* given at Rome, to the bishop of Valence; P. Kehr, *Italia Pontificia,* III, 390, letter n. 410, note, 1088-1099, a privilege to the church of Lucca.

[18] Cf. the previous footnote.

[19] JL 5751, 1088-1099; cf. JL 6894, March 4, 1121, *Sicut iniusta.* given at the Lateran, to Dodo, bishop of Modena (this is a letter of Callistus II).

[20] Canon 2 and 3, Council of Nîmes, Mansi, XX, 934-935. Cf. Fliche, *Histoire,* VIII, 292. Portions of these two canons are found in Gratian, but they are not under Urban's name. Concerning this problem cf. Appendix II, Part I, nn. 33 and 34.

[21] Canon 16, Council of Rome, Mansi, XX, 964: the Collection of Saint-Germain-des-Prés, n. 31, the second Collection of Châlons-sur-Marne, n. 41, and the Collection in Ten Parts, n. 9; not in Gratian. Canon 4, Council of Clermont, according to the *Codex Cencii,* Mansi, XX, 902: the recension "C" of the Collection of Anselm of Lucca, n. 2, the Collection in Nine Books, n. 10, the second recension of the *Collectio Caesaraugustana,* n. 29, the Collection of *Codex Ms. Vaticanus Latinus 1361,* n. 12, and c. 6, C. XVI, q. 16.

in this matter, as much relevant material as possible has been collected. Actually these norms are found both in and out of the cannonical collections.

Among the legislation included in the collections, there was the prohibition which forbade a cleric from retaining two *praebendae* in the same city, or two *dignitates* in the same church.[22] In an effort to overcome the greed which characterized many of the clergy, Urban made frequent denunciations against the buying and the selling of ecclesiastical benefices.[23] Church edifices along with the *bona dotalia* were to be neither held nor administered except by clerics;[24] no ecclesiastical goods could be considered as the hereditary possession of anyone, cleric or lay.[25] The personal property of bishops, of priests and of other clerics was guarded by the law.[26]

To these regulations, the sources as found outside of the collections present similar provisions together with some supplementary rules. The buying and the selling of benefices were forbidden as outright acts of simony.[27] The unlawful seizure of churches, monasteries and other

---

[22] Canons 12 and 14, Council of Clermont, Mansi, XX, 817: the Collection of Saint-Germain-des-Prés, nn. 15 and 17 respectively; canon 14 is also found in the second Collection of Châlons-sur-Marne, n. 23, and in the Collection in Ten Parts, n. 20; neither of the canons is in Gratian.

[23] Canon 1, Council of Melfi, Mansi, XX, 721: the *Collectio Britannica*, n. 47; not in Gratian. Canon 5, Council of Piacenza, Mansi, XX, 805: the Collection in Seven Books, n. 2, the Italian Collection in Three Books, n. 6, the Collection in Nine Books, n. 8, the first and second recension of the *Collectio Caesaraugustana*, n. 5, the Collection of Saint-Germain-des-Prés, n. 31, the second Collection of Châlons-sur-Marne, n. 8, and the Collection in Ten Parts, n. 29; in Gratian at c. 1, C. I, q. 5. Canon 6, Council of Clermont, Mansi, XX, 817: the Collection of Saint-Germain-des-Prés, n. 11; not in Gratian.

[24] Canon 20, Council of Clermont, Mansi, XX, 818: the Collection of Saint-Germain-des-Prés, n. 21, the second Collection of Châlons-sur-Marne, n. 30, and the Collection in Ten Parts, n. 42; not in Gratian.

[25] JL 5407 and 5408: the *Collectio Britannica*, nn. 45 and 46; not in Gratian.

[26] Canon 31, Council of Clermont, Mansi, XX, 818: the Collection of Saint-Germain-des-Prés, n. 29, the second Collection of Châlons-sur-Marne, n. 11, and the Collection in Ten Parts, n. 43; c. 46, C. 12, q. 2, in similar, but it is not a verbatim reproduction of the text in question.

[27] Canon 5, Council of Clermont, according to Ordericus Vitalis, Mansi,

church property by either clerics or laymen was denounced as contrary to all law, human and divine; such invaders were to withdraw at once and do suitable penance.[28] Because of the persistent abuses in the retention and administration of church property, Urban forbade unlawful alienation.[29] All goods and property which had been turned over to the Church were to remain in ecclesiastical hands; recovery was barred to the donor or the potential heirs.[30] In the Council of Nîmes the seizure of the personal property of the clergy by other persons was proscribed again; the last testament of every cleric, especially of bishops, was to be fulfilled to the letter.[31]

Article III. Monasticism

In the same manner as Gregory VII, so Urban also recognized that monasticism and the religious life offered an almost ready-made solution to many of the problems of the Church at the time. Wisely Urban endeavored to employ, to the fullest possible degree, the resources which monasticism presented against the enemies of the Church. Urban's strategy was very positive: the religious formation which was a part of the training of every monk was exactly what Christian society needed to overcome the evil and abuse of that period. Very little of the plan followed by Urban has found its way into the collections. Most of the decrees which became incorporated are in the form of prohibitions.

"*Monachi vagi*" were not welcomed in a diocese, unless they presented testimonial letters.[32] Canons regular, if they decided to

XX, 885; canon 5 of the same council in the version of William of Malmesbury, Mansi, XX, 904; canon 8, Council of Nîmes, Mansi, XX, 936.

[28] JL 5539, 1088-1099, *Lanzonem presbyterum*, to the clergy and faithful of Salerno; JL 5804, May 6, 1099, *Et persona tua*, given at Rome, to the bishop of Valence; P. Kehr, *Italia Pontificia*, VI, pt. I, p. 311, letter n. 252, ca. 1090, concerning the diocese of Brescia; P. Kehr, *Papsturkunden in Spanien*, I, pt. II, p. 281, letter n. 18, 1089-1090, *Venientes nuper*, to the abbot of Thomières.

[29] JL 5780, Jan. 10, 1099, *Religiosis desideriis dignum*, given at the Lateran, to the bishop of Autun.

[30] Canon 14, Council of Nîmes, Mansi, XX, 936.

[31] Canon 5, Mansi, XX, 935.

[32] Canon 10, Council of Melfi, Mansi, XX, 723: the *Collectio Britannica*, n. 47, the second recension of the *Collectio Caesaraugustana*, n. 19; not in Gratian.

become monks, needed the permission of their chapter before they were permitted to make the transfer.[33] Yet according to one canon at least, the authenticity of which has been disputed, a secular cleric could enter the religious life, even contrary to his ordinary's wishes, for the reason that the religious vocation was the higher calling.[34]

During the pontificate of Urban II monks became more and more active in the pastoral ministry; but throughout this evolution the authority of the local ordinary remained supreme. Monastic churches serving the laity were required to have a chaplain, who was appointed to serve as pastor by the bishop upon consultation with the abbot. The spiritual ministry was directly subject to the bishop; the temporal administration was under the supervision of the abbot.[35] Ordinarily no cleric was permitted to serve as chaplain to a lay person without authorization from his own ordinary.[36]

[33] JL 5763: the recension "Bb" of the Collection of Anselm of Lucca, n. 6, the Collection in Nine Books, n. 5, the *Tripartita*, n. 9, the *Decretum*, n. 7, the first recension of the *Collectio Caesaraugustana*, n. 13, the second recension of the *Collectio Caesaraugustana*, n. 15, the Collection of Saint-Germain-des-Prés, n. 32, the second Collection of Châlons-sur-Marne, n. 35, and the Collection in Ten Parts, n. 39; c. 3, C. XIX, q. 3.

[34] JL 5760: the *Polycarpus*, n. 2, the Collection in Seven Books, n. 3, the recension "Bb" of the Collection of Anselm of Lucca, n. 4, the Italian Collection in Three Books, n. 2, the Collection in Nine Books, n. 3, the first recension of the *Collectio Caesaraugustana*, n. 11, the second recension of the *Collectio Caesaraugustana*, n. 13, and the Collection of *Codex Ms. Vaticanus Latinus 1361*, n. 5. Berardi (*Canones*, II, 2, 368-369) regarded this canon as a monastic forgery, quite opposed to the ideas of Urban II. This canon is in Gratian at c. 2, C. XIX, q. 2.

[35] Canon 3, Council of Clermont, according to the peculiar version of the Wolfenbüttel manuscript: the Collection of Saint-Germain-des-Prés, n. 3; this text is also found in the second Collection of Châlons-sur-Marne, n. 32, and in the Collection in Ten Parts, n. 37. This text is also in c. 1, X, *de capellanis monachorum et aliorum religiosorum*, III, 37, Mansi, XX, 819. Canon 4, Council of Clermont (*Codex Cencii*), Mansi, XX, 902: the recension "C" of the Collection of Anselm of Lucca, n. 2, the Collection in Nine Books, n. 10, the second recension of the *Collectio Caesaraugustana*, n. 29, and the Collection of *Codex Ms. Vaticanus Latinus 1361*, n. 12; in Gratian at c. 6, C, XVI, q. 2.

[36] First sentence of canon 18, Council of Clermont, Mansi, XX, 817: the Collection of Saint-Germain-des-Prés, n. 21, the second Collection of

Finally, the collections proscribed the avaricious practice of "renting" churches and altars to religious houses as a kind of benefice whose lease had to be renewed annually. Thenceforth any church held in this manner for a period of thiry years was to cede to the religious who had held it; after the full period of prescription had run its course, the bishop had a right only to the annual *census.* In an effort to prevent more and more churches from passing into the hands of religious, all churches and altars given to religious by benefactors, but not held for the thirty-year period, were ordered to be returned to the supervision and possession of the local ordinary.[37]

To these regulations about the monastic life, the sources outside the collections do not add anything of great importance. There are some points that are not explicitly found within the collections. For example, before his profession the candidate had to be approved by a majority of the members of the community.[38] It has already been mentioned that monks enjoyed the *privilegium fori* and *canonis.*[39] There was a special provision for those monks who were prevented from living according to their rule because of outside interference; the Pope allowed the religious to depart and to resume their regular life at some other monastic house.[40]

Besides the regulations concerning the monastic life itself, norms were frequently given which concerned more the external relations of the communities with the local civil and ecclesiastical rules and with others. Practically all of these rulings are found in the sources outside of the collections.

Châlons-sur-Marne, n. 30, and the Collection in Ten Parts, n. 42; not in Gratian.

[37] Canon 2, Council of Clermont, according to the reading of the Wolfenbüttel manuscript: the Collection of Saint-Germain-des-Prés, n. 2; canon 3, Council of Clermont, according to the *Codex Cencii*, Mansi, XX. 902: the Collection of *Codex Ms. Vaticanus Latinus 1361*, n. 21; also in c. 4, C. I, q. 3.

[38] P. Kehr, *Italia Pontificia*, VI, pt. I, p. 319, letter n. 271, Oct. 16, 1096, *Piae postulatio*, given at Cremona, to Andericus, priest, and his brothers at Brescia.

[39] Cf. *supra*, p. 168.

[40] JL 5711, Nov. 1, 1098, *Audivimus et auditum*, to the brothers of St. Hubert, at Chiny-dans-les-Ardennes.

In Urban's time, monastic exemption had become the rule rather than the exception;[41] yet in matters concerning the *cura animarum,* everyone, including the monks, was under the direct supervision of the local bishop.[42] Frequently too, the bishop was, by the special appointment of the Pope, designated as the arbitrator of disputes, involving the monks.[43] As a general rule, even exempt monasteries depended upon the local ordinary for ordinations, consecrations and some judicial matters, unless by special privilege exemption covered even these items; in the latter case the monks were free to go to the bishop of their choice.[44] Urban frequently extended to a monastery the privilege of being directly subject to the Holy See.[45]

---

[41] Andre-Condis-Wagner, *Dictionnaire de Droit Canonique* (3 vols., Paris: Hippolyte Walzer, Librairie-Editeurs, 1901), II, 174. H. Leclercq, "Exemption monastique," *Dictionnaire d'Archéologie Chrétienne et de Liturgie* (15 vols. in 30, Paris: Librairie Letouzey et Ané, 1907-1953), V, I, 952-962. E. Fogliasso, "Exemption des Religieux," *Dictionnaire de Droit Canonique,* commencé sous la direction de A. Villien et E. Magnin, continué sous la direction de A. Amanieu, publié sous la direction de R. Naz (6 vols. [incomplete], Paris: Librairie Letouzey et Ané, 1924-), V, 646-665.

[42] Cf. *supra,* p. 173. Cf. also P. Kehr, *Italia Pontificia,* VI, pt. I, p. 319, letter n. 271, Oct. 16, 1096, *Piae postulatio,* given at Cremona, to Andericus, priest, and his brothers at Brescia.

[43] JL 5665, August 7, 1096, *Inter Scafusensium,* given at Forcalquier, France, to Gebhard, bishop of Constance; JL 5666, August 7-18, 1096, *Iam dudum,* to the provost and dean of the church at Raitenbuch, Bavaria; JL 5719, ca. 1098, to the abbot of Cluny; JL 5720, ca. 1098, to the archbishop of Lyons; P. Kehr, *Papsturkunden in Spanien,* I, pt. II, pp. 281-288, letters nn. 18-24: n. 18, 1089-1090, *Venientes nuper,* to the abbot of Thomières; n. 19, 1091, *Tanto iam tempore,* to Frotardus, abbot of Thomières; n. 20, 1091, *Inter venerabiles,* to Amatus, archbishop of Bordeaux; n. 21, June 8, 1091 (this is not a letter of Urban II); n. 24, Oct. 28, 1091, *Caritati divinae.*

[44] JL 5479, Jan. 14, 1093, *Ad hoc nos,* given at Salerno, to the monastery at La Cava, Italy; JL 5588, Nov. 19, 1095, *Cum apud Claromontem,* a decree of Urban concerning the bishop of Maguelonne and the abbot of the monastery of the Holy Savior at Aniane; cf. Fliche, *Histoire,* VIII, 280-281.

[45] JL 5587, Nov. 18-28, 1095, given at Clermont, to the monastery of St. Martin at Tours; JL 5590, Nov. 26, 1095, *Iustis votis assensum,* given at Clermont, to the community of St. Mary at Santes, France; JL 5592, Nov. 29, 1095, *Officii nostri nos,* given at Clermont, to the monastery at Auchy-les-Moines; JL 5597, Nov. 29, 1095, *Cum universis sancte,* given at Clermont, to Didacus, abbot of the monastery of Sts. Facundus and

Another frequent privilege granted to monastic communities was papal protection for all of their goods and possessions.[46] This papal protection of property was especially necessary in times when the entire community might be turned out from their cells by an invader. Urban frequently besought such invaders to leave the monks in peace.[47] The local bishop on occasion when requested, intervened on behalf of the monks to make certain that all its former properties were restored to a despoiled monastery.[48]

Article IV. Sacramental Discipline

While it is true that sacramental theology had not reached its high mark in the time of Urban II, there existed at that period definite ideas which became incorporated in later treatises. In the sources of Pope Urban there is no systematic treatment of the sacraments, nor is there much detail concerning any sacramental problem, except that of holy orders.[49]

Concerning the minister of the sacraments, the sources outside of the collections have several items of interest. Sacraments administered by incontinent priests were not questioned, but the faithful were advised to avoid such priests, in order not to encourage the crimes of the latter.[50] Although the faithful were warned to refrain from seeking

---

Primitivus, Sahagun, in the province of León, Spain; JL 5634, March 30, 1096, *Beatum confessorem*, given at Poitiers, to the archbishops and bishops of France.

[46] J. Ramackers, *Papsturkunden in Frankreich*, 1940, Dritte Folge, n. 23, pp. 26-28, letter n. 4, Dec. 3, 1095, *Piae postulatio*, given at Sauxillanges, to Lambert, abbot of the monastery of Saint Benedict, in Artois.

[47] JL 5533, 1094, *Adversus fraternitatem*, to Durranus, bishop of Auvergne; JL 5538, 1094-1095, *Gratias agimus*, to Berengarius, abbot of St. Lawrence at Liège; JL 5711, Nov. 1, 1098, *Audivimus et auditum*, to the brothers of St. Hubert at Chiny-dans-les-Ardennes; P. Kehr, *Italia Pontificia*, V, 156, letter n. 443, Oct. 7, ca. 1096, given at Cremona, to the monks and clerics of the congregation at Vallombrosa; P. Kehr, *Papsturkunden in Spanien*, I, pt. II, pp. 278-279, letter n. 17, Nov. 17, ca. 1089, *Quia religionis tuae*, to Frotardus, abbot of Thomières.

[48] JL 5446, May 7, 1096, *Fraternitatem vestram*, given at Toulouse, to Isnardus, bishop of Toulouse, to Simon, bishop of Agen, to Gerard, bishop of Cahors, and to Raymond, bishop of Lectoure.

[49] Cf. *supra*, pp. 159-161.

[50] Canon 5, Council of Piacenza, according to the résumé of Bernold of Constance, Mansi, XX, 803.

the priestly ministration from a sinful cleric, when there was question of danger of death all restrictions were removed; the faithful could go to any priest. But in this same text, when Urban speaks of those "... *qui extra sunt ... ecclesiam,*" his doctrine reflects close kinship with his teaching regarding sacred ordination *extra ecclesiam*. Apparently Urban denies the full fruitfulness of the sacraments when administered by those outside of the Church (... *formam quidem sacramentorum, non autem virtutis effectum habere profitemur* ...).[51]

Very little discussion was given to baptism in the legislation of Urban, but the few instances discovered were included in the collections of that period. Ordinarily parents were not to baptize their own children, but if the infant was in danger of death a parent could perform the sacred rite.[52] It was sufficient for only one of the *patrini* to receive the child from the baptismal font.[53]

As a reaction to the Eucharistic heresy of Berengarius of Tours, the Blessed Sacramant was ordinarily to be received under only one species, according to a canon included in the collections.[54]

Another canon, which never became included in the collections, clearly

[51] JL 5745, 1088-1099, *Si adulteri*, to the people of St. Vincent at Benevento. The problem involved in this text is exactly the same as the problem of the validity of sacred orders administered by bishops *extra ecclesiam*, when they themselves had been consecrated by an excommunicated prelate. Concerning this whole problem, cf. *supra*, especially pp. 160-161, and the places cited in Saltet, *Les Réordinations*, pp. 218-257, and in Schebler, *Die Reordinationen*, pp. 268-281.

[52] JL 5741: the *Tripartita*, n. 5, the first recension of the *Collectio Caesaraugustana*, n. 7, the second recension of the *Collectio Caesaraugustana*, n. 24, the first Collection of Châlons-sur-Marne, n. 1, the second Collection of Châlons-sur-Marne, n. 36, the Collection of *Codex Ms. Vaticanus Latinus 1361*, n. 14, and the Collection in Ten Parts, nn. 1 and 49; in Gratian at c. 4, C. XXX, q. 3.

[53] JL 5742: the *Tripartita*, n. 6, the first recension of the *Collectio Caesaraugustana*, n. 7, the second recension of the *Collectio Caesaraugustana*, n. 24, the first Collection of Châlons-sur-Marne, n. 2, the second Collection of Châlons-sur-Marne, nn. 2 and 37, the Collection of *Codex Ms. Vaticanus Latinus 1361*, n. 15, and the Collection in Ten Parts, n. 50; in Gratian at c. 6, C. XXX, q. 4.

[54] Canon 28, Council of Clermont, Mansi, XX, 818: the Collection of Saint-Germain-des-Prés, n. 27. Cf. Hefele-Leclercq, *Conciles*, V, I, 403; for the comment of Petrus de Marca on this canon, see Mansi, XX, 894-895.

stated that the Eucharist could not be denied to members of the imperial schismatic group, if they had rightly been reconciled by means of the sacrament of penance.[55]

Likewise, not very many regulations were enacted concerning penance. Within the collections there was a clear rebuke against false penitence; every serious sin had to be included in confession.[56]

From outside the collections there are sources which cautioned against remaining in an occasion of sin, and insisted upon the integrity of the sacrament of penance.[57] Except in extraordinary circumstances, a priest could reconcile only those penitents who had been committed to him by his proper ordinary.[58]

In two cases concerning the validity of a marriage, mentioned again and again in many of the collections and in Gratian, the Pope based his decision upon whether or not consent had been given by both of the parties; the absolute need for such an exchange was stressed.[59] Successively to marry two *commatres* was considered the same as successively to marry two sisters, and was equally for-

[55] Canon 3, Council of Piacenza, according to the summary by Bernold of Constance, Mansi, XX, 803.

[56] Canon 16, Council of Melfi, Mansi, XX, 724: the *Collectio Britannica*, n. 47, the second recension of the *Collectio Caesaraugustana*, n. 27; canon 22, Council of Clermont, Mansi, XX, 818: the Collection of Saint-Germain-des-Prés, n. 23, the first Collection of Châlons-sur-Marne, n. 7, the second Collection of Châlons-sur-Marne, n. 55, and the Collection in Ten Parts, n. 40; neither text is in Gratian.

[57] Canon 1, Council of Piacenza, according to Bernold's summary, Mansi, XX, 803.

[58] Canon 2, Council of Piacenza, according to Bernold, Mansi, XX, 803.

[59] JL 5383: the *Collectio Britannica*, n. 29, the Collection in Nine Books, n. 16, the *Tripartita*, n. 11, the *Decretum* of Ivo, n. 9, the *Panormia*, n. 9, the first recension of the *Collectio Caesaraugustana*, n. 17, the second recension of the *Collectio Caesaraugustana*, n. 21, the Collection of Saint-Germain-des-Prés, n. 34, the second Collection of Châlons-sur-Marne, n. 46, and c. 1, C. XXXI, q. 2. JL 5399: the Collection of *Codex Ms. Vaticanus Latinus 4977*, n. 1, the *Collectio Britannica*, n. 41, the Collection in Nine Books, n. 15, the Collection of *Codex Ms. Bibl. Taurinensis 903*, n. 2, the *Tripartita*, n. 12, the *Decretum*, n. 10, the *Panormia*, n. 14, the first recension of the *Collectio Caesaraugustana*, n. 16, the second recension of the *Collectio Caesaraugustana*, n. 20, the second Collection of Châlons-sur-Marne, n. 47, the Collection in Ten Parts, n. 48, and c. 3, C. XXXI, q. 2.

bidden.[60] A complete carnal union was the foundation for the impediment of affinity; no other mutual sins of impurity had this effect.[61]

From texts not found in the collections several additional points can be included. The spiritual relationship which was an impediment to marriage was contracted by means of a physical contact with the subject during the actual ceremony of baptism as well as confirmation.[62] Whoever married a blood relative within the prohibited degrees was excommunicated;[63] the prohibited degrees extended to the sixth (or seventh) generation.[64] The Council of Nîmes forbade marriage with a public adulterer or with a girl under the age of twelve.[65]

Article V. Other Legislation

This section will deal with other legislation concerning the law of ecclesiastical things covering diverse subjects to which some attention was given. The sources for this legislation are found both in and out of the various collections before Gratian, and cover a rather wide range of topics.

Various regulations are found concerning different aspects of the church year and matters connected with it. For example, there was a definite ruling which forbade marriages to be celebrated during the "closed times." These times, which were enumerated in at

[60] JL 5742: the *Tripartita*, n. 6, the first recension of the *Collectio Caesaraugustana*, n. 7, the second recension of the *Collectio Caesaraugustana*, n. 24, the first Collection of Châlons-sur-Marne, n. 2, the second Collection of Châlons-sur-Marne, nn. 2 and 37, the Collection of *Codex Ms. Vaticanus Latinus 1361*, n. 15, and the Collection in Ten Parts, n. 50; in Gratian at c. 6, C. XXX, q. 4.

[61] JL 5730: the Collection of Turin in Seven Books, n. 1, the *Polycarpus*, n. 4, the *Tripartita*, n. 3, the second recension of the *Collectio Caesaraugustana*, n. 25, the first Collection of Châlons-sur-Marne, n. 4, and the second Collection of Châlons-sur-Marne, n. 16.

[62] JL 5769, 1096-1099, *Neque enim baptizator*, to Rangerius, bishop of Lucca.

[63] Canon 10, Council of Nîmes, Mansi, XX, 936.

[64] Canon 14, Council of Clermont, in the summary of Ordericus Vitalis, Mansi, XX, 885, where the seventh generation is listed; canon 18 of the same council, according to William of Malmesbury, Mansi, XX, 905, where but the sixth generation is mentioned.

[65] Canons 10 and 13 respectively, Mansi, XX, 936.

least one of the pre-Gratian collections, included the period from *Septuagesima* Sunday to the completed octave of Easter, and from the first Sunday of Advent to the completed octave of the Epiphany.[66] Similarly, the collections contained the regulations governing the Ember Week fast.[67] At the Council of Clermont, Urban put the rules for the Ember Days into final form. The *Correctores Romani* cited Urban in this matter.[68]

The sources which were not included in the collections have very similar regulations for the Ember Days.[69] The same sources include the days of Advent and the Rogation Days among the days of fast.[70] Besides the fast for Lent, abstinence also began for all on Ash Wednesday.[71]

The canonical collections made during and after Urban's pontificate have the same regulations for Lent and add that ashes should

[66] Canon 4, second part, Council of Benevento, Mansi, XX, 739: the Collection in Seven Books, n. 4; this canon is not in Gratian.

[67] Canon 14, Council of Piacenza, Mansi, XX, 806: the Italian Collection in Three Books, n. 11, and the Collection in Nine Books, n. 14; in Gratian at c. 4, D. LXXVI. Cf. Sdralek, pp. 24-25.

[68] Canon 1, Council of Clermont, according to the special series of canons found in the Collection of Saint-Germain-des-Prés, n. 1; this canon is also found in the second Collection of Châlons-sur-Marne, n. 44, and in the Collection in Ten Parts, n. 5. See also the notes of the *Correctores* at c. 2, D. LXXVI; the canon cited by the *Correctores* is not among the ones found in Lambert's version; cf. Sdralek, pp. 24-25.

[69] Canon 27, Council of Clermont (Lambert's account), Mansi, XX, 818; canons 7 and 10 of the same council, according to Ordericus Vitalis, Mansi, XX, 885; canon 13 in the account of William of Malmesbury, Mansi, XX, 904.

[70] Canon 10, Council of Clermont, according to the summary of Ordericus Vitalis, Mansi, XX, 885; canons 10 and 14, of the same council, in the résumé of William of Malmesbury, Mansi, XX, 904. These two do not completely agree in every detail.

[71] Canon 6, Council of Clermont (Ordericus Vitalis), Mansi, XX, 885; canon 9 of the same council (William of Malmesbury), Mansi, XX, 904.

[72] Canon 4, Council of Benevento, Mansi, XX, 739: the recension "Bb" of the Collection of Anselm of Lucca, n. 3; canon 23, Council of Clermont, Mansi, XX, 818: the Collection of Saint-Germain-des-Prés, n. 24, the second Collection of Châlons-sur-Marne, n. 43, and the Collection in Ten Parts, n. 4; neither canon is in Gratian.

be received on Ash Wednesday.[72] The fast on Holy Saturday was ordered to be prolonged "*circa noctem.*" [73]

Another matter which came up for consideration was ecclesiastical tithes. The collections themselves contain some rules, especially in an effort to determine with exactness the righful recipient of the tithes. With a view to overcoming much of the abuse in this matter, it was determined that the parish church, where Mass was attended and the sacraments habitually received, had a prior right to the tithes of its people.[74] To spell out the implications of this decree, Urban forbade abbots and others from accepting tithes which lawfully belonged to some one else.[75]

The sources as found outside of the collections contain the same basic rules for tithes, but add nothing new.[76]

The collections contain a few directives governing the right of sanctuary, which could be invoked either in a church or at a roadside cross. Any guilty person who took refuge was spared life and limb, but was ordered to be turned over to the lawful authorities for punishment.[77]

Another matter given some attention was the *treuga Dei.* This truce was undertaken as a measure against the frequent private warfare which was so often engaged in by the feudal barons

[73] Canon 26, Council of Clermont, Mansi, XX, 818: the Collection of Saint-Germain-des-Prés, n. 26, the second Collection of Châlons-sur-Marne, n. 45, and the Collection in Ten Parts, n. 6; not in Gratian.

[74] Canon repeated at the Council of Melfi, Mansi, XX, 726; actually this canon was first promulgated in canon 19, Council of Châlon-sur-Saône, 813, Mansi, XIV, 97: found in the Collection Nine Books, n. 6; cf. 46, C. XVI, q. 1, and the *notationes Correctorum* at that place.

[75] Canon 5, Council of Melfi, Mansi, XX, 723: the *Collectio Britannica*, n. 47; repeated as canon 15, Council of Rome, Mansi, XX, 963-964: the Collection of Saint-Germain-des-Prés, n. 31, the second Collection of Châlons-sur-Marne, n. 39, and the Collection in Ten Parts, n. 3; canon 16, Council of Rome, Mansi, XX, 964: the Collection of Saint-Germain-des-Prés, n. 31, the second Collection of Châlons-sur-Marne, n. 41, and the Collection in Ten Parts, n. 9; none of these canons is in Gratian.

[76] Canon 20, Council of Clermont (Ordericus Vitalis), Mansi, XX, 885, and canon 23 of the same council, in the summary of William of Malmesbury, Mansi, XX, 905; canon 6, Council of Nîmes, Mansi, XX, 935.

[77] Canons 29 and 30, Council of Clermont, Mansi, XX, 818: the Collection of Saint-Germain-des-Prés, n. 29; not in Gratian.

and knights of the middle ages.[78] Urban was the first pontiff to extend the "peace" to the whole of Christendom.[79] The general regulations of the "peace" are found in at least one of the collections of that time. For all monks, clerics and women, every day was regarded as a day of peace; for others, only the last four days of the week. A day of peace meant that no fighting was permitted.[80] All animals were also included under the "peace" except the horse.[81]

From sources not found in the collections some additional facts can be drawn. Urban first proclaimed the "peace" on a limited scale at the Councils of Melfi and Troia.[82] The same regulations for the "peace" are found in the *Codex Cencii* version of the Council of Clermont.[83] The institution of the *treuga Dei* was given final form in the three general councils held at the Lateran in 1123, 1139 and 1179.

Two canons included in contemporary collections contain the teaching of the juridic value of an oath. Both of these directly concern marriages in which the partners were accused of close consanguinity or affinity. The principle invoked was direct and at the same time simple: if the charge of "*propinquitas*" could

[78] For a background to the *pax Dei*, see Daniel Rops, *Cathedral and Crusade*, translated by J. Warrington (London: J. M. Dent and Sons Ltd., 1957), pp. 274-280; Mourret, *History*, IV, 281-282; Fliche, *Histoire*, VIII, 283; R. Parsons, *Studies in Church History*, Vol. II (2 ed., New York: Pustet and Company, 1906), 258-265. There is every reason to believe that one of the motivating reasons behind Urban's calling the first Crusade was to offer to the numerous professional soldiers of his day a substitute for the local pillaging, plundering and murder that was so frequent; in this regard, cf. Setton-Baldwin, *A History of the Crusades*, I, 231 and 242.

[79] "The canon [of Clermont], which proclaimed the Truce of God, might be regarded as papal confirmation of the peace movement, which up to this time had been a matter of regional action. . . . "—Setton-Baldwin, *A History of the Crusades*, I, 237.

[80] Canon 1, Council of Clermont, Mansi, XX, 816: the Collection of Saint-Germain-des-Prés, nn. 6 and 7; not in Gratian.

[81] Canon 5, Council of Clermont, according to the special version of the acts of that council as found in the Collection of Saint-Germain-des-Prés, n. 5; not in Gratian; cf. Sdralek, p. 25.

[82] Fliche, *Histoire*, VIII, 282, and canon 2, Council of Troia, Mansi, XX, 789.

[83] Canon 9, Mansi, XX, 902-903.

be supported by the oath of close relatives or other reliable witnesses, the parties were forced to separate; if the allegation could not be sustained under oath, the spouses were permitted to remain together.[84] Any oath extracted under duress was null.[85]

The first concession of a plenary indulgence was made by Urban to all those who partook in the first Crusade for unselfish reasons.[86]

[84] JL 5388: the *Collectio Britannica*, n. 35, the Collection in Nine Books, n. 17, the *Tripartita*, n. 13, the *Decretum*, n. 11, the *Panormia*, n. 15, the first recension of the *Collectio Caesaraugustana*, n. 18, the second recension of the *Collectio Caesaraugustana*, n. 22, the Collection of Saint-Germain-des-Prés, n. 35, the second Collection of Châlons-sur-Marne, n. 50, the Collection of *Codex Ms. Vaticanus Latinus 1361*, n. 16, and the Collection in Ten Parts, n. 51; in Gratian at c. 3, C. XXXV, q. 6. Canon 1, Council of Troia, Mansi, XX, 789-790: the Collection of *Codex Ms. Vaticanus Latinus 3829*, n. 2, the *Tripartita*, n. 14, the *Decretum*, n. 12, the first recension of the *Collectio Caesaraugustana*, n. 8, the second recension of the *Collectio Caesaraugustana*, n. 23, the Collection of Saint-Germain-des-Prés, n. 33, the second Collection of Châlons-sur-Marne, n. 51, and the Collection of *Codex Ms. Vaticanus Latinus 1361*, n. 17; in Gratian at c. 4, C. XXXV, q. 6.

[85] JL 5423: the first recension of the *Collectio Caesaraugustana*, n. 10, and the second recension of the same collection, n. 12; not in Gratian.

[86] Canon 2, Council of Clermont, Mansi, XX, 816: the Collection of Saint-Germain-des-Prés, n. 8. "C'est un véritable nouveauté que l'apparition de cette *indulgence* au sens strict du mot, comportant rémission de la *pénitence* de tous les péchés confessés. Car elle est le premier exemple que connaisse le droit canon d'une indulgence plénière digne d'être notée." —M. Villey, *La Croisade* (Paris: Librairie Philosophique J. Vrin, 1942), p. 143; cf. also pp. 141-151, and Setton-Baldwin, *A History of the Crusades*, I, 245-246.

CHAPTER III

The Law of Penalties

Article I. General Notions

By actual count the legislation which concerns ecclesiastical crimes and their punishment is not extensive. Yet the Pope was called upon frequently to invoke ecclesiastical penalties, in order to deter those who were especially malicious in their contempt for the sacred canons.

Excommunication was the most common penalty threatened; Urban's regulations concerning this penalty, its effects and its excusing causes, became an established part of the later law in this matter, and were included in many of the collections.[1] Usually an excommunication was preceded by a private admonition.[2] When the ordinary inflicted excommunication upon one of his subjects, the remission of the penalty was reserved to that prelate; others were forbidden to absolve from it without the bishop's leave.[3]

One of the principal effects of excommunication in medieval times was the complete social ostracism which the penalty entailed. The sources outside the collections offer some details of the effects of excommunication. All association or social contact with others was

---

[1] JL 5393: the Collection in Two Books, n. 2 (whole letter), the *Collectio Britannica*, n. 38, the recension "C" of the Collection of Anselm of Lucca, n. 3, the Collection of *Codex Ms. Vaticanus Latinus 3829*, n. 1, the *Tripartita*, nn. 1 and 7, the *Decretum* of Ivo, nn. 3 and 14, the *Panormia*, n. 10, the first and second recension of the *Collectio Caesaraugustana*, n. 2, the first Collection of Châlons-sur-Marne, n. 3, the second Collection of Châlons-sur-Marne, nn. 12 and 52, the Collection in Thirteen Books, n. 1, and the Collection in Ten Parts, n. 45. Fragments of this letter are found at c. 110, C. XI, q. and c. 4, C. IX, q. 1. Cf. Mourret, *History*, IV, 245-246; Hefele-Leclercq, *Conciles*, V, I, 342.

[2] JL 5471: the Collection of Saint-Germain-des-Prés, n. 38; not in Gratian.

[3] Canon 15, Council of Melfi, Mansi, XX, 724: the *Collectio Britannica*, n. 47; not in Gratian.

forbidden.[4] Ecclesiastical burial and attendance at the "divine offices" was denied to persons under censure.[5]

The effects of excommunication are spelled out in some detail in one canon of the pre-Gratian collections which is attributed to Urban II. When the members of a parish had been placed under excommunication, the censure meant that no sacred rite or public prayer could be performed in the parish church; the ritual of Christian burial could not be carried out, although penance and the Holy Eucharist were not to be denied to the sick, and baptism could be conferred as usual.[6] Among those upon whom rested the threat of excommunication, the collections mention the so-called "*canonum contemptores*"[7] and persons involved in an incestuous marriage.[8] Soldiers were forbidden to serve under the command of an excommunicated count.[9] Thus the excommunicate was the outcast of the whole of society. Because of the severe consequences of the penalty, as long as there was real doubt concerning his guilt, the offender was given the benefit of the doubt.[10]

[4] JL 5712, ca. Nov., 1098, *Dolemus pro vobis*, to the clergy and people of Liège.

[5] H. Wiederhold, *Papsturkunden in Frankreich*, Beiheft, 1907, pp. 62-64, letter n. 6, May 1, 1099, *Piae postulatio*, given at St. Peter's, Rome, to Fulconus, abbot of the monastery of St. Peter in the diocese of Nîmes. Canon 16, Council of Nîmes, Mansi, XX, 937.

[6] This canon cannot be identified positively; it is attributed to Urban II in the second recension of the *Collectio Caesaraugustana*, n. 30; it is not found in Gratian.

[7] JL 5611: the *Decretum* of Ivo, n. 1; this canon is not in Gratian.

[8] Canon 1, Council of Troia, Mansi, XX, 789-790: the Collection of *Codex Ms. Vaticanus Latinus 3829*, n. 2, the *Tripartita*, n. 14, the *Decretum*, n. 12, the first recension of the *Collectio Caesaraugustana*, n. 8, the second recension of the *Collectio Caesaraugustana*, n. 23, the Collection of Saint-Germain-des-Prés, n. 33, the second Collection of Châlons-sur-Marne, n. 51, and the Collection of *Codex Ms. Vaticanus Latinus 1361*, n. 17; in Gratian at c. 4, C. XXXV, q. 6.

[9] JL 5724: the Collection in Nine Books, n. 12, the *Panormia*, n. 11, the first recension of the *Collectio Caesaraugustana*, n. 9, the second recension of the *Collectio Caesaraugustana*, n. 11, the second Collection of Châlons-sur-Marne, n. 53, the Collection of *Codex Ms. Vaticanus Latinus 1361*, n. 20, and the Collection in Ten Parts, n. 46; this fragment is in Gratian at c. 5, C. XV, q. 6.

[10] JL 5363: the *Collectio Britannica*, n. 16, the first Collection of

Occasional references to interdict are found in the sources of Urban in the collections.[11]

Outside the collections the most frequent mention of interdict occurred in connection with the grants of privileges to monastic groups. Monks were frequently exempted from interdicts leveled by the local ordinary. With this privilege the monks could continue the liturgical functions "*ianuis clausis.*" [12]

A persisent problem for Urban to face concerned the remission of penalties. It was necessary for the Pope to censure severely the unlawful remission of penalties by anyone other than the one who had imposed them, or by the latter's delegate.[13] At times, however, Urban permitted the reconciliation to be effected by one other than the delinquent's superior.[14] There are also instances in which the Holy Father extended delegated power to lift both excommunication and interdict.[15]

Prague, n. 1, the *Decretum* of Ivo, n. 15, the *Panormia*, n. 12, the second Collection of Châlons-sur-Marne, n. 54, and the Collection in Ten Parts, n. 47; in Gratian at c. 3, C. XXIV, q. 2.

[11] JL 5368: the *Collectio Britannica*, n. 19; not in Gratian. JL 5423: the first recension of the *Collectio Caesaraugustana*, n. 10, the second recension of the *Collectio Caesaraugustana*, n. 12; not in Gratian. Canon 32, Council of Clermont, Mansi, XX, 818: the Collection of Saint-Germain-des-Prés, n. 30, the second Collection of Châlons-sur-Marne, n. 14, and the Collection in Ten Parts, n. 44; not in Gratian.

[12] J. Ramackers, *Papsturkunden in Frankreich*, 1940, Dritte Folge, n. 23, pp. 38-40, letter n. 5, May 17, 1099, *Petis a me*, given at Rome, to Bernold, provost of the Church of St. Mary, Watten, France. For the extension of this same privilege to Cluny, see JL 5682, April 17, 1097, *Quoniam abundante*, given at the Lateran, to Hugh, abbot of Cluny. Also cf. JL 5659, July 22, 1096, *Sicut iniuste*, given at Avignon in the monastery of St. Andrew, to the monastery of St. Giles, Nîmes.

[13] Canon 15, Council of Nîmes, Mansi, XX, 936; JL 5636, ca. March, 1096, *Auditum est apud*, to Richerius, archbishop of Sens; JL 5773, April 4, 1097-1099, *Beati Aegidii monasterium*, given at the Lateran, to Raymond, bishop of Nîmes; P. Kehr, *Papsturkunden in Spanien*, I, pt. II, p. 281, letter n. 18, 1089-1090, *Venientes nuper*, to the abbot of Thomières; canon 2, Council of Troia, Mansi, XX, 789.

[14] JL 5768, 1088-1099, *Religionis vestrae petitionis*, to Gualcelinus, abbot.

[15] JL 5712, ca. Nov., 1098, *Dolemus pro vobis*, to the clergy and the people of Liège; JL 5746, 1088-1099, *Episcopalis officii interest*, to Aribertus, bishop of Avignon; JL 5774, April 24, 1097-1099, *Carissimi filii*, given at the Lateran, to Manasses, archbishop of Reims.

Article II. Some Specific Delicts

In this section three particular crimes will be examined, simony, clerical incontinence and contemptuous disobedience toward ecclesiastical regulations. These three crimes were rampant during the pontificate of Urban II, and a rather extensive portion of his letters and councils dealt with overcoming these evils. This section will conclude with some brief remarks about other offenses to which Urban directed his attention.

Of all the evils which infected the Church in the time of Urban, none was attacked with greater frequency than simony. The contemporary canonical collections contain constant pleas and threats. From the very start of his offensive, Urban insisted that his views were those of the Fathers of the Church.[16] In an effort to strike at the very core of the problem, the Pope declared that every simoniacal contract and transaction was invalid.[17] All commerce in churches and benefices was proscribed without reservation, even when parents engaged therein on behalf of their unsuspecting sons.[18] But just as Urban tolerated those who unwittingly had

[16] Canon 1, Council of Melfi, Mansi, XX, 721: the *Collectio Britannica*, n. 47 (not in Gratian); canon 1, Council of Piacenza, Mansi, XX, 805: the Collection in Seven Books, n. 2, the Italian Collection in Three Books, n. 5, the Collection in Nine Books, n. 7, the first and second recension of the *Collectio Caesaraugustana*, n. 5 (in Gration at c. 5, C. I, q. 3); this canon was repeated at Council of Rome, canon 1, Mansi, XX, 961: the Collection of Saint-Germain-des-Prés, n. 31. Cf. portions of JL 5743: the Recension "C" of the Collection of Anselm of Lucca, n. 1, the Italian Collection in Three Books, n. 4, the Collection in Nine Books, n. 11, the Collection of *Codex Ms. Vaticanus Latinus 1361*, n. 1, and at c. 8 and c. 12, D. XXXII.

[17] Canon 2, Council of Piacenza, Mansi, XX, 805: the Collection in Seven Books, n. 2, the Italian Collection in Three Books, n. 5, the Collection in Nine Books, n. 7, the first and second recension of the *Collectio Caesaraugustana*, n. 5; repeated in canon 2, Council of Rome, Mansi, XX, 961: the Collection of Saint-Germain-des-Prés, n. 31, the second Collection of Châlons-sur-Marne, n. 4, the Collection in Ten Parts, n, 23, and c. 5, C. I, q. 3.

[18] Canons 5, 6 and 7, Council of Piacenza, Mansi, XX, 805: the Collection in Seven Books, n. 2, the Italian Collection in Three Books, n. 6, the Collection in Nine Books, n. 8, the first and second recension of the *Collectio Caesaraugustana*, n. 5; repeated as canons 5, 6 and 7, Council of Rome, Mansi, XX, 961: the Collection of Saint-Germain-des-Prés, n. 31.

permitted themselves to be ordained by heretics and simoniacs, so he was equally indulgent to those whose offices or benefices had been bought, without the knowledge of the incumbent, by payment from a third party.[19] Inasmuch as the clergy as a class enjoyed great prospects of material gain and worldly influence, simoniacal ordinations became a regular occurrence. The situation was not helped by the members of the imperial faction, which openly opposed everything which the Holy See stood for and favored. Special attempts were made in an effort to stamp out simoniacal ordinations.[20]

Among other measures enacted to strengthen the offensive against simony was the emphasis put upon the bishop's exclusive right to distribute ecclesiastical benefices. This regulation aimed at curbing the indiscriminate distribution of benefices, especially by laymen, to the highest bidder.[21] Likewise Urban corrected the popular notion that benefices, like other properties, were hereditary. This false idea also encouraged the lax concept with reference to clerical celibacy among many of the clergy.[22]

In the matter of the reconciliation of simoniacs, several regulations were enacted. Generally in this matter the bishop was given discretionary powers, so that his judgment determined some of the requirements demanded of repentant clerics.[23] A demanded con-

the second Collection of Châlons-sur-Marne, nn. 8-10, the Collection in Ten Parts, nn. 29-32 and c. 1, C. I, q. 5; the paraphrase of canon 6, Council of Clermont, Mansi, XX, 817: the Collection of Saint-Germain-des-Prés, n. 11 (this last canon is not in Gratian).

[19] JL 5386 and 5396: the *Collectio Britannica*, nn. 33 and 39 respectively; neither text is in Gratian.

[20] Canon 2, Council of Piacenza, Mansi, XX, 805: the Collection in Seven Books, n. 2, the Italian Collection in Three Books, n. 5, the Collection in Nine Books, n. 7, the first and second recension of the *Collectio Caesaraugustana*, n. 5; repeated in canon 2, Council of Rome, Mansi, XX, 961: the Collection of Saint-Germain-des-Prés, n. 31, the second Collection of Châlons-sur-Marne, n. 4, and the Collection in Ten Parts, n. 23; in Gratian at c. 5, C. I, q. 3.

[21] JL 5407 and 5408: the *Collectio Britannica*, nn. 45 and 46. The first sentence of canon 15, Council of Clermont, Mansi, XX, 817: the Collection of Saint-Germain-des-Prés, n. 18; not in Gratian.

[22] JL 5407: the *Collectio Britannica*, n. 45; not in Gratian.

[23] JL 5404: the *Collectio Britannica*, n. 42: not in Gratian.

dition in almost every case was that the cleric relinquish the simoniacally obtained church or benefice.[24] At times pardon was extended to a guilty cleric on the condition that he subject himself to the monastic life as a form of penance.[25]

Attempts were also made to eradicate simony in connection with the consecration of a bishop and the blessing of an abbot,[26] the making of religious profession,[27] the reception of baptism or of confirmation, and the conducting of burial services.[28]

The sources not found in the collections forbade simony in conjunction with the payment or reception of tithes, with the consecration of the holy chrism, and especially with the bestowal of ecclesiastical burial.[29] The same rebukes against simoniacs who retained ecclesiastical offices and benefices are found in the sources outside of the collections.[30]

---

[24] JL 5740: the Collection of *Codex Ms. Vaticanus Latinus 3829*, n. 3, the *Tripartita*, n. 6, the first recension of the *Collectio Caesaraugustana*, nn. 4 and 7, the second recension of the *Collectio Caesaraugustana*, nn. 4 and 24, the first Collection of Châlons-sur-Marne, n. 2, the second Collection of Châlons-sur-Marne, nn. 2 and 37, the Collection of *Codex Ms. Vaticanus Latinus 1361*, n. 15, and c. 2, C. I, q. 5.

[25] JL 5396: the *Collectio Britannica*, n. 39; not in Gratian.

[26] Paraphrase of canon 4, Council of Rome, Mansi, XX, 961: the second Collection of Châlons-sur-Marne, n. 7 and the Collection in Ten Parts, n. 27; not in Gratian.

[27] First part of canon 17, Council of Rome, Mansi, XX, 964: the Collection of Saint-Germain-des-Prés, n. 31 and the Collection in Ten Parts, n. 28; the first part of this canon is found in canon 7, Council of Melfi, Mansi, XX, 723, and in Gratian at c. 3, C. I, q. 2.

[28] Canon 13, Council of Piacenza, Mansi, XX, 806: the *Polycarpus*, n. 1, the Italian Collection in Three Books, n. 10, the Collection in Nine Books, n. 13, the first and second recension of the *Collectio Caesaraugustana*, n. 5; repeated in canon 12, Council of Rome, Mansi, XX, 963: the Collection of Saint-Germain-des-Prés, n. 31, the second Collection of Châlons-sur-Marne, n. 38, and the Collection in Ten Parts, n. 2; not in Gratian.

[29] P. Kehr, *Papsturkunden in Spanien*, II, pt. II, p. 284, letter, n. 13, May 4, 1098, *Piae postulatio*, given at the Lateran to the monastery of Jesus Nazarenus, in Huesca, Spain; canon 9, Council of Piacenza, according to the summary of Bernold of Constance, Mansi, XX, 803; JL 5678, ca. Jan. 9-March 4, 1097, *Quod de Guapicensi*, to Hugh, archbishop of Lyons; JL 5775, 1097-1099, *Mortuorum qui*, to Godfrey, bishop of Maguelonne, France. Concerning this last letter, cf. the note of the *Correctores Romani* at c. 12, C. XIII, q. 2.

[30] For example, JL 5442, Feb. 1, 1090, *Gaudemus filii*, given at Benevento,

The special tolerance which Urban granted to those who had unknowingly benefited by the simony of a third party is also referred to in the sources outside of the collections.[31] Reinstatement was possible to an erring cleric who was truly penitent. Explicit provision was made for repentant bishops.[32]

An evil which infected the Church with very much the same intensity and with equally dire consequences was incontinence among major clerics. Clerical incontinence was not merely a vice among some of the clergy; it was a deep-rooted, pernicious practice based on the assumption that celibacy was unnatural, impossible and unreasonable. In one of the first councils convoked during his pontificate, at Melfi in 1089, Urban let his position on this matter be known; his formulation of what the law was became incorporated in contemporary collections again and again.[33] The Pope threatened incontinent clerics with suspension; clerics in major orders, if they took wives for themselves, suffered loss of benefice and office, and

to Lanzo and Rudolph, abbots, to Adalbero, *primicerius*, and to the archdeacons, clergy and faithful of Metz; JL 5631, March 29, 1096, *Bonorum omnium*, given at Poitiers, to the church of St. Martin of Tours; canon 1, Council of Nîmes, Mansi, XX, 933; P. Kehr, *Italia Pontificia*, VIII, pt. II, p. 91, letter n. 175, 1093, to the patriarch of Grado; J. Ramackers, *Papsturkunden in Frankreich*, 1940, Dritte Folge, n. 23, pp. 26-38, letter n. 4, Dec. 3, 1095, *Piae postulatio*, given at Sauxillanges, to Lambert, abbot of the monastery of St. Benedict.

[31] JL 5409, ca. Sept., 1089, *Super quaestionibus*, to Pibo, bishop of Toul; canon 8, Council of Clermont, according to the compendium of William of Malmesbury, Mansi, XX, 904.

[32] JL 5486, July 18, 1093, *Accusationem simoniacae*, to the clergy and faithful of Amiens; JL 5718, ca. 1098, *Sic apud bonis*, to Bernard, abbot of St. Martin at Tours.

[33] Canon 12, Council of Melfi, Mansi, XX, 724: the Collection of *Codex Ms. Vaticanus Latinus 4977*, n. 2, the *Collectio Britannica*, n. 47, the *Panormia*, n. 6, the second recension of the *Collectio Caesaraugustana*, n. 7, the Collection of Saint-Germain-des-Prés, n. 36, the second Collection of Châlons-sur-Marne, n. 26, the Collection of *Codex Ms. Vaticanus Latinus 1361*, n. 3, the Collection in Ten Parts, n. 22, and c. 10, D. XXXII; canon 2, Council of Melfi, Mansi, XX, 723: the *Collectio Britannica*, n. 47; repeated in canon 13, Council of Rome, Mansi, XX, 963: the Collection of Saint-Germain-des Prés, n. 31; this canon is not in Gratian. Cf. also, canon 9, Council of Clermont, Mansi, XX, 817: the Collection of Saint-Germain-des-Prés, n. 12, and the second Collection of Châlons-sur-Marne, n. 27; not in Gratian.

unless their amendment was timely, their wives faced bondage at the hand of the local civil authority. Any bishop who consented to clerical disregard for chastity could expect to be deprived of his office. In the same vein, Urban wrote to the bishop of Metz that, as long as major clerics remained in their wretched condition, they were to be deprived of the exercise of ecclesiastical powers (". . . nullam suae ordinationis potestatem in ecclesiam habere permittas.")[34]

In the sources not included within the collections, the same norms are found.[35]

Already a great deal has been said about deliberate disregard for the laws of the Church. Here the writer will seek to list some of the penalties, specific in nature, which could be incurred in consequence of such contempt. Most of the examples cited come from outside the collections.

Anathemas were frequently leveled against those bishops who allied themselves with the imperial schismatic faction.[36] There were instances in which bishops had to be urged under pain of censure to attend councils.[37] Likewise presentation to the Holy See could be commanded under pain of censure.[38] Monks too were not immune from punishment for deliberate and malicious contempt and disobedience.[39] In an effort to regain for the Church the administration of properties rightfully

[34] JL 5381: the *Collection Britannica*, n. 26, the *Panormia*, n. 8, the Collection of *Codex Ms. Vaticanus Latinus 1361*, n. 2, and the Collection in Ten Parts, n. 26; not in Gratian.

[35] JL 5409, ca. Sept., 1089, *Super quaestionibus*, to Pibo, bishop of Toul; canon 4, Council of Clermont, according to the summary of Ordericus Vitalis, Mansi, XX, 885; canon 12, Council of Nîmes, Mansi, XX, 936.

[36] Canon 7, Council of Piacenza, in the version of Bernold of Constance, Mansi, XX, 803; JL 5538, 1094-1095, *Gratias agimus*, to Berengerus, abbot of St. Lawrence at Liège.

[37] Cf. the prologue to the Council of Piacenza, Mansi, XX, 801; JL 5531, to Rainaldus, archbishop of Reims; JL 5570, August 15, 1095, *Noverit dilectio*, given at Le Puy-en-Velay, to Lambert, bishop of Arras; JL 5571, ca. August, 1095, to the same Rainaldus; JL 5636, ca. March, 1096, *Auditum est apud*, to Richerius, archbishop of Sens.

[38] P. Kehr, *Italia Pontificia*, III, 89, letter, n. 403, 1099, to Bernard, abbot of Vallombrosa.

[39] JL 5605, Dec. 29, 1095, *Carissimus noster in*, given at Limoges, to Ademerus, bishop of Angoulême.

hers, Urban declared what the sacred canons proposed and he attached excommunication and interdict to those who by seizing every kind of church property, disregarded the established norms.[40] Those who were guilty of theft or who set up a false patrimonial claim to ecclesistical property faced the same penalty.[41]

Within the collections there existed several norms which should be mentioned here. There was a general reproof of those who contemptuously ignored the sacred canons.[42] Excommunication awaited the cleric who seized the possessions of another cleric, especially if the latter was a bishop.[43] Clerics guilty of having received lay investiture were penalized with deposition and excommunication.[44]

Among the penalties threatened for other delicts, the collections of the pre-Gratian period reflect a few. For example, those who disregarded the privilege of the canon in regard to bishops were

[40] JL 5517, March 31, 1094, *Noverit dilectio*, given at Rome, to Amatus, archbishop of Bordeaux, to Peter, bishop of Poitiers, and to Ramnulfus, bishop of Les Saintes; JL 5666, August 7-18, 1096, *Iam dudum*, to Odalricus, provost, and Manegoldus, dean of the church at Raitenbuch in Bavaria; JL 5711, Nov. 1, 1098, *Audivimus et auditum*, to the brothers of St. Hubert at Chiny-dans-les-Ardennes; JL 5739, 1088-1099, *Lanzonem presbyterum*, to the clergy and people of Salerno; P. Kehr, *Italia Pontificia*, V, 156, letter, n. 443, Oct. 7, 1096, given at Cremona, to the monks and lay brothers at Vallombrosa; *ibid.*, VI, pt. I, p. 311, letter n. 252, ca. 1090, Urban excommunicated Obertus, invader of the diocese of Brescia.

[41] JL 5458, Jan. 28, 1092, *Venerunt ad*, given at Anagni, to Gebhard, bishop of Constance, to Welf, duke of Bavaria, to Berthold, duke of Swabia, and to Burchard, count of Wellenburg; canon 7, Council of Nîmes, Mansi, XX, 935.

[42] JL 5611: the *Decretum* of Ivo, n. 1; not in Gratian.

[43] Canon 31, Council of Clermont, Mansi, XX, 818: the Collection of Saint-Germain-des-Prés, n. 29, the second Collection of Châlons-sur-Marne, n. 11, and the Collection in Ten Parts, n. 43; this canon is related to c. 46, C. XII, q. 2.

[44] Canon 8, Council of Melfi, Mansi, XX, 723: the *Collectio Britannica*, n. 47; not in Gratian.

[45] Canon 32, Council of Clermont, Mansi, XX, 819: the Collection of Saint-Germain-des-Prés, n. 30, the second Collection of Châlons-sur-Marne, n. 14, and the Collection in Ten Parts, n. 44; JL 5423: the first recension of the *Collectio Caesaraugustana*, n. 10, the second recension of the *Collectio Caesaraugustana*, n. 12; not in Gratian.

declared perpetually infamous.[45] One year of penance was meted out to a cleric who allowed himself to be ordained *per saltum*.[46]

The sources found outside of the collections also indicate that any violation of the *privilegium canonis* entailed ecclesiastical censures.[47] Bishops faced deposition, if they ordained clerics who lacked the proper age.[48] Any cleric, if on his own authority he acted as a chaplain to a layman, laid himself open to possible deprivation of office and benefice.[49] The violating of a cemetery could invite the incurring of a penalty.[50] Urban made the violation of the *treuga Dei* punishable with excommunication.[51] Brigands, when killed in the act of pillaging, were denied Christain burial; Holy Mass could not be offered for them.[52]

The collections include some final norms with reference to specific misdemeanors. Accidental homicide by a cleric did not bring the ordinary penalty of suspension.[53] The full rigor of ecclesiastical punishment was not inflicted upon those who had killed excommunicated persons because of zeal for the Church; Urban maintained that such a deed was not the equivalent of homicide.[54]

[46] JL 5734: the second recension of the *Collectio Caesaraugustana*, n. 18; not in Gratian.

[47] For example, JL 5584, Nov., 1095, *Venerabilem fratrem*, to Guarnerius, son of Pontio; JL 5585, Nov., 1095, *Audivimus Guarnerium*, to Richerius, archbishop of Sens; canon 11, Council of Clermont, according to Ordericus Vitalis, Mansi, XX, 885, and canon 15 of the same council, in the summary of William of Malmesbury, Mansi, XX, 904. Cf. also, canon 4, Council of Nîmes, Mansi, XX, 935.

[48] Canon 6, Council of Clermont, according to the *Codex Cencii*, Mansi, XX, 902.

[49] Canon 2, Council of Benevento, Mansi, XX, 739.

[50] JL 5684, April 29, 1097, *Cum in Ausciensi*, given at Rome, to Raymond, archbishop of Auch, France.

[51] Canon 2, Council of Troia, Mansi, XX, 789.

[52] Canon 11, Council of Nîmes, Mansi, XX, 936.

[53] JL 5724: the *Panormia*, n. 9, the second recension of the *Collectio Caesaraugustana*, n. 8, the second Collection of Châlon-sur-Marne, n. 49, and the Collection in Ten Parts, n. 36; in Gratian at c. 37, D. L.

[54] JL 5536: the first Collection of Prague, n. 2, the *Tripartita*, n. 15, the *Decretum*, n. 13, the *Panormia*, n. 16, the first recension of the *Collectio Caesaraugustana*, n. 19, the second recension of the *Collectio Caesaraugustana*, n. 28, the second Collection of Châlons-sur-Marne, n. 48, the Collection of *Codex Ms. Vaticanus Latinus 1361*, n. 19, and the Collection in Ten Parts, n. 52; in Gratian at c. 47, C. XXIII, q. 5.

BIBLIOGRAPHY

MICROFILMS OF MANUSCRIPTS

Municipal Library, Châlons-sur-Marne, France

Bibliothèque municipale 47: the First Collection of Châlons-sur-Marne.

Bibliothèque municipale 75: the Second Collection of Châlons-sur-Marne.

Municipal Library, Douai, France

Bibliothèque municipale 584: the *Panormia* of Ivo of Chartres.

National Library, Paris

Bibliothèque nationale latin 3858B: the *Tripartita* of Ivo Chartres.

National Library, Munich

Bayerische Staatsbibliothek lateinische 4545: the *Panormia* of Ivo of Chartres.

Vatican Library, Rome

Latinus Barberinus 535: the Recension "Bb" of the Collection of Anselm of Lucca.

Latinus Barberinus 897: the First Recension of the *Collectio Caesaraugustana.*

Latinus Bibliothecae S. Petri C. 118: the Collection in Nine Books.

Latinus 1346: the Collection in Seven Books.

Latinus 1354: the *Polycarpus.*

Latinus 1357: the *Decretum* of Ivo of Chartres.

Latinus 1361

Latinus 3829

Latinus 3831: the Italian Collection in Three Books.

Latinus 3832: the Collection in Two Books.

Latinus 4977

Latinus 4983: the Recension "C" of the Collection of Anselm of Lucca.

Latinus 5715: the Second Recension of the *Collectio Caesaraugustana.*

National Library, Vienna

Österreichische Nationalbibliothek 2178 (juris canonici 91): the Collection in Ten Parts.

PAPAL REGISTERS

Jaffé, Philippus, *Regesta Pontificum Romanorum ab condita ecclesia ad annum post Christum natum MCXCVIII*, 2. ed. curaverunt S. Loewenfeld, F. Kaltenbrunner, P. Ewald, 2 vols., Lipsiae: Viet et Comp., 1885-1888.

———, *Bibliotheca Rerum Germanicarum*, Vol. II, *Monumenta Gregoriana*, Berolini: apud Weidmannos, 1865.

Loewenfeld, S., *Epistolae Pontificum Romanorum ineditae*, Lipsiae: Veit et Comp., 1885.

Pflugk-Harttung, J. von, *Acta Pontificum Romanorum inedita*, 3 vols., Vol. I, Tübingen: Verlag und Druck von Franz Fues, 1881, Vols. II and III, Stuttgart: Verlag von W. Kohlhammer, 1884-1886.

Italy:

Kehr, P., *Italia Pontificia*, 8 vols. in 9, Berolini: apud Weidmannos, 1906-1935 with the supplementary materials of the same author in *Nachträge zu den Papsturkunden Italiens*, in *Nachrichten von der [königl.] Gesellschaft der Wissenschaften zu Göttingen*, philologisch-historische Klasse, I-IX, Göttingen, 1905-1924.

Germany:

Brackmann, A., *Germania Pontificia*, 3 vols. in 4, Berolini: apud Weidmannos, 1910-1935.

France:

Wiederhold, H., *Papsturkunden in Frankreich*, in *Nachichten von der königl. Gesellschaft der Wissenschaften zu Göttingen*, philologisch-historische Klasse, Beiheft, 1906, 1907, 1910, 1911 and 1913.

Meinart, H., *Papsturkunden in Frankreich*, Neue Folge, I, *Champagne und Lothringen*, in *Abhandlungen der Gesellschaft der Wissenschaften zu Göttingen*, philologisch-historische Klasse, Dritte Folge, nn. 3 and 4, Berlin, 1932-1933.

Ramackers, J., *Papsturkunden in Frankreich*, Neue Folge, II *Normandie*, in *Abhandlungen der Gesellschaft der Wissenschaften zu Göttingen*, philologisch-historische Klasse, Dritte Folge, n. 21, Göttingen, 1937.

———, Neue Folge, III, *Artois*, Dritte Folge, n. 25, Berlin, 1940.

———, Neue Folge, IV, *Picardie*, Dritte Folge, n. 27, Göttingen, 1942.

———, Neue Folge, V, Dritte Folge, n. 35, Göttingen, 1956.

Spain:

Kehr, P., *Papsturkunden in Spanien*, I, *Katalanien*, in *Abhandlungen der Gesellschaft der Wissenschaften zu Göttingen*, philologisch-historische Klasse, Neue Folge, Vol. XVIII, n. 2, Berlin, 1926.

———, II, *Navarra und Aragon*, Neue Folge, Vol. XXII, n. 1, Berlin, 1928.

Portugal:

Erdmann, C., *Papsturkunden in Portugal*, in *Abhandlungen der Gesellschaft der Wissenschaften zu Göttingen*, philologisch-historische Klasse, Neue Folge, Vol. XX, n. 3, Berlin, 1927.

England:

Holtzmann, W., *Papsturkunden in England*, I, *Bibliotheken und Archive in London*, in *Abhandlungen der Gesellschaft der Wissenschaften zu Göttingen*, philologisch-historische Klasse, Neue Folge, Vol. XXV, Berlin, 1930-1931.

———, II, *Die kirchlichen Archive und Bibliotheken*, Dritte Folge, nn. 14 and 15, Berlin, 1935-1936.

———, III, in *Abhandlungen der Akademie der Wissenschaften zu Göttingen*, philologisch-historische Klasse, Dritte Folge, n. 33, Berlin, 1952.

The Lowlands:

Ramackers, J., *Papsturkunden in den Niederlanden* (Belgien, Luxemburg, Holland und Französisch-Flandern), in *Abhandlungen der Gesellschaft der Wissenschaften zu Göttingen*, philologisch-historische Klasse, Dritte Folge, nn. 8-9, Berlin, 1933-1934.

OTHER SOURCES

Antiquae Collectiones Decretalium, ed. Antonio Agustín, editionis licentia et approbatio post tertiam collectionem queratur, Ilerdae, 1576.

Baluze, E., *Miscellanea*, 7 vols., Parisiis, 1678-1715.

Corpus Iuris Canonici, ed. Lipsiensis 2. post Aemilii Ludovici Richteri curas . . . instruxit Aemilius Friedberg, 2 vols., Lipsiae: ex Officina Bernhardi Tauchnitz, 1879-1881; editio anastatice repetita, Lipsiae: Tauchnitz, 1928.

Decretales D. Gregorii Papae IX, suae integritati una cum glossis restitutae, cum privilegio Gregorii XIII, Pont. Max., et aliorum principum, Romae, 1582.

Decretum Gratiani emendatum et notationibus illustratum cum glossis, Gregorii XIII, Pont. Max., iussu editum, 2 vols., Romae, 1582.

Duchesne, L., ed., *le Liber Pontificalis*, 2 vols., Paris: Ernest Thorin, Editeur, 1886-1892.

Hinschius, Paulus, ed., *Decretales Pseudo-Isidorianae et Capitula Angilramni*, Lipsiae: ex Officina Bernhardi Tauchnitz, 1863.

Labbé, P.-Cossart, G., *Sacrosancta Concilia*, 15 vols. in 16, Parisiis, 1672.

le Provost, Auguste, ed., *Orderici Vitalis Historiae Ecclesiasticae Libri Tredecim*, 5 vols., Parisiis: apud Julium Prenouard et Socios, 1840-1855.

Mansi, Ioannes Dominicus, *Sacrorum Conciliorum Nova et Amplissima Collectio*, 53 vols. in 60, Parisiis, Arnhem, Lipsiae, 1901-1927.

Migne, J. P., ed., *Patrologiae Cursus Completus, Series Latina*, 221 vols., Parisiis, 1844-1864.

Monumenta Germaniae Historica, Leges, Sectio IV, *Constitutiones et Acta Publica Imperatorum et Regum*, Vol. I, ed., L. Weiland, Hannoverae: Impensis Bibliopoli Hahniani, 1893.

Monumenta Germaniae Historica, Scriptores, Vol. V, ed., G. Pertz, Leipzig: Verlag Karl W. Hiersemann, 1925.

Quinque Compilationes Antiquae nec non Collectio Canonum Lipsiensis, ed., Aemilius Friedberg, Lipsiae, 1882; reprint, Graz: Akademische Druck -u. Verlagsanstalt, 1956.

Ryan, J. J., *Saint Peter Damiani and his Canonical Sources*, The Pontifical Institute of Mediaeval Studies, Studies and Texts, n. 2, Toronto, 1956.

Schroeder, H. J., *Disciplinary Decrees of the General Councils*, St. Louis: B. Herder Book Company, 1937.

Sdralek, Max. *Wolfenbüttler Fragmente*, in the series *Kirchengeschichtliche Studien herausgegeben von Dr. Knöfler, Dr. Schrörs, Dr. Sdralek*, Band I, Heft II, Münster i. W.: Verlag von Heinrich Schöningh, 1891.

Stubbs, William, ed., *Willelmi Malmesbiriensis Monachi De Gestis Regum Anglorum*, Rerum Britannicarum Medii Aevi Scriptores (Rolls Series), 2 vols., London, 1889.

Thaner, F., ed., *Anselmi Episcopi Luccensis Collectio Canonum una cum Collectione Minore*, 2 vols. in 1, Oeniponte: Librariae Academicae Wagnerianae, 1906-1915.

Watterich, I. M., ed., *Pontificum Romanorum Vitae*, 2 vols., Lipsiae: Sumptibus Guilhelmi Engelmanni, 1862.

REFERENCE WORKS

Berardi, C., *Gratiani Canones geniuni ab apocryphis discreto*, 3 parts in 4, Venetiis: ex Typographia Petri Valvasensis, 1777.

Brooke, Z. N., *The English Church and the Papacy*, 2, ed., Cambridge: at the University Press, 1952.

Cantor, Norman F., *Church, Kingship and Lay Investiture in England, 1089-1135*, Princeton Studies in History, Volume 10, Princeton, New Jersey: Princeton University Press, 1958.

Cappello, F., *Tractatus Canonico-Moralis de Sacramantis*, Vol. IV, *De Sacra Ordinatione*, 3. ed., Taurini: Marietti, 1951.

Daniel-Rops, H., translated by J. Warrington, *Cathedral and Crusade*, London: J. M. Dent and Sons, Ltd., 1957.

Fliche, A.-Martin, V., eds., *Histoire de l'Église*, Vol. VIII: A. Fliche, *La Réforme grégorienne et la Reconquête chrétienne (1057-1123)*, Paris: Bloud et Gay, 1944.

Fournier, P.-Le Bras, G., *Histoire des collections canoniques en Occident depuis les fausses décrétales jusqu'au Décret de Gratien*, 2 vols., Paris: Recueil Sirey, 1931-1932.

Fournier, P., *Les Collections canoniques attribuées à Yves de Chartres* (a separately published reprint of an article from the *Bibliothèque de l'École des Chartes*, Vols. LVII and LVIII, 1896-1897), Paris: Librairie d'Alphonse Picard et Fils, 1897.

———, *Un Groupe de Recueils Canoniques Italiens des Xe et XIe Siècles*, Paris: Imprimerie Nationale, 1915.

Fuchs, V., *Der Ordinationstitel von seiner Entstehung bis auf Innozenz III*, Kanonistische Studien und Texte herausgegeben von Dr. Albert M. Koeniger, n. 4, Bonn: Kurt Schroeder Verlang, 1930.

Gams, P. *Series Episcoporum Ecclesiae Catholicae*, reprint of the edition of 1873-1886, Graz: Akademische Druck -u. Verlagsanstalt, 1957.

Hefele, C.-Leclercq, H., *Histoire des Conciles*, 11 vols., in 21, Paris: Letouzey et Ané, Editeurs, 1907-1952.

Heintschel, D., *The Medieval Concept of an Ecclesiastical Office,* The Catholic University of America Canon Law Studies, n. 363, Washington, D. C.: The Catholic University of America Press, 1956.

Journet, C., *The Church of the Word Incarnate,* Vol. I, *The Apostolic Hierarchy,* New York and London: Sheed and Ward, 1955.

Lennerz, H., *De Sacramentis Novae Legis in Genere,* 3. ed., Romae: apud Aedes Universitatis Gregorianae, 1950.

Many, S., *De Sacra Ordinatione,* Parisiis: apud Letouzey et Ané, Editores, 1905.

Marca, Petrus de, *De concordia Sacerdotii et Imperii,* 4 vols., Neapoli, 1771.

Mourret, F., *A History of the Catholic Church,* Vol. IV, St. Louis, B. Herder Book Company, 1941.

Parsons, R., *Studies in Church History,* Vol. II, 2. ed., New York: Pustet and Company, 1906.

Rosati, M., *La Teologia Sacramentaria nella lotta contro la Simonia e l'Investitura laica del Secolo XI,* Dissertatio ad Lauream in Facultate Theologica Pontificae Universitatis Gregorianae, Tolentino: Tipografia S. Nicola, 1951.

Reiss, J., *The Time and Place of Sacred Ordination,* The Catholic University of America Canon Law Studies, n. 343, Washington, D. C.: The Catholic University of America Press, 1953.

Runciman, S., *The History of the Crusades,* 3 vols., Cambridge: at the University Press, 1951-1954.

Saltet, L., *Les Réordinations,* Paris: J. Gabalda et Cie., 1907.

Schebler, A., *Die Reordinationen in der "altkatholischen" Kirche unter besonderer Berücksichtigung der Anschauungen Rudolph Sohms,* Kanonistische Studien und Texte herausgegeben von Dr. Albert M. Koeniger, n. 10, Bonn: Ludwig Röhrscheid Verlag, 1936.

Setton, K.-Baldwin, M., eds., *History of the Crusades,* Vol. I, *The First Hundred Years,* Philadelphia: the University of Pennsylvania Press, 1955.

Stickler, A., *Historia Iuris Canonici Latini,* Vol. I, *Historia Fontium,* Augustae Taurinorum: apud Custodiam Librorum Pontificalis Athenaei Salesiani, 1950.

Theiner, A., *Disquisitiones Criticae in praecipuas canonum et decretalium collectiones,* Romae: in Collegio Urbano, 1836.

Van Hove, A., *Prolegomena,* Vol. I, Tom. I of the *Commentarium Lovaniense in Codicem Iuris Canonici,* editum a Magistris et Doctoribus Universitatis Lovaniensis, 2. ed., Mechliniae: H. Dessain, 1945.

Villey, Michel, *La Croisade,* Paris: Librairie Philosophique J. Vrin, 1942.

DICTIONARIES AND ENCYLOPEDIAS

Cottineau, L. H., *Répertoire topo-bibliographique des Abbayes et Prieurés,* 2 vols., Macon: Protat Frères, 1935-1937.

Dictionnaire d'Archéologie Chrétienne et de la Liturgie, 15 vols. in 30, Paris: Librairie Letouzey et Ané, 1907-1953.

Dictionnaire de Droit Canonique, eds. André, Condis and Wagner, 3 vols., Paris: Hippolyte Walzer, Librairie-Editeurs, 1901.

Dictionnaire de Droit Canonique, commencé sous la direction de A. Villien et E. Magnin, continué sous la direction de A. Amanieu, publié sous la direction de R. Naz, 6 vols. completed thus far, Paris: Librairie Letouzey et Ané, 1924-

Dictionnaire de Théologie Catholique, 15 vols., Paris: Librairie Letouzey et Ané, 1903-

Du Cange, C., *Glossarium mediae et infimae Latinitatis*, ed. of Niort, 1883-1887 reprinted, 10 vols., Paris: Librairie des Sciences et des Artes, 1937.

Enciclopedia Cattolica, 12 vols., Città del Vaticano: Ente per l'Enciclopedia e per il Libro Cattolico, 1948-1954.

ARTICLES

Amman, E., "Réordinations," *Dictionnaire de Théologie Catholique*, XIII, 2416-2421.

Ehrle, F., "Zu Bethmanns Notizen über die Hanschifen von St. Francesco in Assisi," *Archiv für Litteratur -und Kirchengeschichte des Mittelalters*, I (1885), 471-481.

Ewald, P., "Die Papstbriefe der Brittischen Sammlung," *Neues Archiv der Gesellschaft für ältere deutsche Geschichtskunde*, V (1879-1880), 277-414, 501-596.

Feine, H., "Studien zum langobardisch-italischen Eigenkirchenrecht, III Teil," *Zeitschrift der Savigny-Stiftung für Rechtsgeschichte*, kanonistische Abteilung, XXXII (1943), 64-190.

Fournier, P., "Le 'Décret' de Burchard de Worms. Ses caractères, son influence," *Revue d'Histoire ecclésiastique*, XII (1911), 451-473, 670-701.

———, "Études critiques sur le Décret de Burchard de Worms," *Nouvelle Revue historique de Droit Français et Étranger*, XXXIV (1910), 41-112; 213-221; 289-331; 564-584.

———, "Observations sur diverses recensions de la collection canonique d'Anselme de Lucques," *Annales de l'Université de Grenoble*, XIII (1901), 427-458.

Kuttner, Stephan, "Bulletin for 1957 of the Institute of Research and Study in Medieval Canon Law," *Traditio*, XIII (1957), 463-514.

———, "Bulletin for 1958 of the Institute of Research and Study in Medieval Canon Law," *Traditio*, XIV (1958), 457-512.

Levison, W., "Aus Englischen Bibliotheken II: Englische Handschriften des Liber Pontificalis," *Neues Archiv der Gesellschaft für ältere deutsche Geschichtskunde*, XXXV (1909-1910), 392-395.

Pflugk-Harttung, J. von, "Eine grosse Fälschung von Canones," *Zeitschrift für Kirchenrecht*, XIX (Neue Folge, IV, 1884), 361-372.

Schulte, F., "Über drei in Prager Handschriften enthaltene Canonen-

Sammlungen," *Sitzungsberichte der philosophisch-historischen Classe der kaiserlichen Akademie der Wissenschaften* (of Vienna), LVII (1868), Heft 1, 175-221.

PERIODICALS

Abhandlungen der [königl.] Gesellschaft der Wissenschaften zu Göttingen, philologisch-historische Klasse, Göttingen and Berlin, Neue Folge, 1896-1931; Dritte Folge, 1932-

Annales de l'Université de Grenoble, Grenoble, 1889-1923.

Archiv für Litteratur -und Kirchengeschichte des Mittelalters, Berlin, 1885-1900.

Nachrichten von der [königl.] Gesellschaft der Wissenschaften zu Göttingen, philologisch-historische Klasse, Göttingen, 1894-1933; Neue Folge, 1941-

Neues Archiv der -Gesellschaft für ältere deutsche Geschichtskunde, Hanover and Berlin, 1876-1935.

Nouvelle Revue historique de Droit Français et Étranger, Paris, 1877-1921.

Revue d'Histoire ecclésiastique, Louvain, 1900-

Sitzungsberichte der philosophisch-historischen Classe der kaiserlichen Akademie der Wissenschaften, Vienna, 1848-

Traditio, New York, 1945-

Zeitscrift der Savigny-Stiftung für Rechtsgeschichte, kanonistische Abteilung, Weimar, 1911-

Zeitschrift für Kirchenrecht, Berlin, 1861-1889.

ALPHABETICAL INDEX

BIOGRAPHICAL NOTE

Francis Joseph Gossman was born on April 1, 1930, in Baltimore, Maryland. He received his elementary education at the parochial school of the Shrine of the Little Flower in the same city. In September, 1944 he entered St. Charles College, Catonsville, Maryland where he completed high school and two years of college education. In June, 1950 he graduated from St. Charles and was appointed to St. Mary's Seminary to pursue his studies in philosophy; in June of 1952 he graduated and received the Bachelor of Arts degree. Thereupon he was sent to the North American College, Rome, Italy to undertake his studies in Sacred Theology. In July, 1954 he received the Baccalaureate in Sacred Theology from the Pontifical Gregorian University in Rome. On December 17, 1955 he was ordained to the Priesthood for the Archdiocese of Baltimore by His Excellency, Martin J. O'Connor, Rector of the North American College in the College chapel in Rome. In June, 1956 he received the Licentiate in Sacred Theology from the same Gregorian University and returned to the United States. In September of the same year he entered the School of Canon Law of the Catholic University of America, Washington, D. C., from which he received the Baccalaurate in Canon Law in June, 1957, and the Licentiate in Canon Law in June, 1958.

CANON LAW STUDIES *

402. Chyang, Rev. Peter B., M. A., J. C. L., Decennial faculties for ordinaries in quasi-dioceses.
403. Gossman, Rev. Francis J., B. A., S. T. L., J. C. L., Pope Urban II and canon law.
404. Love, Rev. Paul L., A. B., J. C. L., The penal remedies of the Code of canon law.
405. McLeaish, Rev. Donald C., A. B., S. T. L., J. C. L., The laws of the State of Texas affecting church property.
406. Rodriguez, Rev. Manuel J., Ph. B., S. T. L., J. C. L., The laws of the State of New Mexico affecting church property.
407. Sampon, Rev. Robert G., Ph. B., S. T. L., J. C. L., A comparative study of the First Provincial Council of Milwaukee and the Code of Canon Law.
408. Schreiber, Rev. Paul F., A. B., J. C. L., Canonical precedence.
409. Welsh, Rev. Maurice L., M. A., J. C. L., The laws of the State of Nevada affecting church property.

* For a complete list of the available numbers of this series apply to the Catholic University of America Press, 620 Michigan Ave, N. E., Washington (17), D. C., for a general catalogue.

www.ingramcontent.com/pod-product-compliance
Lightning Source LLC
LaVergne TN
LVHW050241080826
844660LV00012B/573

* 9 7 8 0 8 1 3 2 2 5 6 3 0 *